DATE DUE

Designing a Polity

Designing a Polity

America's Constitution
in Theory and Practice

James W. Ceaser

ROWMAN & LITTLEFIELD PUBLISHERS, INC.
Lanham • Boulder • New York • Toronto • Plymouth, UK

Published by Rowman & Littlefield Publishers, Inc.
A wholly owned subsidiary of The Rowman & Littlefield Publishing Group, Inc.
4501 Forbes Boulevard, Suite 200, Lanham, Maryland 20706
http://www.rowmanlittlefield.com

Estover Road, Plymouth PL6 7PY, United Kingdom

British Library Cataloguing in Publication Information Available

Library of Congress Cataloging-in-Publication Data
Ceaser, James W.
  Designing a polity : America's Constitution in theory and practice / James W. Ceaser.
    p. cm.
  Includes index.
  ISBN 978-1-4422-0790-5 (cloth : alk. paper) — ISBN 978-1-4422-0792-9 (electronic)
  1. United States—Politics and government. 2. Constitutional history—United States. I. Title.
  JK31.C43 2011
  320.973—dc22   2010030132

∞™ The paper used in this publication meets the minimum requirements of American National Standard for Information Sciences—Permanence of Paper for Printed Library Materials, ANSI/NISO Z39.48-1992.

Printed in the United States of America
ACC LIBRARY SERVICES AUSTIN, TX

Contents

Part IV   The American Way of Life

Preface

The modern discipline of political science lacks a single, commonly accepted term to designate the central object of political inquiry. That object is known variously—the list is incomplete—as a "political order," "regime," "constitution" (with a small "c"), "form of government," "political system," and "polity." No matter which word is used, the concept in question refers to how a society is arranged or shaped with a view to who governs and how power is allocated, for what basic purposes, and to generate what general way of life. The nature of this concept comes most clearly into focus at moments of revolution or "regime change." It is then that the entire face of the political and social organization of a society may change, as occurred, for example, in the nations of Eastern Europe following the fall of communism in 1989. No one at such times questions that the regime is the most important fact about politics, if only because those acting inside political life regard it as such. Stakes rarely appear higher, and people are often prepared to risk all—to sacrifice their lives, their fortunes, and their sacred honor—either to save the old form or to institute a new one.

For the title of this work, I opted for the lesser-used "polity," in part because it avoids some of the distracting connotations of the other terms. "Polity," derived from the original Greek word *politeia*, places the core elements of the concept front and center. America's Founders used it in this sense when they spoke of the "ancient polity," the "feudal polity," or the "commercial polity," by which they had in mind not only the arrangement of political offices but also animating ideas, general objectives, and a way of life.

In this vein, I begin the study of America's polity by considering the nation's "foundation," meaning its first principle or guiding idea of right. The nation, it is usually said, was constituted by its embrace of an explicit foundation deriving from "nature"—"the Laws of Nature and Nature's God," in the words of the Declaration of Independence. Although some historians question whether so abstract a foundation ever meant much to the general public, there is no doubt that it was central to the thinking of the most important Founders. They emphasized this foundation together with, or over and against, previous foundations that sought the idea of right in the cherished beliefs of our (English) ancestors and their old customs and charters—for example, the Magna Carta. Since the time of the Founding, deliberate efforts have been undertaken to alter or change the foundation in nature and replace it with other principles. Some of the great theoretical-political struggles in American politics—in the approach to the Civil War and in the Progressive era—have dealt with exactly this question. The three chapters in this first section of the book explore the theme of foundations, asking about the character of the original foundation, how it has been challenged, what its current status is, and whether America still needs or is well served by having a foundation of any kind.

I turn in the next section to more conventional aspects of the polity that deal with constructing the actual framework of government. This task in America was the work originally of constitution writers, first at the state level and then at the national level. The book that explained and defended the Constitution, *The Federalist*, is almost universally considered to be the greatest American work of political science. One of its achievements was helping to revive political science as a body of knowledge that actively guided political life, above all in the task of constitution-making. The lead chapter in this section examines the character of this science as it is outlined in *The Federalist* and considers the authors' defense of political science against two rival sciences—natural history (or biology) and philosophy of history—that others were promoting at the time as a superior substitute for directing political life. The key to the other sciences was the explication of politics by pre- or nonpolitical factors, in the first case climate or racial characteristics and in the second an automatic process built into the flow of history. For the Founders, the core of political science was the polity and how it shaped political life. While the determination of which polity existed was influenced by many factors, it was also partly a matter of choice, a choice that could be informed by the "science of politics." *The Federalist* puts this proposition directly to the test by its own recourse to political science to explain the Constitution in the effort to help secure its ratification. The book put into practice what it preached.

The chapter on *The Federalist* is followed by two others that detail the Founders' application of political science to two of the most important challenges of constitution-building: controlling the "arts of popularity" or "demagoguery" in the pursuit and exercise of power—which the classical writers on politics, Plato and Aristotle, judged to be the single greatest threat to maintaining a popular form of government—and properly dividing and allocating powers among the governing institutions—which the greatest modern writers, Locke and Montesquieu, considered the key to establishing successful constitutional polities. Here the Founders show how political science operates: how it analyzes a problem and how it weighs and considers the solution. All three topics of the chapters in this section—the character and status of political science, the means by which political leaders solicit office and seek to persuade public opinion, and the division of power between the president and Congress—remain great issues of contemporary politics.

In the third section, I shift attention to the two major organizing bodies of thought of our own era: conservatism and liberalism. The focus is more on conservatism, for, as the name suggests, it is the body of thought that has been more directly concerned with the question of what should be conserved, which is a main theme of this book. Conservatism, like liberalism (only more so), is comprised of different strands that, at least for many of the intellectual leaders, come close to advocating distinct first principles or foundations. Despite their differences, the four strands of the modern conservative coalition—traditionalists, libertarians, neoconservatives, and religious conservatives—remain together, with all of their tensions, because of their greater opposition to modern liberalism. The chapter on the conservative movement is followed by a second one that concentrates on the political figure who was most responsible for reviving the fortunes of conservatism in modern American politics and who succeeded better than any politician before or after in skillfully holding together the four parts of the coalition: Ronald Reagan. Liberals and conservatives over the past three decades have in large measure been defined in the public mind—and have defined themselves—by how they have judged and evaluated Ronald Reagan. The reputation of Ronald Regan is such important political property that both sides have invested heavily in efforts to control his public image—conservatives to build it up, liberals to tear it down. The chapter on Ronald Reagan has as its special theme the struggle by a species of intellectual, called "legacy managers," to "construct" an historical reputation of a political leader and his public philosophy in order to serve their party's immediate political purposes. The efforts of these managers to spin a legacy for the sake of bolstering a political cause represent an application of the popular arts to the realm of ideas. It offers the latest twist in the age-old practice of intellectual demagoguery.

The final section, consisting of a single chapter, turns to the last aspect of a polity, which is the way of life generated by a society's political principles and governing institutions. A full exploration of this theme would obviously need to consider vast quantities of material from the disciplines of sociology, economics, and cultural studies and would require more than a single volume of its own. One good way to pose a synoptic view of the basic issues involved in this question is to present some of the sweeping generalizations about the American way of life that are the core of the body of thought known as "anti-Americanism." Anti-Americanism has evolved into a kind of full-scale ideology, arguably the only ideology of our day that has a worldwide reach. It has perfected the technique of boiling down everything about America to a series of formulae depicting American civilization in its most frightful or demeaning light. These formulae draw on an entire discourse about America that stretches back over two centuries, a discourse that was developed by high-level intellectuals and philosophers, sometimes for the purpose of building a symbol to fit into larger theories about the development of Western civilization. It is an old principle of pedagogy that one can often learn as much from examining what is distorted or false in an image as from trying to paint a true picture. Every American confronted with the astonishing images found in this discourse will likely feel compelled to begin thinking about the actual way of life in this country. For this reason, an inquiry into the intellectual origins of anti-Americanism serves as a fitting conclusion to the effort to better understand the American polity.

Much of this work traces the political development of the American polity, meaning the changes that have taken place since the Founding with respect to its three main elements—its foundation, its framework of government, and its way of life. The purpose of studying the American polity's development is not so much to explain its causes as to consider a central question that emerges, so to speak, from the fact of development itself. To an extent greater than most other nations, America's polity was fashioned by the conscious acts of political leaders in the "long decade" that ran from the outbreak of the Revolution in 1775 to the ratification of the Constitution in 1789. Because of this rational aspect of our Founding, one cannot embrace subsequent development just because it has taken place without, in effect, expressing indifference to something that was deliberate.

Development, of course, is of different kinds. Some of it is unplanned, resulting from events and the piecemeal and unorganized responses to them (of things just "growing," as is sometimes said), and some of it is a result of deliberate attempts to redesign huge parts of the polity (although these efforts often produce unintended consequences). Whatever the source of development, the main question concerns its relation to the character of the original design. Development can sometimes fulfill and improve on the original design, according even to the designers' own criteria, but it can also undermine and destroy it. If the original design is deemed worthy, as something to cherish, then only development that accords with it should be initially welcomed. It is understood by all that there will always be change—nothing in history remains frozen—so that conserving in any reasonable sense cannot mean keeping everything intact. A polity is not a museum, and much development is compatible with the spirit if not always the letter of the original design. As for development beyond or in conflict with the original design, it should bear a heavy burden of proof, equal at least to the level of scrutiny that the Founders employed in constructing the polity in the first place. To assist readers in making such judgments is the primary aim of this book.

Most of the chapters in this volume draw on essays that have been previously published in different venues, and I would like to acknowledge the University of Michigan Press, Johns Hopkins University Press, ISI Press, and the University of Kentucky Press for kindly granting permission to reprint. All of these essays have been revised to take account of subsequent developments and to fit with the content of other chapters in this book. My thanks also go to Rebecca Rine and Patricia Stevenson for their able assistance in editing the manuscript and to the editors of Rowman & Littlefield, especially Jon Sisk, for affording me the opportunity over the years to reach such a wide audience of readers.

I

POLITICAL
FOUNDATIONS

1

✛

The Doctrine of Political Nonfoundationalism

One of the greatest threats to America today comes from a theoretical doctrine that has been offered in all sincerity as the savior of liberal democracy. The doctrine appears under a number of different names—"neo-pragmatism," "anti-essentialism," and "public reason"—but it is perhaps most accurately described by the term "political nonfoundationalism." Advocates of this position, which include some of the most celebrated thinkers of our era, hold that liberal democracy is best maintained by renouncing public reliance on any kind of first principle (or "foundation") that claims to embody an objective truth—something, for example, like the "laws of nature" invoked in the Declaration of Independence. Political life should instead be neutral toward such principles or exclude them altogether. Adopting the doctrine of political nonfoundationalism, according to its proponents, will not require any constitutional amendments or new laws, except perhaps in the case of excluding references to religion. It will be sufficient to encourage a new way of thinking called "reasonableness" or "irony," which fortunately is already in the process of trickling down from the intelligentsia to the people.[1] Nonfoundationalism is the wave of the future, on the side of history. Once it succeeds in shaping the public mind, there will be no going back. People will regard the introduction of first principles into politics as retrograde (because all foundations are fictions), divisive (because not all persons share the same first principles), or undemocratic (because a truth is held to be self-subsisting and thus beyond our own making).

The doctrine of political nonfoundationalism has drawn its support from, among others, the philosophers Richard Rorty, Jacques Derrida,

3

John Rawls, Jürgen Habermas, and Gianni Vattimo. Each of these men created his own school of thought, known respectively as "anti-essentialism," "political deconstructionism," "the doctrine of public reason," "deliberative democracy," and "weak thinking" (*il pensiero debole*). By no means are these positions in perfect agreement on theoretical issues, with some defending a thoroughgoing skepticism and others insisting that certain positions can be objectively established.[2] Regardless of these differences, however, nonfoundationalists join together in seeking to erect a high wall of separation between foundations and politics.

To put a clearer face on the doctrine of political nonfoundationalism, it would mean an end in America to public discourse about the "transcendent law of nature and nature's god" that has been invoked since the Founding.[3] "Metaphysical ideas" or "comprehensive doctrines" of this sort should have no place in the public discussions of an advanced liberal democracy. They are, in a word, and the word is Richard Rorty's, "useless."[4] "A liberal society," he writes, "is badly served by an attempt to supply it with philosophical foundations. For the attempt to supply such foundations presupposes a natural order of topics which is prior to, and overrides the results of, encounters between old and new vocabularies."[5] A nation without foundations can move more easily from one language game to the next, free of the vexing constraints imposed by claims of truth. A nonfoundationalist public philosophy, Rorty continues, is a boon to liberal democracy; it "chimes . . . with the spirit of tolerance that has made constitutional democracy possible."[6] John Rawls, in the aftermath of his famous "turn" from metaphysical thinking in the 1980s, argued along much the same lines: "A constitutional regime does not require an agreement on a comprehensive doctrine: the basis of social unity lies elsewhere."[7]

The doctrine of nonfoundationalism would likewise exclude public acknowledgment of any sort of religious basis of America's political system and civilization. Shortly before his death, Jacques Derrida contrasted contemporary European public philosophy, characterized by its exclusion of religion from sanctioned public discourse, with the backward views found in America, where "despite the separation in principle between church and state, [there is] a fundamental biblical (and primarily Christian) reference in its official public discourse and the discourse of its political leaders."[8] Derrida lamented the fact that American currency still displays the motto "In God We Trust" and that presidents regularly invoke the Almighty in their public speeches. Just as Rorty had urged the abandonment of metaphysical foundations, so Derrida called on American political elites to dispense with anachronistic references to religion. Americans should follow the lead of advanced European nations in embracing nonfoundationalist secularism.

No observer can fail to remark on the highly political use to which the doctrine of nonfoundationalism was put in recent times, especially during the years of George W. Bush's presidency. Almost alone among the Western liberal democracies, America exhibits strong foundationalist elements in its political discourse. This is a source of American exceptionalism. Nonfoundationalists roundly criticized President Bush for relying on foundational concepts to help explain or justify certain positions in foreign policy. Jürgen Habermas, probably Europe's most important contemporary philosopher, has argued that the kind of "universalism" invoked by Americans is of no help in spreading liberal democracy. The alternative, embodied in contemporary European nonfoundationalist philosophy, is predicated "on an equality that demands . . . one step outside of one's own viewpoint in order to put it into relationship with the viewpoints adopted by another, which are to be regarded as equal."[9] Pierre Rosanvallon, one of France's most prominent social scientists, has taken Habermas's thinking a step further, distinguishing between America's "dogmatic [or foundational] universalism," which is "characterized by an intolerable arrogance that is only made more so by its spontaneous naïveté," and Europe's "pragmatic" or "experimental universalism," which makes no foundational claims.[10]

In studying these criticisms, it is hard to say to what degree they are based on an objection to tone or packaging (a repulsion, for example, to the forwardness many found in George W. Bush's demeanor), or on a genuine theoretical difference. President Bush's successor, Barack Obama, has sought to evade the problem by expressing regrets about America's "arrogance" and by largely avoiding explicit references to a foundation of natural right. But when the occasion calls for it, such as when he accepted the Nobel Peace Prize in 2009, he has been ready to invoke "aspirations that are universal" and refer to "the inherent rights and dignity of every individual."[11] Does nonfoundationalism allow for universalist formulations of this kind, just as long as one uses softer words like "aspirations" and "dignity" and avoids dreaded terms like "nature" or "truths"? Is nonfoundationalism in the end just a rhetorical pose? Given the prominence of the philosophers involved and the earnestness and insistence with which they have addressed the problem, it is impossible to believe that this could be the case. Nonfoundationalism may indeed be used or nuanced to decry one side (conservatives) while somehow supporting the other (liberals), but in the end it stands as a theoretical position that deserves to be taken at its word. Nonfoundationalism means that there should be no foundations, pure and simple.

The increasing advocacy of political nonfoundationalism in America, where it still represents a minority position, marks a dramatic departure from the past. The change can be appreciated by juxtaposing two statements. The first comes from a speech by Abraham Lincoln delivered in

New Haven, Connecticut, in 1860, in which he reflected on how a democratic system must operate: "Whenever this question [i.e., the question of
slavery] shall be settled, it must be settled on some philosophical basis.
No polity that does not rest upon some philosophical public opinion can
be permanently maintained."[12] Contrast this position with the nonfoundationalist claim of Richard Rorty: "The idea that liberal societies are
bound together by philosophical beliefs seems to me to be ludicrous."[13]
And he went on to insist that "philosophy is not that important for politics."[14] Of course, if philosophy were as inconsequential as Rorty claims, it
is difficult to understand why he wasted so much of his career inveighing
against it. His central point is this: a polity that rests upon a philosophical
foundation cannot long endure.

The doctrine of political nonfoundationalism in its full-blown form is a
product of the recent past. This assertion may sound strange in light of the
fact that so many (though not all) nonfoundationalists are skeptics, a type
of thinker as old as philosophy itself. But, to paraphrase Edmund Burke,
boldness in public was not formerly the character of skeptical thinkers.
Despite their doubts about truth, skeptics of old ordinarily agreed that a
political community needed a firm foundation. If no truths existed, it was
necessary to act publicly as if they did. Political nonfoundationalists, by
contrast, hold that advanced societies could easily do away with any kind
of foundation and would be much better off for doing so. Political nonfoundationalism accordingly goes much further than skepticism, although it has
been welcomed by many contemporary skeptics who now feel liberated to
say in public what their predecessors once only dared to utter in private.

It might seem overly academic to characterize a theoretical view as a
danger to America when there are more tangible threats, like the menace
of terrorism, all around us. But if Auguste Comte was correct when he
observed that "ideas govern the world, or throw it into chaos," then it is
proper to begin with intellectual doctrines.[15] The effects of ideas, though
less visible than the effects resulting from practical disasters, can be more
enduring. Such is the case in this debate. This is so even though nonfoundationalists do not call for a revolutionary change in the formal character
of liberal democracy, but support the seemingly "conservative" objective
of maintaining and improving it. Nonfoundationalists are no Jacobins.
Their moderate posture nevertheless hides a more radical project. The
American polity today is not defined entirely by its formal political model
(liberal democracy)—no polity ever is—but just as much by its animating
spirit. That spirit includes devotion to a version of natural right and reliance, at least indirectly, on faith. An American populace that embraced
the doctrine of political nonfoundationalism would therefore be a very
different kind of people than the one that exists today. A change in the
character of the people is exactly what nonfoundationalists seek.

THE CHARACTER OF FOUNDATIONAL
CONCEPTS IN AMERICA

To understand what is at stake in the current debate, nonfoundational-ism must be compared with what it aims to replace. Nonfoundationalists have deliberately obscured this understanding by trying to define the terms of the discussion to favor their position. As they frame the issue, their doctrine is a substitute for a parallel doctrine they call "founda-tionalism." But "foundationalism," to the extent that any such notion previously existed, was never considered a doctrine, but merely a for-mal property of any polity. What mattered was *which* foundation was adopted. Foundations could be as different (to refer to the situation that Lincoln confronted) as the claim of right made by the vice president of the Confederacy, Alexander Stephens, that "the negro is not the equal of the white man [and] that slavery—subordination to the superior race—is his natural and normal condition," and Lincoln's proposition that "no man is good enough to govern another man without the other's consent."[16] Viewed in this light, the important choice that confronts America today is not between nonfoundationalism and the recently coined abstraction of "foundationalism"; it is rather between nonfoundationalism and a particular foundation (or combination of foundations). In other words, it is almost a diversion to defend foundationalism per se.

The proper mode of theoretical inquiry is therefore to commence by considering the concept of a foundation and to examine its different types. A foundation is a first principle that explains or justifies a general political orientation; it is offered as an authoritative standard or a fundamental idea of right. A foundation may be proposed initially by a movement or party, but with the aim ultimately of becoming accepted or "authoritative" for the nation as a whole as the common ground or idea that holds a society to-gether. In John Stuart Mill's words, a foundation is "a recognised principle . . . which no one could either fear or hope to see shaken."[17]

A political foundation is not just an analytic concept invented by schol-ars to study politics from the outside, but a phenomenon of political life itself. Foundations are generally most apparent to political actors at criti-cal moments. The concept—even the term itself—was present in America at the outset, when it arose in a seminal debate of the Continental Con-gress in 1774 on the justification for the colonial policy toward Britain. As recorded by John Adams, the great question confronting Congress was the "*foundation* of right" that should be adopted: "We very deliberately considered and debated . . . whether we should recur to the law of nature" along with the historical foundations of the tradition, such as the "com-mon law" and "the charters" or "the rights of British subjects."[18] Partici-pants in the debate considered not only which foundational concept was true in theoretical terms, but also which one might best meet the political objective of effectively mobilizing people and binding them together. While political foundations are generally proclaimed publicly as "pure" truths, they have a certain function to perform in the political realm.

An example is worth a thousand arguments, so the listing of a few statements may help to illustrate what a foundation is:

Progress! Did you ever reflect that that word is almost a new one? No word comes more often or more naturally to the lips of modern man, as if the things it stands for were almost synonymous with life itself. . . . We think of the future, not the past, as the more glorious time in comparison with which the present is nothing. Progress, development—those are modern words. The modern idea is to leave the past and press onward to something new. (Woodrow Wilson, 1912)[19]

We had no occasion to search into musty records, to hunt up royal parchments, or to investigate the laws and institutions of a semi-barbarous ancestry. We appealed to those of nature, and found them engraved in our hearts. (Thomas Jefferson, 1824)[20]

It concerneth New England always to remember that they are originally a plantation religious, not a plantation of trade. The profession of the purity of doctrine, worship and discipline is written upon her forehead. . . . [W]orldly gain was not the end and design of the people of New England but religion. (John Higginson, 1663)[21]

These examples of particular foundations allow the analyst to consider, in the abstract, the different general sources from which they derive. These can be grouped into three general types, according to whether the claim they raise is based on History, nature, or faith. Each source needs to be further specified.

1

A foundation in History offers ultimate justification by reference to what takes place in the flow of time. Something is said to be right or good because it conforms to the past and our tradition, which is deemed almost sacred or unassailable. This view may be called "Customary History." Alternatively, something is known to be right because it accords with the direction in which the historical process as a whole is going, which can be downward (decline) or, as has more usually been the case, upward (progress). This view is known as "Philosophy of History." The use of History in this grandiose sense to supply a standard of right should be distinguished from "ordinary" history (with a small *h*) of the sort we usually encounter—what Winston Churchill once defined, in one of his more cheerful moods, as "mainly the record of the crimes, follies and miseries of mankind."[22] History in this sense recounts and analyzes the past, but it makes no pretense of supplying the grounds for making ultimate judgments.

In America, Customary History played the central role in the early stages leading up to the break with Britain, until it was largely replaced on the eve of the Revolution by an appeal to nature. The particular form of Customary History derived its idea of right from the ancient sources of the tradition—from the great British charters such as the Magna Carta, or, still further back, from the Gothic constitution originating in the "native wilds and woods in the north of Europe."[23] This idea stressed the individual's rights and the limited role of government. History was reintroduced as a major foundation in the 1830s. It appeared in two forms. The Whig Party embraced Customary History, while Democrats adopted Philosophy of History. The Whigs, especially those in New England, sought to build an American tradition that relied heavily on the Puritan Fathers, whose merits were extolled in an attempt to create a doctrine of "two foundings," one at Plymouth and the other in Philadelphia. This turn to Customary History was undertaken in part under the influence of the conservative reaction in Europe to the French Revolution, where thinkers beginning with Edmund Burke worried about the radical consequences flowing from appeals to abstract philosophical principles. Some Whigs saw similar dangers in the excesses of Jacksonian democracy. Unlike European conservatives, however, American Whigs did not seek to replace natural right (which, after all, was central to America's tradition), but instead to add History to it in a new synthesis. In addition to curbing Jacksonianism, the synthesis would promote some of the virtues that Whigs thought were being shunted aside in the unfolding of various strands of "Lockean" thought. [24]

The Democrats turned to Philosophy of History to supplement the standard of nature. They connected universal progress to American democracy and to its expansion (Manifest Destiny). One of the best expressions of this view is found in the writings of the historian George Bancroft, who was also a prominent Democratic advisor and speechwriter. A student of Hegel who sought to democratize the Hegelian system, Bancroft famously wrote, "The voice of the people is the voice of pure Reason." He continued, "Everything is in motion for the better. The last system of philosophy is always the best. . . . The last political state of the world likewise is ever more excellent than the old."[25] Each political party maintained an uneasy mix of the two foundations of History and nature until the 1850s, when History acquired the upper hand in both parties. What remained of the Whig Party appealed to tradition, while northern Democrats, following Stephen Douglas, grounded the party in their idea of progress. A defense of natural right was then taken up by a new party, the Republicans, and given classic voice by its leader Abraham Lincoln.

There is no mystery about the basic foundational principle that dominated the Progressive Era. Progressivism, as its etymological root ("progress") indicates, subscribed to Philosophy of History. Progressives understood progress to be not merely a hope or sustaining faith, but an objective fact discernible through the study of history. They drew eclectically on different statements of this idea, taking pieces from German idealistic philosophy (mostly from Hegel), from adaptations of Charles Darwin's evolutionary theory, and, most important, from the positivist approach of Comte and Condorcet. It was Condorcet, the good friend of Jefferson, who provided the classic definition of Philosophy of History as "a science that can foresee the progress of humankind, direct it, and accelerate it."[26] This understanding became one of the bases of Progressivism. History, in this view, moved largely on its own. Its direction was fixed, but those conscious of its laws were needed to help superintend its movement. Otherwise, humankind could fall back. The task of directing progress now fell to the pragmatic philosophers and social scientists. A new era of governance that relied on the assistance of these experts, operating beyond all partisanship, was in the offing.

2

A foundation in nature provides justification by reference to something in the structure of reality as it can be accessed by reason. Nature designates a rational, that is, a scientific or philosophical, approach that humans can grasp without the direct need of divine revelation. Different understandings of science as applied to politics may therefore produce alternative conceptions of nature. Think, for example, of the contrast between accounts that come from current theories of sociobiology, with its laws of movement and adaptation based on the machinations of the little selfish gene, and the account of the "laws of nature" invoked above by the Founders, which supplied a permanent standard of right.

The American republic was the first to bring the concept of nature down from the realm of theory and introduce it into the political world as the functioning foundation of a large nation. The turn from History to nature marked a revolution in the intellectual world comparable in importance to the political revolution that commenced at Lexington and Concord. Not myth, mystery, or History, but philosophy or science—the two terms were then synonyms—could serve, perhaps in a simplified version, as a public foundational concept. There could be "public philosophy." The "laws of nature" were taken by the Founders to be derivations from rational inquiry. For some of them, this investigation relied on forms of Christian rationalism ("natural law"), while for others it derived from a new science that combined inquiry into human nature ("psychology") with rational political analysis. The science that was derived from this combination became the basis for articulating the idea of natural rights or the rights of man.

Because the Founders' general version of natural right was solemnly promulgated in official public documents, it earned a "privileged" position in America and was often identified as *the* view of nature. Those holding contrary views of nature therefore had to consider whether to present their position as an alternative account of nature, or to attack the standard of nature outright. Both strategies have been followed. An early challenge to the Founders' view of nature drew on the science of ethnology (or "natural history") in support of a position of racial hierarchy. Proponents of this science promoted their position as the truly natural one—that is, based on science—while dismissing the Founders' view as nonempirical. Following the Civil War, the favored science became evolutionary biology ("Darwinism"). Darwinists likewise offered a version of a natural standard of right (or of necessity). They stressed the notion of struggle, which was observed first in the lower species. In the words of the sociologist William Graham Sumner, "The social order is fixed by laws of nature precisely analogous to those of the physical order . . . the law of the survival of the fittest was not made by man and cannot be abrogated by man."[27]

Progressive theorists launched the most sustained attack on the foundation of natural right and in some cases embraced the tactic of denying the very idea of a natural standard. According to John Dewey, natural right was a concept "located in the clouds . . . whose falsity may easily be demonstrated both philosophically and historically."[28] Criticism of the idea of permanency in nature, especially in human nature, was needed to sustain the most robust notion of progress, for the idea of an unchangeable human nature set limits to the possibilities of development. Dewey took the further step, so important for future philosophical development, of claiming that *any* philosophical proposition that implied a theoretical hierarchy or an idea of right is supportive of authoritarian political rule, because it proclaims a standard of right outside of what the people decide. A view that is "committed to a notion that inherently some realities are superior to others, are better than others . . . inevitably works on behalf of a regime of authority, for it is only right that the superior should lord it over the inferior."[29] For Dewey, true democracy is foundationless. Implicit in this view is a "metaphysical" position of its own. Only if nature is understood as matter in motion possessing no natural hierarchy is democracy safe.

3

A final source for a foundation derives from faith. For the earliest Puritan communities, the "plantation[s] religious" were established "for the Glory of God and Advancement of the Christian Faith." Foundations of faith in the West are rooted chiefly in the Bible and Christian doctrine. They appear in two basic forms: either as commands or deductions that state a permanent law or teaching, or as interpretations of the course of God's plan for redeeming the world—that is, Providence. As an example of the first, the faithful in the prerevolutionary period and Founding era subscribed overwhelmingly to the view that modern scholars label "religious republicanism."[30] Proponents of this view held that the Bible clearly taught the superiority of republican government and enjoined believers to establish civil liberty as a religious obligation. In Benjamin Rush's words, "Republican forms of government are the best repositories of the Gospel."[31] As an example of the second, adherents of the "Social Gospel" movement of the late nineteenth century sought to orient American politics by what they understood as God's plan to establish his Kingdom on this earth. For many in this movement, such as the economist Richard Ely, the Kingdom was to be realized by progressive-style programs: "God works through the State in carrying out his purposes more universally than through any other institution."[32]

By the time of the American Founding, the faithful had largely relinquished claims to make a religious idea serve as the primary foundation for political life. This position was based partly on religious grounds—that it was not the proper function of religion to run political life—and partly on the realization that revelation is something to which all do not have access. Foundations deriving from faith became part of a "second constitution" that operated in the culture. These foundations were invoked to support (or sometimes almost to merge with) other foundations, beginning with the phrase in the Declaration of "the laws of nature and nature's God." Religious foundations have received public recognition and acknowledgment in the platforms of parties, the campaign speeches of candidates, and in the addresses and official pronouncements of American presidents.

FOUNDATIONS IN THE MODERN ERA

The authority of America's major foundational ideas came under challenge beginning in the early twentieth century. In a first phase, just noted, progressive intellectuals guided by a positivist spirit rejected the concept of natural right as pure "metaphysics" (in the pejorative sense). They continued, however, to embrace the idea of progress, not as a theoretical supposition, but as a fact established by the science of history. Progress was understood to consist chiefly of economic development, technological advancement, greater equality, and the spread of liberal democracy.

In a second phase, which began in the 1930s, the idea of progress itself came under assault as being itself a "metaphysical" proposition. Confidence in the idea of progress was shaken on the plane of politics by the emergence of Fascism and Communism, which directly challenged liberal democracy. It was by no means evident in the 1930s, as had been thought earlier in the century, that liberal democracy represented the wave of the future. On a theoretical plane, the idea of progress was challenged by the arrival in America of the powerful nexus of ideas labeled "historicism." Historicism held that there was no permanent standard for making judgments; instead, all values derived from the shifting and contingent views that held sway in the era in which one lived. The idea of progress, only recently considered to be an objective truth, was now said to be merely an opinion of the age. The historian Charles Beard, who began the century as a progressive, shifted ground in his presidential address to the American Historical Association in 1933, titled, significantly, "Written History as an Act of Faith." Beard declared the notion of a "science of history embracing the fullness of history" to be an "illusion." Each era—each historian within each era—had to choose a frame of reference, which ultimately was a "subjective decision."[33] Like many other American intellectuals, Beard opted for progress, but on the basis of nothing more than "an act of faith."

In a well-known account of the development of Western thought in the twentieth century, the French philosopher Francois Lyotard in 1979 traced the emergence of what he called "the postmodern condition." Postmodernity is an intellectual situation in which philosophy renders untenable belief in any grand "metanarrative" or permanent truth.[34] Thus, for Lyotard, Western thought had entered a postfoundational age. Lyotard's analysis bore certain similarities to a set of earlier assessments made in the United States in the 1950s and 1960s by Leo Strauss and Walter Lippmann. Besides describing this "condition," which they labeled "historicism," these thinkers did not hesitate to diagnose it as a "crisis" that would have dire consequences for liberal democracy in general and for American liberal democracy in particular. The abstract philosophical crisis translated on the political level into a crisis of foundations. In Strauss's words, "a society which was accustomed to understand itself in terms of a universal purpose cannot lose faith in that purpose without becoming completely bewildered."[35] In the immediate context of their day, both men worried whether America could sustain its efforts for liberal democracy in the struggle against an ideology (Communism) that was unscrupulous in its means and that, for the moment, professed greater surety about its future.

There have been two major theoretical responses in American politics to this condition of postmodernity: an effort to revive natural right and an attempt to embrace the doctrine of political nonfoundationalism. The first can be traced back in large part to the writings of Strauss and Lippmann.[36] Despite their analysis of the powerful trends in modern thought that produced historicism, neither thinker judged it to be a permanent condition or an unalterable fate. Time and philosophy did not for them stop in the middle of the twentieth century. Strauss made an appeal to reopen the theoretical question of natural right, and he suggested that the very crisis into which the West had fallen had the salutary effect of prompting such an inquiry. Lippmann went further and, perhaps prematurely, began to sketch his idea of "the public philosophy," which was a kind of program to implement natural law. Since the 1970s, relatively small but important parts of the American intellectual community have sought to recover the underpinnings of natural right thinking from the classical philosophers, the scholastic natural law theorists, and the American Founders. This investigation has achieved the status of a full-scale theoretical project that has lent support to a reintroduction of the idea of natural right in American political life. The intellectual situation in America today accordingly bears only partial resemblance to the one that Strauss and Lippmann described a half-century ago. The change has been in large part a result of their efforts.

The second response has been the doctrine of political nonfoundationalism, many proponents of which stress its direct connection to the condition of postmodernity. After all, if no theoretical foundations are available, then political nonfoundationalism would seem to be the best fit with the times in which we live. It would convey a false impression, however, to suggest that nonfoundationalists all greeted postmodernity in a spirit of glum resignation, as a condition that contemporary man and woman had reluctantly to bear. Just the contrary, in fact, has often been the case. Nonfoundationalists have regarded postmodernity as a great liberating moment, a gift of fate that they celebrated in a mood reminiscent of one famously described by William Wordsworth: "Bliss was it in that dawn to be alive / But to be young was very heaven!" Postmodernity has placed the advanced portion of humanity in a much better position both politically and morally—politically because nonfoundationalism provides the first theoretical basis for the establishment of full and genuine democracy, and morally because people now face the world as it really is, without the illusions once supplied by philosophical and religious foundations. Despite their formal contention that all "vocabularies" are relative to the age in which one happens to live, none any better than another, many postmodernists seem to think that we live in a "privileged" time when our vocabulary provides access to the world as it really is.

The striking fact is, then, that nonfoundationalists are heavily invested in the condition of postmodernity, so much so that they cannot seem to contemplate ever letting it go. It is Richard Rorty's "hunch" that "Western social and political thought may have had the last conceptual revolution it needs."[37] Although nonfoundationalists formally reject Philosophy of History as a meta-narrative, many seem very close to having embraced something like it in fact. History culminates in nonfoundationalism.[38] Only this attitude can explain the nonfoundationalists' unwillingness to entertain the possibility of a new period of thought—that is, a *post*-postmodern era. As to what has been happening recently in America, with the widespread return to discussion of foundational ideas, many treat it as a weird aberration, a temporary return to "fundamentalism," that cannot represent a genuine theoretical development. Still, the growing uneasiness of many nonfoundationalists about where history is going is all too evident, as seen by the rising chorus of their harsh attacks on "foundationalism." If the horse is really dying, why keep flogging it so unmercifully?

There has been a parallel development in America to the revival of natural right. It is a renewal in some quarters of religious faith. This change has, if anything, been even more unexpected than the shift that has taken place in philosophy. At roughly the same time as the emergence of the idea of historicism in the West, when philosophical foundations were counted as moribund, religion was also declared to be entering into its last stage. Max Weber's famous pronouncement of a growing "disenchantment of the world" in his *Protestant Ethic and the Spirit of Capitalism* (1904) helped give birth to the thesis of secularization, which held that religion in the West was fated to lose its influence over the sphere of public life and to begin to die out altogether. For years, all evidence confirmed the veracity of this thesis, and the expected trends have continued in most Western democracies. But in the United States, there has been a reaction in the form of a religious movement in politics, which formed to contest the political arm of the secularist cause. It has sought to win a place for religious faith inside public life and has promoted a religious foundation as a supporting element to the other foundations. America once again stands out as the exceptional case among the Western democracies.

POLITICAL NONFOUNDATIONALISM
AND MODERN AMERICAN POLITICS

If examined strictly on the basis of its formal properties, there is no reason why nonfoundationalism should be on one side of the political spectrum in America today. Yet as matters now stand, most nonfoundationalists are found on the Left. A partial explanation is that most of those who stress foundations today are clustered on the Right, which has induced nonfoundationalists to join the other side. The reverse may be equally as true. Either way, it appears today that the theoretical dispute about foundations, independent of all other causes, has contributed to the political division among elites in America.

It is too simplistic, however, to think that the theoretical debate perfectly correlates with the political division or that it is the only cause. While the Right is home to most of those who espouse foundations, it contains elements that approach a kind of nonfoundationalism, although usually not in name. Of all of the foundational concepts mentioned earlier, Customary History, which has a significant constituency among conservatives today in the form of traditionalism, is clearly the "weakest" kind of foundation. Customary History, which grew up in part after the French Revolution to counter explicit philosophical foundations, celebrates the particular, that is, our tradition and our History, against the universal. This position is only one small step from the conclusion that if we have "our" tradition that is right for us, everyone else has "their" tradition that is right for them. There is no standard higher than traditions or cultures. For this reason, Customary History in the nineteenth century may be said to have contributed to the rise of historicism and thus indirectly to postmodernism. Still, for all this, Customary History is not the same as nonfoundationalism. Conservatives revere tradition and often mix it with other foundations. Finally, a part of the Right in America today takes its bearings from neoclassical economics, which, as Francis Fukuyama has argued, "is basically a kind of anti-foundationalism. The whole tradition that begins with Alfred Marshall's marginalism takes individual preferences as essentially sovereign; the job of the government is not to shape individual preferences, it's simply to aggregate them."[39]

The situation on the Left is interesting, although in a different way. Given that so many on the intellectual Left today embrace some form of nonfoundationalism, it has become almost the public face of the Left. At the same time, as all acknowledge, there is no dearth of expression of broad values and ideals on the Left, such as social justice, human dignity, and humanitarianism. And every so often, when the situation is fitting, the political leaders of the Left will speak of "aspirations that are universal" or "universal values," though without dwelling on where they come from. The result is that the Left today is characterized by the curious combination of a scrupulous denial of foundations together with a persistent affirmation of values, a position that might best be described as "idealistic nonfoundationalism." Whether the Leftist program is salable to a broad public on this basis has concerned some nonfoundationalists.

They surmise that American opinion, at this point, is not ready for the real medicine, as Americans cling stubbornly to their foundations. To help rally the faithful to the political cause, Richard Rorty has recommended the mild opium of "spinning . . . narratives of social hope" that will "tell a story about how things get better."[40] This task, to be performed by novelists, journalists, and artists, will supply the needed solidarity for a liberal democratic people. It is to be supplemented by a sentimental education that cultivates compassion or the "recognition of a common susceptibility to humiliation [as] the only social bond that is needed."[41]

NONFOUNDATIONALISM: AN ASSESSMENT

Political nonfoundationalism has been widely accepted by the intellectual class in America, which now considers it to be virtually a self-evident truth. Nonfoundationalism appeals to this class's belief in the dogma of theoretical relativism while offering simultaneous assurances that nothing in this position endangers the promotion of the same class's cherished progressive values. Although the support for this doctrine by intellectuals is impressive, the intelligentsia has been known on occasion to err, as when it prostrated itself for so long before the idol of Marxist ideology. The only honest way to proceed is to consider the doctrine of political nonfoundationalism on its own merits, testing the strength of the arguments and weighing its likely consequences. By these criteria, there are a number of reasons to doubt the wisdom of embracing this new product of modern philosophy.

First, the doctrine rests on a simplistic binary schema that falsely collapses all thought into the categories of foundationalism and nonfoundationalism. All ideas labeled "foundationalist," which include almost all first principles ever conceived before the birth of John Dewey or John Rawls, are treated as part of a supposed class of things that is said to share certain important properties. This step allows nonfoundationalists to impute qualities of the most dangerous or odious of foundations to the most reasonable of them. Thus, the concept of natural right and the Marxist idea of History, though obviously not the same thing, are grouped together as instances of "foundationalism"; they therefore participate in the same sin of intellectual rigidity, preempting "encounters between old and new vocabularies" and working "on behalf of a regime of authority." By this technique, a purely academic distinction between foundationalism and nonfoundationalism is used to obscure the real political distinction between free societies and regimes of authority.

And what of the category of nonfoundationalism? Proponents of this position almost never speak of the variety of its possible political manifestations, but identify it with the single form of a liberal democratic doctrine while arguing that "foundationalism" has supported authoritarian systems. But what is good for the goose should be good for the gander. Nonfoundationalist theory has served as a nursery for authoritarian systems. The list of philosophers who have embraced theoretical nonfoundationalism includes such figures as Martin Heidegger, Ernst Jünger, and Michel Foucault, all of whom favored nonliberal positions, whether of the Right or the Left. While the premises of nonfoundationalism may "chime with the spirit of tolerance" for thinkers today, they have often tolled for tyranny in the past.

None of this is meant to call into question the intentions of contemporary proponents of nonfoundationalism, who are generally tolerant of others' views (except insofar as they support foundations). The real issue, however, is not the sincerity of nonfoundationalist thinkers, but whether their doctrine is sustainable and supportive of liberal democracy. Nonfoundationalism creates a vacuum in the public realm with regard to the truth of first principles. It claims, with no experience to prove it, that a polity of this kind will be stable. But is not the circumstance of an empty public square the most fertile soil in which holistic political religions and ideologies are most likely to take hold? Did not the destruction of real religion among the elites in France in the eighteenth century prepare the way for the creation of the political religion of the Revolution, in much the same fashion as the promotion of nihilism in the early part of the twentieth century helped prepare the way for Fascism and Communism?

Second, political nonfoundationalism trades on false hopes to win adherents. The binary distinction demarcates not only two categories of thought, but also, seductively, two epochs of history. Political nonfoundationalists maintain that, for centuries, the nations of the West suffered under a politics plagued by continuous conflicts among incompatible foundations. Now, with the emergence of nonfoundationalism, the West is ready to enter a new era, likely to be the final one, in which a new kind of logic will prevail. Political life will be delivered from its past woes. The essentialist will lie down with the historicist; neither will there be strife anymore. Despite the nonfoundationalist's denials of History, this extravagant "narrative of hope" would seem to have little to separate it from what used to be called Philosophy of History.

Third, the doctrine of political nonfoundationalism has been constructed from abstract philosophical propositions, not from actual inquiry into political life. The source of theorizing about "essentialism" and "foundationalism" originally had nothing to do with politics, but derived from pure philosophy and the interpretation of literary texts. The transfer of these categories to politics came as an afterthought. Instances can certainly be cited in which the application of a concept from another field to politics has produced an intellectual payoff—the biological notion of organic development might be one such example—but this result has always required that the concept in question prove its utility as a tool of real political analysis. This test has not been met in this case—far from it. Pages, nay, volumes, have been written, filled with airy generalizations about the dangers of foundationalism. But which thinkers have taken the trouble to investigate the record of foundations in order to assess how they have performed in American history? Certainly not John Rawls, who is systematic to the point of painfulness about everything except the exploration of the actual performance of foundations. A quick look, for example, at the index of his *Political Liberalism* shows that he has discussed "Adams" once, but it is a contemporary academic, Robert Adams, not John. Thomas Jefferson appears twice, once in a footnote. Lincoln makes only a cameo appearance. Nor was Richard Rorty ever especially well known for the depth of his historical inquiries. His brief historical forays exhibited all of the charming casualness of invented narratives. And why not, for, as he notes, "there is no nonmythological . . . way of telling a country's story. . . . Nobody knows what it would be like to try to be objective when attempting to decide what one's country really is, what its history really means."[42]

If the concern of nonfoundationalists is with the performance of political foundations, they should have found it instructive to examine the role played in America by the foundation of the "law of nature" supported by an invocation of faith. No doubt such an examination would have pointed to certain difficulties, enough so that many at different points made attempts to supplement or alter this synthesis. But would this investigation demonstrate, as nonfoundationalists would have us think, that the doctrine of nature and nature's God has on balance thwarted liberal democratic development? Was this foundation an impediment to the Revolution in the 1770s, to the fight against slavery in the 1860s, to the struggle for civil rights in the 1960s, or to the efforts in Eastern Europe to overthrow Communist tyranny in the 1980s? Where, exactly, is the evidence of the millions who have suffered under its iron boot? It is a well-regarded counsel of prudence that no system should be overthrown for "light and transient causes," and certainly not until there is an alternative that offers the prospect of a better result. Have nonfoundationalists followed this counsel, or for that matter even considered it?

If a real examination of the record has been lacking, one must nevertheless concede the existence of a highly imaginative "discourse" adamant in its opposition to natural right. In one typical and prominent version, it is argued that all essentialist thought, including the natural rights thinking of the American founders, creates a "logic of identity" that "denies or represses difference."[43] Foundationalism has thus been linked over the past quarter-century with opposition to progressive positions on issues of race and gender. As Shelby Steele has explained, "America was a foundational nation, but we were hypocritical. . . . Many people argued that foundational principles were really a pretext for evil, out of which came this darker evil—the West—that dominated the world and oppressed people." To the rescue comes the saving doctrine of nonfoundationalism, whose proponents claim the moral high ground. In Steele's words, "They're saying, we're not partaking of that hypocrisy and we've got new things like diversity and tolerance that don't have any foundational basis and aren't grounded in principle. They're just grounded in wonderfulness."[44]

Fourth, the doctrine of political nonfoundationalism is a cover for a (sub)regime change that seeks to alter the character of the American people. When speaking in a pragmatic vein, proponents of nonfoundationalism often claim to rest their case on the political ground that their doctrine is best for promoting liberal democracy. Nonfoundationalists, by this argument, have nothing against religion or natural right per se; it is just that these foundations turn out to be unhealthy for liberal democracy. But even the most superficial acquaintance with the thought of some of the leading nonfoundationalists reveals the disingenuousness of this argument. It comes far closer to the mark to say that nonfoundationalists believe in the "moral" superiority of nonfoundationalism and that their political argument is advanced for the sake of promoting their moral positions. They lavish praise on the "ironic" or "reasonable" personality, while dismissing the rigid or dogmatic one, and they generally make no secret of their support for secularism over the promotion of religion.

Even if it were the case, however, that the doctrine of nonfoundationalism promoted greater safety for liberal democracy, there might be sound reason to reject it. The reason why many in America have favored a liberal democratic system is not merely to cultivate "pure" liberal democracy. Liberal democracy as a political form is not the full American regime. Liberalism supplies the "floor" of the system, meaning its fundamental political premises and the rules that must not be violated. What a people choose to construct above that floor, so long as it is not inconsistent with the principles of liberalism, can rightly be considered an integral part of the full polity. Americans have sought to maintain the recognition of faith, supported in forms of public discourse and by incidental forms of public acknowledgment, as a central element of the political order. Nonfoundationalism, which demands public neutrality concerning faith and nonbelief, aims at a profound alteration of the character of the polity.

Finally, the doctrine of political nonfoundationalism would promote listlessness in the American public. Without a foundational principle—without the moral energy that derives from efforts to establish foundational principles—a community ceases to exist in a deep or meaningful sense, and without this energy, a nation will be unable to extract the added measure of devotion and resolve from its members that is needed to undertake important projects and to assure its survival. People will sacrifice for a truth, but in what measure will they do so for a "narrative"? Embracing a public philosophy of nonfoundationalism would lead to an evacuation of spiritedness and a denial of any notion of exceptionalism. Nonfoundationalists will doubtless reply that many nations today are happily dispensing with foundations while blazing new paths to a higher form of liberal democracy. But even if this assessment should prove correct, which is by no means clear, it would hardly be dispositive for the United States. Fate sometimes assigns different roles to different nations. Western civilization today confronts two great challenges: saving itself from a new barbarism that aims to destroy it and sustaining the faith that helped to give it birth. As the world's leading power, the United States has responsibilities in meeting these challenges that are of a different kind than those faced by countries like Luxembourg or Canada or France.

If the seductive doctrine of nonfoundationalism is resisted, the reward will come in the form of averting an enormous danger. It is in such terms that victories in politics are often counted. The benefit will nonetheless be real: it will allow America to return to the perennial challenge of seeking foundational remedies to the problems most incident to foundational thinking.

2

+

Political Foundations in Tocqueville's *Democracy in America*

Alexis de Tocqueville was one of the first thinkers in the nineteenth century to challenge the prevailing historical account of the American Founding. According to that account, which was well on the way to becoming solidified when Tocqueville visited the United States in 1831, America's polity or regime was established in the period that began with the Revolutionary War and ended with the ratification of the Constitution. The principal leaders during this time, referred to as "Founders" or "Fathers," were celebrated for having decisively shaped the character of America's way of life. An illustration of this position can be found in Timothy Pitkin's widely read *A Political and Civil History of the United States*, published in 1828. Pitkin begins by promising "a more intimate knowledge and recollection of the difficulties which their political fathers had to overcome," so that his readers might better appreciate the "great charter of their union, as their best and only security against domestic discord and foreign force."[1]

Tocqueville, by contrast, presents an account of the Founding that identifies not one but *two* formative moments. The New England–Puritan tradition, in his view, was every bit as consequential in constituting America as the Founding of 1775–1789. From the Puritan colonies came "the two or three principal ideas [that] were combined [and that] today form the bases of the social theory of the United States." New England's "civilization"—Tocqueville helped introduce this sense of the term to America—was like one of those "fires" set on a high slope whose light "still tinge[s] the furthest reaches of the horizon."[2]

These two interpretations of America's origins are strikingly different. Although it is possible to imagine how Tocqueville might have brought them more closely together, perhaps by refining the meaning of the concept of "founding," he made no effort to do so. Without either acknowledging or criticizing the prevailing view, Tocqueville proceeded simply to sketch his own narrative, with the evident aim of having it modify or replace the existing one. His version will be referred to here as the "two-founding thesis."[3]

Tocqueville introduced the two-founding thesis near the beginning of *Democracy in America*, in a chapter titled "On the Point of Departure and Its Importance for the Future of the Anglo-Americans," which reads as if it is providing a straightforward *historical* explanation of how America developed. Yet further analysis reveals that something else, something more important than historical explanation, was also at stake. Tocqueville, it will be argued, introduced the two-founding thesis in order to promote a new *theoretical* position for the proper kind of political foundation for modern liberal democratic government. The prevailing view at the time, derived from the entire tradition of Enlightenment thought, was that a political foundation should rest on a public doctrine of philosophy, such as natural law theory. Foundations of this kind, Tocqueville thought, endangered the cause of liberty. His alternative was a foundation based not on philosophy, but on "customary history."[4] The two-founding thesis was Tocqueville's version of customary history crafted specifically for America. In offering this foundation, Tocqueville was furthering a great project inaugurated by his chief mentor, Montesquieu, and designed to alter the way in which political philosophy entered into and influenced political life.

The exploration of this argument requires treating a number of interlocking issues. I begin by identifying the major theoretical implications that flow from adopting the two-founding thesis and presenting evidence for the claim that Tocqueville intentionally favored this position in order to promote a new political foundation. After defining—with help from Tocqueville's thought—the analytical concept of a political foundation, I turn next to a discussion of the original theoretical project for customary history as sketched by Montesquieu in his *The Spirit of the Laws*. Finally, I examine Tocqueville's adaptation of Montesquieu's theory to America, concluding with a few comments intended to help assess Tocqueville's position on foundations.

THE THEORETICAL PREMISES OF
THE TWO-FOUNDING THESIS

The two-founding thesis is linked to a number of arguments or conclusions that become evident when considered against the backdrop of the prevailing view of a single founding. Five points are worth mentioning.

First, the idea of two founding moments has the inevitable effect of diminishing the Founders' status, for the simple reason that they are no longer *the* Founders. To be sure, Tocqueville speaks of the men of 1775–1789 with great admiration, praising them for both their "patriotism" in coming to the nation's aid at a critical moment and for their "courage" in instructing the public, somewhat against its inclinations, about how to protect and maintain freedom.[5] His comments nevertheless display a certain reserve concerning the magnitude of their accomplishment. He ascribes the victory in the Revolutionary War more to America's "[geographical] position than to the valor of its armies or the patriotism of its citizens"; he praises the Convention for including "the finest minds and noblest characters that had ever appeared *in the New World*"; and he describes *The Federalist* as a "fine book . . . though special to America."[6] These judgments hardly seem calculated to create an aura of greatness around the Founders. Tocqueville never ranks them with the famous lawgivers of antiquity, such as Lycurgus or Numa, which is a comparison that the Founders themselves invited.[7] Indeed, Tocqueville never directly refers to them as "Founders," reserving that term for New England's leaders ("first founders").[8]

Second, the two-founding thesis fits with Tocqueville's cultural or sociological approach that considers "mores," which derive mostly from inherited dispositions and customs, to be more important in the formation of a regime than constitutional forms and arrangements.[9] This approach, too, has the effect of reducing the Founders' status by assigning more weight to tradition—in this case, to the practices deriving from the New England colonies—than to the Constitution. Tocqueville directly addresses his readers to tell them that they will "find in the present chapter [on the Point of Departure] the seed [*germe*] of what is to follow and the key to almost the whole work."[10] The two-founding thesis thus also reverses an implicit premise of the standard historical account that divides American history into the colonial and modern eras, an account that has the effect of relegating the colonial period to a kind of prehistory. For Tocqueville, by contrast, colonial history is every bit as important as what has occurred since the Revolution. His presentation likewise directs attention away from the Founders' handiwork—the Constitution—to the practices within the states: "The great political principles that govern American society today were born and developed in the *state* . . . it is therefore the state that one must know to have the key to all the rest."[11]

Third, and following directly from the last point, the two-founding thesis diminishes the importance of the doctrine of natural rights, what *The Federalist* refers to as the "transcendent law of nature and nature's god."[12] This doctrine was the theoretical basis that the Founders adopted to justify the Revolution and supply the criteria for the fundamental ends of legitimate government. In Tocqueville's account, the preexisting mores, not this foundation, were the key to the development of republican government in America.

Fourth, the two-founding thesis depreciates the understanding of founding as a conscious act of "making" or construction that draws on models conceived by reason. "Making" according to reason best expresses what was usually meant in the eighteenth century by the term "natural," as in establishing a government in accord with natural law. Tocqueville introduced another understanding of the natural based on the notion of organic development, as seen in his account of the growth of a nation: "Peoples always feel the effects of their origins. The circumstances that accompanied their birth and served to develop them influence the entire course of the rest of their lives"; these origins are the "first cause" of a people's "prejudices, habits [and] dominant passions," and comprise a "national character" that continues to evolve partly on its own.[13]

Present-day political theorists often stress the connection between the idea of organic development and reactionary thinkers, such as Joseph de Maistre, who mistrusted the use of science or reason in political affairs.[14] But as Tocqueville's case makes clear, this connection did not hold across the board. There were many organic liberals fully open to reason. Tocqueville, in fact, was renowned for his advocacy of a "new political science" meant to "instruct democracy" and "substitute little by little the science of affairs for its inexperience." What is noteworthy about his political science, however, is that it subjected the role of rationalism in public life to critical inquiry, including the question of whether the cause of liberty is best promoted by a public understanding of founding as a wholesale remaking on the basis of a theoretical model. Whatever Tocqueville's answer to this scientific question, his two-founding version of American history clearly removes the period of 1775–1787 from consideration as an example of a full-blown rationalist founding. He presents it more as a reform than a founding: "The form of the federal government of the United States appeared last; it was only a modification of the republic, a summary of the political principles spread through the entire society before it and subsisting independently of it."[15]

Fifth and finally, the two-founding thesis seems to have been calculated to influence people's "mental habits," a key concept for Tocqueville that refers to the epistemological premises that people use to process reality. A nation's mental habits will be influenced by how its citizens conceive of their origins. In the measure that Americans embraced the two-founding thesis, then, they would abandon thinking primarily in terms of abstract models of politics. Instead, they would concentrate on the content of their tradition, exploring the question of "who are we?" This approach fits well with Tocqueville's understanding of how best to introduce basic standards of right or good into society, including aspects of natural right (the idea that certain things are just by nature and accessible to human reason). The idea of right, Tocqueville thought, was best taught not through public philosophical doctrines, which lead to extremes and utopian notions, but through being discovered as embedded within historical experience. The task of instructing people about natural right is best undertaken by the analytical historian (like Tocqueville), who sifts through a tradition, indicates the practices of right, and offers corrections to specific aspects of the national character.

ON DISCERNING TOCQUEVILLE'S INTENTION

These five points taken together add up to what looks to be a full theoretical position on the character of founding. But did Tocqueville *intend* to set forth a general theory, or is this "theory" just the result of his effort to recount America's historical origins? There are certainly grounds for favoring the last position. *Democracy in America*, after all, does not proceed in the manner of a theoretical treatise that sets out different possible conceptions of origins and then weighs their respective merits. Furthermore, Tocqueville makes clear his interest in historical explanation, announcing that one of the reasons for writing the book is to understand the rise of the democratic revolution by studying the American case. At the same time, however, Tocqueville presents *Democracy in America* first and foremost as a work of political science intended to promote free government. The question therefore becomes whether, in the event that these two aims are not in perfect harmony, Tocqueville would somehow have "adjusted" his historical explanations to promote an objective commanded by political science.

Tocqueville unfortunately never directly commented on this issue, either in his published works or his notes. A judgment can accordingly only be reached by inference, which will be investigated here in a slightly roundabout manner. In an important article written over a decade ago, Thomas West identified what he called a major "flaw" in *Democracy in America*: its omission of any mention of the doctrine of natural rights in the context of the Founding. Tocqueville, according to West, failed to note the decisive fact that "in our founding we Americans understood ourselves to be dedicated to the truth that all men are created equal, and that this dedication, and this truth, are what justified the break with Britain and made us a nation."[16] Indeed, as West points out, Tocqueville never so much as mentions America's seminal document, the Declaration of Independence.

Setting aside for the moment whether this omission was a "flaw," West's observation is striking, perhaps even more so than he makes

out. Classic accounts of America written in a comparative perspective
have often characterized the United States as a "propositional" or a
"creedal" nation, referring to Americans' core belief in rights and equality grounded in the laws of nature. G. K. Chesterton, one of the first to
develop this theme, argued that Americans were bound by the "creed
. . . set forth with dogmatic and even theological lucidity in the Declaration of Independence."[17] Gunnar Myrdal followed in the same line in
The American Dilemma, in which he speaks of American history as "the
gradual realization of the American Creed." Finally, Samuel Huntington,
whose book *Who Are We?* restates Tocqueville's two-founding thesis, felt
obliged to contrast his position with what he acknowledged is a widely
held "creedal" understanding of the American polity, a position to which
he himself had previously subscribed in an earlier work.

If *Democracy in America* meant to provide a comprehensive historical account of America's origins, it is fair to ask how a thinker of Tocqueville's
rank could have missed so fundamental a point. Was his omission an
oversight of some kind—an instance of Homer nodding—or must it be
explained as a deliberate act undertaken with a "strategic" purpose in
mind? Published scholarship on Tocqueville only touches on this question.[18] Turning for help to the work of historians, there are two possible
responses that can be drawn. One, relying on arguments of the "republican" school of historiography, might almost excuse Tocqueville's oversight on the grounds that—contrary to what most have long thought—
the doctrine of natural rights was not very significant at the time of the
Founding; indeed, one historian has gone so far as to title an article "The
Irrelevance of the Declaration of Independence."[19] Only with Lincoln and
the rise of the Republican Party in the 1850s, this argument continues, did
the foundation of natural rights become central to American political life,
after which historians made the mistake of reading its importance back
into the Founding era. The other response, based on the views of many
recent historians, makes it almost inconceivable that Tocqueville could
have overlooked the doctrine of natural rights. Perhaps, say these historians, the doctrine was not quite as central as older historians, like Carl
Becker, claimed, but it was still very important.[20] In addition, it had re-
emerged as a topic of debate in the 1820s, just before Tocqueville arrived
in America, in conflicts about property rights and labor issues.[21] By this
account, Tocqueville's omission of any reference to natural right would
have been intentional; something besides pure history must be going on
in his developmental account in *Democracy in America*.

Other considerations lend further support to this last position. From an
examination of Tocqueville's correspondence from the period of his visit,
it is clear that he was acutely aware of the Declaration and its importance.
In one letter, written to his friend Ernest de Charbol, Tocqueville mov-

ingly describes a July 4 celebration that he attended in Albany at which the Declaration of Independence was read in full. The ceremony made a strong impression on him: "there was in all of this something deeply felt and truly great."[22] Could Tocqueville have forgotten this "great" moment when he wrote *Democracy in America*? Even more compelling is the fact that Tocqueville was a close reader of Jefferson's writings. *Democracy in America* includes more citations to Jefferson than to any other source. Tocqueville's judgment of the importance of Jefferson's thought speaks for itself: "I consider him to be the most powerful apostle that democracy has ever had."[23] As much as anyone else, Tocqueville knew the central place that Jefferson gave to the foundation of natural rights as an "expression of the American mind."[24] Can his omission, then, have been anything other than deliberate?

Yet, if one is to charge Tocqueville with the crime of being selective in his historical account, it is necessary to supply a motive. Tocqueville, it may be surmised, sought to make America's success appear less dependent on a foundation of abstract natural right than most claimed, because of the dangerous effects of "public philosophy." He developed his objections to philosophical foundations in his book *The Old Regime and the Revolution*, when discussing the disastrous role that intellectuals played in preparing the way for the French Revolution. "The men of letters," as he called them, all began their thought from the same "point of departure": "they all think that it would be good to substitute basic and simple principles, derived from reason and natural, for the complicated and traditional customs which ruled the society of their time."[25] According to Tocqueville, theorizing in this way leads to excess and encourages mental habits that abstract and simplify, when what is needed to promote liberty are habits that recognize particularities and complexity. Tocqueville expressed the same concern about "general ideas in political affairs" in *Democracy in America*, though without explicitly mentioning natural rights doctrine.[26]

THE CONCEPT OF POLITICAL FOUNDATION

The contemporary term "political foundation" is not one that Tocqueville used, but his analysis of what transforms a collection of discreet individuals into a political community treats the same concept. A community, by Tocqueville's account, only comes into being where certain ideas are shared: "without common ideas there is no common action, and without common action men still exist, but a social body does not."[27] Scattered throughout his work are examples of the kinds of ideas that perform this function. Three types stand out.

First, in a well-known passage on patriotism, Tocqueville identifies customary thinking as the traditional source of attachment to the nation. Whereas the modern concept of patriotism stresses the individual's rational calculation of a stake in the community, the older form rested on an "instinctive love of country." This mode of attachment, which once dominated in Europe, was based on what Tocqueville described as "a taste for old customs, the respect for ancestors and the memory of the past." Traditional patriotism, Tocqueville emphasized, had nothing philosophical about it. Neither was it essentially religious, though in some nations custom contained elements of Christianity. Rather, traditional patriotism was "itself a sort of religion, it does not reason at all; it feels, it believes, it acts."[28]

Second, Tocqueville identified a genuinely religious basis of solidarity. The prime example he cites was found in the original New England communities. These were formed by their devotion to *"an idea"* (his emphasis) to fulfill a sacred mission.[29] There was nothing customary in this idea, which called for a clear and active commitment of ongoing faith. Christian thought, Tocqueville indicates, also had an allied idea in the form of the doctrine of Providence that could contribute to forming the common ground of a community.

Finally, Tocqueville spoke of plans to make philosophical doctrines the basis of community. He noted the efforts by intellectuals in the eighteenth century to introduce ideas of natural law as the main political foundation of the new order, and he identified in his own time another philosophical idea, pantheism, which combined the laws of the natural physical processes with a vague progressive historical movement. These instances illustrate the central role that modern thinkers ascribed to philosophical doctrines in politics, which would become active as a political force in the name of philosophy (or science) and supply the bond to hold modern societies together. Philosophy also held out the hope of providing an impartial and objective standard of political right that might eventually supersede the disparate standards deriving from particular histories, partisan views of justice, or different religious beliefs.

"Political foundation" is the term used here to designate the central idea (or set of ideas) that is proposed to supply the commonality of a political community, assuming that there is some such core idea. A foundation, as noted in the last chapter, refers to a general idea, whether explicit or implicit, of right or good, and ultimately to the source or authority that sanctions that idea. By this account, there are many specific political foundations, nearly as many as there are different communities (nearly, because some communities may adopt virtually the same foundation as others, as was the case, for example, in various Communist regimes). For purposes of analysis, foundations can best be categorized on the basis of their respective *sources* for the understanding of right. Reorganizing slightly Tocqueville's list, these sources may be located in religion, nature, and History (capitalized here to distinguish it from ordinary narrative accounts). In the case of religion, God or scripture fixes a standard of right, or shows where history is going; in the case of nature, right is found in a permanent or eternal standard discovered by philosophical (or scientific) investigation; in the case of History, right is known from something that occurs in time, whether from what is old or ancestral (Customary History) or from knowledge of where history is going (Philosophy of History). These sources are parallel to categories used in discussions of philosophy or theology, but as *political* foundations they have special reference to ideas that are capable of moving large numbers of people and supplying the solidarity for what Tocqueville called a "social body."

THE THEORY OF CUSTOMARY HISTORY

With the help of the concept of political foundations, the theoretical project embedded in Tocqueville's two-founding thesis can now be more fully described. Tocqueville sought to replace the theoretical foundation preferred by modern philosophers with a foundation in Customary History. The revival of this historical approach, which is most often associated today with Hume, Burke, and Guizot, originated with Montesquieu, and it is in his thought that the character of this project comes most clearly to sight.[30]

The fact that Customary History had to be revived in the modern era meant that its properties had to change. In a world already altered by the introduction of philosophy, Customary History could not assume the form of the naïve and unconscious "instinctive patriotism" that Tocqueville described. It required something new and more rational. For one thing, the premises underlying Customary History needed to be elaborated theoretically, if not for a general audience, then at least for those who would be engaged in the project of bringing it back. For another, the modern mind could no longer readily accept legend and fable. Customary History had at least to appear to meet the standard of genuine history, in Gibbon's sense of "apply[ing] the science of philosophy to the study of facts."[31]

Montesquieu began the task of creating modern Customary History in his famous chapter on the English constitution, the longest in *The Spirit of the Laws* (11:6).[32] The English constitution, which had political liberty as "its direct end," was Montesquieu's preferred regime for his time (11:5). Most of the chapter is taken up with a description of the constitution's animating structural principle of the separation of powers. But near the end, Montesquieu abruptly shifts focus and raises the question of the origins of this constitution. From Tacitus's work on "the mores of the Germans," Montesquieu observes, it becomes clear that "it is from them [the Germans] that the English took their idea of political government. This beautiful system was founded in the woods" (11:6).

The discovery of the origin of modern liberty in the "forests of Germany" was the basis of the celebrated Gothic (or barbarian) thesis, which was subsequently embraced in one form or another by so many thinkers, including Gibbon, Guizot, and Tocqueville (30:18). For Montesquieu, it was the Goths, those "valiant people," who taught men the worth of liberty (17:5). The Gothic thesis remained a major theme of historiography until the world wars of the twentieth century, when the German forests lost much of their luster along with their foliage. Nearly all of the American historians who established the professional discipline of history in the latter part of the nineteenth century embraced this thesis.[33]

The challenge that the Gothic thesis posed for modern political philosophy could not have been greater. Instead of the origin of liberty being found in the philosophical abstraction of the state of nature, Montesquieu located it with "our ancestors" in their ancient historical condition. What a remarkable slight to philosophy, and, for that matter, to theology! According to this view, the principles of liberty did not originate with philosophy, or indeed with rationalist thought. Liberty derived from the mores of a barbarian people who originally knew neither philosophy nor Christianity. Montesquieu here also initiated a new method for investigating political right: not deductive or geometric reasoning from abstract premises, but the tracing of things to their origin or "germ" and the observation of their subsequent development. The mental habits encouraged in society by this approach also differ from those that flow from rationalist philosophy. Individuals develop a disposition to look to the past with appreciation, rather than to dismiss everything that is old as a "prejudice." With this explanation, the modern idea of Customary History was born.

Following his treatment of the English constitution, Montesquieu turns in the next chapter to the "monarchies we are acquainted with," meaning the earlier monarchies found on the continent (11:7). This form of government differs slightly from the English constitution in that it had honor or glory rather than liberty as its direct end—a fact that did not, however, make it less able to secure liberty. It is result, not intention, that matters, and in the world of politics the two often differ. These older monarchies also derived from the German forests, making them cousins of the English regime, and Montesquieu here takes the occasion to develop further the Gothic thesis by tracing their development (11:8). Originally, the German tribes were each able to assemble in pure republican fashion, in the manner that Tacitus recounted. But after they conquered much of Europe, the process of popular consultation could only continue by developing a system of representation. In addition, having initially enslaved those whom they conquered, which created ranks in society, the rulers eventually took steps to grant certain civil liberties to all.

At the end of this process, the old-style European monarchy emerged—the "gothic government among us"—with its institutions of representation, its different orders, and its complex balances. Montesquieu pronounces his judgment on this system: "I do not believe there has ever been on earth a government so well tempered." He concludes the chapter as follows: "it is remarkable that the corruption of the government of a conquering people formed the best kind of government that men could imagine" (11:8).

It is unclear whether Montesquieu is asserting that the Gothic monarchy is the simply best regime—that is, forever—or whether it was the best that men could imagine *until that time*. No matter. If the main question of political theory is the character of the best regime, Montesquieu in this brief chapter—indeed, in three sentences—provides his response to classical political philosophy. The contrast is striking, even more in the method recommended for investigating how to determine the best regime than in the exact character of that regime itself. For the classics, the best regime is discovered by reason and has the form of an eternal model. For Montesquieu, the best regime is a gift of historical accident that is tied to a particular context, not a product of something intentionally constructed by thought. The best regime is a product of unconscious development inside of actual history, in this case even of a falling away (a "corruption") from an original form. Before the best regime came to be, it could not have been known.

This difference accounts for the otherwise curious placement of the next chapter (11:9), titled "Aristotle's Manner of Thinking." Montesquieu faults Aristotle for the incompleteness of his treatment of the different kinds of monarchy, one form of which, absolute kingship of the best person, arguably represents Aristotle's conception of the best regime. Montesquieu's deepest criticism of Aristotle is not that he erred in constructing the best regime that reason could discern, but that he held that reason had the capacity to construct the best regime in the first place. The "ancients"—this would include Plato—"who did not know about the distribution of powers in the government by one, could not form a just idea of monarchy." They could not form this idea, because monarchy in its best form had not yet come into being. The classics' "manner of thinking" overestimated what pure theory can know.

In Montesquieu's presentation of Customary History—I will refer to it now as his doctrine—reason plays a role in political life, but its scope is limited in comparison to what modern political philosophy envisaged. (In comparison to classical political philosophy, Montesquieu, as just noted, also offered a more modest view of what *theorizing* about politics could discover, though classical political philosophy, unlike its modern counterpart, never embraced a project of trying to actualize the best regime.) Under Montesquieu's doctrine, political philosophy entered political life in a new way, abjuring the modern approach of openly proclaiming the authority of philosophical doctrines and of encouraging people to think of starting society anew. Instead, political philosophy should be introduced more indirectly. It should be inserted into society by thinkers who engage in concrete political analysis and by historians. These historians will look for the good in what has come to be, extracting and refining ideas of right in the process of their analysis. The good, contained in part in the original germ, carries with it a measure of authority deriving from the usual social disposition, perhaps created or perhaps innate, to respect the original, the old, and one's own. Cultivating and encouraging the "historical sense," as distinct from the "metaphysical sense," in turn promotes the weight of the customary within society.[34] Finally, historically minded thinkers, unlike Enlightenment theorists, will not try to usurp the role of political actors, but will appear to defer to them, serving as their counselors. Political philosophy will encourage moderation.

Underlying this view of history is a premise, for which Montesquieu perhaps never fully accounted, that what unfolds or develops on its own, so long as it is not violently interfered with by vast rational plans, tends to work out well (19:5, 19:6). This process of unfolding is not teleological, in the sense of development toward a single known end (and ultimately toward a perfect and universal model). It is "organic" or "natural," in a sense reminiscent of biological beings that follow a slow and not perfectly defined process of growth, with each particular being having its own "genius," or "spirit." Montesquieu's insertion of this premise into Customary History did as much as anything else to define and shape the modern alternative to the Enlightenment concept of rationality.

Montesquieu helped invent the idea of what we today call "tradition," referring to that which grows insensibly and which is worthy of respect. Tradition is the antidote to the modern philosophic animus against the past. A tradition is presented as something already there, as a natural fact that all recognize, but in fact it may be something that the artful poet or historian must find and articulate. Authors who discover a tradition would of course be reluctant to announce their invention, as any claim of originality undermines the purpose of the project. Montesquieu presents the Gothic thesis as the real—that is, the historically actual—path of evolution in Europe, a proposition he labors to prove in the second half of *The Spirit of the Laws* by detailing the development of European constitutions and jurisprudence. (Tocqueville proceeds in a similar manner, claiming no act of invention in articulating the Puritan tradition.) Still, it would be hard for scholars today to acknowledge the Gothic thesis as fully historical. There seems to be more than a touch of artifice in Montesquieu's discovery of it as "our" tradition.

Customary History envisages a new way of introducing natural right into the political world. Right is brought in piecemeal and judged in specific contexts, as these can be examined in the unfolding of history. As practices enter history, the "historian" (Montesquieu) selects them and pronounces on their worth. This approach is the forerunner of Burke's concept of "prescription," where the historian modestly judges what has proven its merit, calling on history to serve as the lead witness. Montesquieu's wish, by his own account, was to promote "moderation," which he praises as a great virtue (29:1). Moderation is arguably the best emulator of prudence, the classical political virtue par excellence. But moderation is not prudence, which on occasion demands boldness and immoderation. This consideration prompts one to ask whether Montesquieu's doctrine represents the best way to introduce right in the political world, or the best way to do so *now*, even with its limitations, in an era in which all viable positions must be offered as doctrines, even one as seemingly anti-doctrinal as Customary History. Prudence no longer has the resources it once had to stand on its own, but needs the backing of a doctrine to provide the space within which it can operate.

Classical political philosophy was modest in its political aims, urging great caution in the political application of philosophy. It was maintained that philosophy should never be introduced in an unmediated fashion as public doctrine or foundation. The limited role that political philosophy prescribed for itself was for the purpose, first, of promoting the political good, since philosophical teachings about right were too complicated to be made into doctrines, and, second, of protecting philosophy itself, since philosophy might be endangered by becoming directly embroiled as a claimant to authority. By Montesquieu's day, however, the classical approach was effectively foreclosed, in large part because of a new path that philosophy had chosen. Philosophy was now engaged in a project of wholesale reconstruction of the political world. Whatever the reasons or motives for this new disposition—whether to rescue the world from theology, to serve the interests of the many rather than the few, to construct a new defense for free inquiry, or to make use of philosophy's new powers of control (perhaps for the sheer pride of exercising power)—the consequence, for Montesquieu, was not in doubt. Philosophy had become unfriendly to the cause of political liberty and was serving as chief supporter of a new absolutism known as "enlightened despotism."

Customary History was a counterdoctrine to modern philosophy. It was believed that in a contest with the philosophic idea of nature, tradition would be more than able to hold its own. Customary History also offered some powerful new theoretical arguments. It emphasized the *fact*—making it perhaps more of a fact than it was—of an existent substance: the "spirit" of a nation or a civilization. The staying power of this "spirit," above all its resistance to being altered or engineered, encouraged a kind of moderation. Respecting what has developed, correcting or reforming its ways without attempting to begin anew, is not only the milder and wiser policy but also the one in accord with how things are. It is "realistic." Montesquieu answers Machiavellian (and philosophical) realism by a realism of his own making. Modern philosophy overestimated the plasticity of political matter and thus exaggerated its capacity to shape political matter. It was "utopian."

On a theoretical plane, the doctrine of Customary History introduced a new and rival understanding of nature. What is natural is what is unique to each being, with a "being" in politics now referring not just to an individual person, but also—and especially—to collectivities, such as nations and civilizations. Each unit lives and unfolds on its own in interaction with an environment. Each nation develops its own "general spirit" (19:4), or what Tocqueville called a "national character." This view of the natural contrasted with the most common view of modern philosophy, where the natural meant the human discovery or construction of laws that account for the movement and properties of the things around us. Customary History also promised great appeal as a rival political doctrine, as people have generally displayed a strong inclination to look back to the past with veneration.

Two final observations may be offered about Montesquieu's doctrine. The first is that "tradition" is, of course, a general idea or an abstraction. There are only particular traditions—unless there would develop a universal tradition that applied to the whole world, which is the basis for Hegel's concept of "spirit." While Montesquieu counsels respect for tradition as such—that is, as a general rule—he shows along the way that there are many cases in which a prevailing tradition has little to recommend it. In such instances a full-scale attempt at renewal might not be unreasonable, even if the chances that it will occur are unlikely and the chances that it will succeed are less likely still. For the sake of his doctrine, however, he does not take his general bearings from these cases, but presents the normal course of development as tending to work in a salutary direction. This approach serves to bolster moderation and to dampen the impulse to remodel societies.

Second, although Montesquieu adopts a rather "traditional" stance in politics, it does not follow that he held to a traditional view of philosophy. He opposed one doctrine (that philosophy should direct and control politics by the introduction of theoretical models) with another (that Customary History should be society's point of departure). His doctrine was a philosophical innovation that was as bold, and as much of a construction, as anything that modern philosophy had ever attempted. Or, as he obliquely acknowledged, "And I too am a painter" (preface).

Montesquieu's political goal was to foster a disposition to moderation, which in his age required a new theoretical doctrine. No act of theoretical intervention, he taught, is ever without unforeseen consequences. This law of unforeseen consequences would obviously apply to his own doctrine. Whatever the risks involved, Montesquieu must have concluded that they were worth running, given the destructive consequences of prevailing theoretical views. It remains an open question whether the project he launched ultimately produced the moderation that he hoped for.

TOCQUEVILLE'S APPLICATION OF
CUSTOMARY HISTORY TO AMERICA

Tocqueville cited three thinkers—Pascal, Montesquieu, and Rousseau—who were most influential for him while writing *Democracy in America*, of whom Montesquieu seems to have been the most important.[35] Tocqueville continued Montesquieu's theoretical project, though with major innovations, by fashioning a Customary History for America. Insofar as he intended America as a model for the modern world, akin to Montesquieu's presentation of England in the previous century, his account was also meant to offer instruction for how to establish and maintain liberal democratic government. Europeans, of course, would have a different Customary History than Americans, but the example of the American case, as Tocqueville presented it, might provide a template for how Europeans could treat their own past.

It is reasonable to ask why Tocqueville chose to anchor his Customary History in Puritan New England rather than in some other tradition in America. Other options were open. The colonies in New England, in fact, were not the first English colonies—Virginia was—but Tocqueville quickly dismissed the Southern tradition, with its slave regime, from the center of the America he wanted to discuss. *Democracy in America* was above all a book that was meant "to instruct democracy."[36] Tocqueville might also have chosen the same Customary History that Montesquieu used, tracing American liberty back to the Goths. Strange as it sounds, many Americans before Tocqueville (including, for a time, Jefferson) had adopted this approach, and, in a development that would almost certainly have surprised Tocqueville, it was to enjoy a huge revival among intellectuals following his visit. For his part, Tocqueville subscribed to the Gothic thesis *for Europe*. He referred to Tacitus and the "political institutions of

our fathers, the Germans," whose influence may very well have constituted "the fertile seed (*germe*) of free institutions [that] had already entered
profoundly into English habits" (and thus formed the colonists' idea of liberty).[37] But Tocqueville went no further, thinking it unlikely that those who
left the Old World would be interested in linking themselves to the forests
of Germany.[38] To be effective, Customary History now had to appear as
fully rational. This possibility could be realized in America, indeed only in
America, because its history was, so to speak, visible from the beginning. It
is the "only country . . . where it has been possible to specify the influence
exerted by the point of departure on the future of states."[39] Tocqueville
could rely on documents and known sources, avoiding the inventions that
opened the Gothic thesis to serious questions.

Most of the historians whom Tocqueville met in America were from
New England, and the greater part of historical work in America at that
time concentrated on that region.[40] Locating the essential point of departure in New England thus had the advantage of being accurate, or at least
plausible, on historical grounds: "New England's principles spread at
first to the neighboring states; later, they gradually won out in the most
distant ones and . . . penetrated the entire confederation."[41] But historical
considerations aside, Tocqueville found in New England the kernel of the
principles of right needed to sustain modern democracy. New England
history contained three fundamental components of free government and
liberty: self-regulating individuals, political liberty (civic participation),
and, eventually, private rights.

Developing self-regulating individuals depended on sound mores,
which were best cultivated by religion. New England became the basis
for Tocqueville's famous judgment in favor of combining "*the spirit of religion* and *the spirit of freedom*."[42] The spirit of religion, which was ignored
or rejected in modern philosophical doctrines of right, was also absent in
Gothic Customary History, which is another reason why New England
represented for Tocqueville a more attractive point of departure than
Germany. Tocqueville modified Montesquieu by substituting the Puritans for the Goths and by bringing religion into the equation.[43] New England demonstrated the reciprocal and reinforcing relationship between
Christianity and democracy. To be sure, the original Puritan theocratic
community had to undergo changes before it could become compatible with modern liberty. Its "tyrannical" excesses had to be purged.[44]
Tocqueville introduced considerations of natural right by approving the
devolution (or "corruption," as Montesquieu might have called it) from the
original regime and its change to a more modern form. Like Montesquieu,
Tocqueville elected to introduce natural right teachings piecemeal, inside
of a historical account, rather than to offer a sweeping philosophical doctrine to remodel the entire society.

Political liberty is a second essential element of a modern liberal democratic regime. Those living in democratic times, Tocqueville stressed, need to learn the habits of taking part in governing, not only to protect themselves from the growth of an all-encompassing central state, but also to promote their personal development as human beings. The roots of this participatory theory, which were largely absent from modern philosophical doctrines, could be found in New England. Puritanism "was almost as much a political theory as a religious doctrine. . . . Democracy such as antiquity had not dared to dream of sprang full-grown and fully armed" in New England.[45] In the New England communities, Americans learned the skills of self-government, becoming citizens in a meaningful sense.

Finally, the third element—private rights—developed in the course of time in New England. This idea held that "man is free and owes an account of himself only to God."[46] Private rights were an aspect of liberty that was promoted in modern philosophical doctrines, although Tocqueville also made clear that the sentiments and energy that supported securing private rights depended heavily on cultivating the first two forms of liberty. Liberty, for Tocqueville, consisted in a combination of different principles that are arrayed in a complex and uneasy balance.

Nothing in Tocqueville's account suggests that he was a proponent of a progressive view of the movement of history, according to which matters tend to evolve for the good. His muted account of "growth" in New England is not part of a general theory of development. As for his overall view of history, Tocqueville invoked "Providence" to seal the argument for the movement of modernity to a stage of equality, which he thought held the potential to being the most just era man had known. But he saw nothing in this dispensation that assured a beneficial result. His argument rather was in the other direction: left on its own, modernity was trending to one form or other of democratic despotism. To forestall this outcome, he emphasized the need to employ "art" or "political science." Reason was required to help shape and guide society, but it was reason of a different kind than the model of rationalist reconstruction developed by modern philosophy. It was the reason of political science.

Likewise, in cautioning against establishing political foundations based on modern natural law doctrines, Tocqueville was not rejecting natural right. He referred often to what is "by nature" or according to the "the order of nature."[47] In a reversal of the modern philosophical view, however, his understanding of what was right by nature led him to be wary of public doctrines of right, including modern natural rights doctrines, which are inevitably oversimplifications. Natural right is best seen when expressed in particular cases, through different and shifting notions of conventional right. In recounting a Customary History, the theorist-historian can purge national character of its excesses while assuring that the core of that character remains intact.

Many other thinkers in America at the time, especially in the Whig party, were engaged in a similar project of creating an American Customary History. Their aim was to combat what they saw as the materialism and easy progressivism of modern philosophical doctrines—problems they often attributed, rightly or wrongly, to the philosophy of John Locke. Customary History, usually offered in combination with a natural rights teaching, was meant to correct the philosophical foundation of the Founding. One of the most thoughtful writers in this school was the New England Whig leader Rufus Choate. In a series of orations in the 1830s and 1840s, including one titled "The Age of the Pilgrims, Our Heroic Period," Choate called for new histories to celebrate the resolute qualities of our earliest "fathers."[48] Choate sought to cultivate the historical sense—a disposition to look back with reverence to what is old and one's own—that was being threatened by a rationalist mind-set that led each individual, to use Tocqueville's description, to "take tradition only as information . . . [and] to call only on the individual effort of his reason."[49] For Choate, this way of thinking was insufficient to hold a society together and promote the virtues of a free people.

STATESMANSHIP AND POLITICAL FOUNDATIONS

How should Tocqueville's two-founding thesis be judged? Thomas West, in the article referenced earlier, does not hesitate to provide an answer. West's concern, it turns out, is not chiefly with Tocqueville's historical error, but with what West regards as his theoretical error of downplaying natural rights doctrine. For West, that doctrine is the fundamental source of protection of liberty in America and the core of the regime. Any flaws that have developed in American politics since the Founding are not attributable to that doctrine, but owe their origins to other, and unrelated, theoretical sources. Nor would it make sense, by West's reasoning, to close the door to all philosophical doctrines in order to block the dangerous ones: the good would only be thrown out with the bad. However admirable *Democracy in America* may be in other respects, West regards it as defective on the central point of mistaking America's political foundation.

Some have defended Tocqueville's omission of the doctrine of natural rights by claiming that his audience was chiefly among Europeans, not Americans. Attempts to promote natural rights theory with moderate Europeans at that time, it is argued, would only have been dismissed, as the lesson they had drawn from the French Revolution was that its excesses resulted from its philosophical foundations.[50] Natural law doctrines were considered to be dangerous. Furthermore, any effort to distinguish a moderate, Lockean version of natural law from a more radical one—supposing even that Tocqueville had been so inclined—was too refined an argument to make headway in public. The French, going back to 1776, had interpreted the American Revolution and its doctrine of natural law in the radical sense of giving full license to completely remaking society: "The Americans . . . gave substantial reality to what we were dreaming about."[51] The practical choice in Europe was between a foundation that was based on philosophical doctrine and one that relied on Customary History.

This argument about audience, if true, still leaves unanswered the question of what effect Tocqueville's two-founding thesis might have on *Americans*. If his concern was exclusively for Europeans, he might be charged with endangering the cause of good government in America in order to promote good government in Europe, or, on a more charitable interpretation, with helping Europe while doing no harm to America. Americans, by this last reading, would never abandon their cherished founding principles just because a well-intentioned foreigner failed to assign the Declaration the credit it deserved.

An alternative position would claim that Tocqueville intended *Democracy in America* to instruct *all* readers, Americans as well as Europeans. His teaching about the danger of theoretical doctrines in political life was therefore meant to have an effect within the American context, and it seemed in fact to bolster the aforementioned body of thought at the time, calling for a corrective to the Lockean natural rights doctrine. Versions of the two-founding thesis subsequently became a major theme of American historiography.[52] Others were in accord with Tocqueville's *general* position of promoting Customary History, but they rejected the two-founding thesis, with its New England–Puritan narrative, on the grounds that it was inaccurate historically (it undervalued the Founding), spoke only to one locality (most Americans did not regard the Puritans as their "fathers"), and presented a dangerous model (religious themes were too deeply enmeshed in politics). They offered alternative versions of Customary History that were more national in scope. The leading candidate located the "germ" of liberty within the Founding era (1775–1787), although now on customary as much as philosophical grounds. This approach, adumbrated in *The Federalist* (no. 49), sought to place the "prejudices of the community on the side" of law and to inculcate a "reverence" and "veneration" for the Constitution and the Founding. Rufus Choate came around to this approach by 1845 in his celebrated "Speech to the Harvard Law School," in which he commemorated the general idea of law, crediting the constitutions of the Founding era, national and state, as the source of American liberty.[53] Earlier, a young and unknown Whig politician from Illinois, Abraham Lincoln, introduced a similar account, proposing to make obedience to the laws, attached to the memory of the Founding, into "the political religion of the nation."[54]

Tocqueville's argument for Customary History thus connects *Democracy in America* with the general "Whig" approach in America that urged a foundation based on a synthesis of national rights theory and Customary History. Tocqueville, of course, went further than any of the Whigs in his silence about the Founders' natural rights doctrine, which they acknowledged. But Tocqueville at one point appeared to concede the effectiveness of this doctrine *in America*, when he noted that Americans never displayed "as blind a faith [as the French] in the goodness and absolute truth of any theory."[55] Americans had a philosophical foundation that worked, in part because they applied it with a large dose of prudence. A theoretical foundation so hedged might satisfy the demands of good government.

To argue that Tocqueville intended his theory of the Founding to instruct American democracy refutes the criticism that he was concerned only with a European audience. But it does so by strengthening Thomas West's objection, because Tocqueville now can be charged with deliberately downplaying the natural rights doctrine. For West, any approach that veils or qualifies, let alone omits, "the abstract principle" at the core of the Founding undermines the cause of liberty.

There remains, therefore, an unresolved issue, not only of intellectual history, but also of political theory and of "practical" politics today. What political foundation is best for America, and how does one even approach answering a question of this kind? Searching for a simple determination of the "one best foundation" may go beyond what political philosophy can furnish. An alternative is to proceed in a more "political" fashion by considering the merit of foundational ideas as judged in part by their effects in different contexts. This approach recognizes a role for what amounts to "statesmanship" in determining the proper application of political ideas. Statesmanship, as Tocqueville explains, involves making judgments that abjure a strict adherence to laws or formulae, on the grounds that the changing character of political life demands varying methods to achieve certain fixed ends.[56] The form in which political foundations are expressed must therefore take account of different circumstances, not in the ordinary sense of the shifting political situation, but, since fundamental ideas generally outlast such situations, in the much broader sense of great changes of context that bear on the character of the nation.

The historical experience of the United States since Tocqueville's visit obviously provides new material for judging the question of the best presentation of foundational ideas. The slavery crisis of the 1850s made it evident that the "general spirit of the nation" could not be expressed without acknowledging the centrality of the foundation of natural rights.

There are reasons to think that Tocqueville himself, in his responses both in public and private to the slavery crisis—he died in 1859—was already moving in this direction, as he was searching for a clear doctrinal expression of right to oppose slavery and its expansion.[57] In any case, following the Civil War and the refounding of America's polity, the context of American political life changed, and it became impossible thereafter to ignore the thought of America's most important statesman at its most critical moment.

If the essence of the doctrine of natural rights is to state a truth, then it must be asserted in this form—that is, as a truth—and not merely as a useful idea for its day, much less a helpful myth. To say, however, that it is a truth does not deny that it may be less than the whole truth. Incompleteness can lead to distortion and error, which suggests the need for an ongoing process of adjustment or supplementation. This process can take place through a creative interpretation of the natural rights doctrine or by introducing other foundational principles to qualify and complement it. Tocqueville's *Democracy in America* remains the indispensable text for guiding us in this difficult task.

3

✦

American Political Foundations in the Thought of Leo Strauss

Leo Strauss is widely acknowledged today by both his admirers and his critics as one of the most important political philosophers of the twentieth century. The range of topics and thinkers that he treated spanned the whole of the Western tradition, from the Hebrew scriptures to modern historicism and from Heraclitus to Heidegger. Yet what, if anything, did this thinker, who came to America at mid-life in 1937, have to say specifically about American political thought? Part of the answer can be found in an examination of the introduction to Strauss's most widely read book, *Natural Right and History* (1953), in which he offered his most extensive treatment of the question of America's political foundations.

For the unbiased American of the 1950s—a citizen who was not directly subject to the influence of modern philosophy or social science—the encounter with Leo Strauss's *Natural Right and History* must have been unsettling and perplexing. (It is appropriate to speak of an "encounter," because the book is based on a series of lectures that Strauss delivered in Chicago in 1949 in which he began by directly addressing his audience.) His tone was ominous, raising the specter of an impending, though unspecified, crisis. First citing the Declaration of Independence (Jefferson) and then alluding to the Gettysburg Address (Lincoln), Strauss asked whether "the nation" still "cherish[es] the faith" and holds fast to its original principles.[1]

The old America to which Strauss referred was forged in two moments: in an original founding (1775–1789) based on a foundation of natural right, and in a refounding (1861–1865) that rekindled the original principles. The second moment supported the idea of natural right by appealing not only to reason, but also to tradition, evoking reverence for the original founding. The second moment was therefore partly a "romantic" event, blending an appeal to Customary History with an appeal to reason.[2]

The political foundation of the old America, Strauss concluded, had been all but abandoned, at least by intellectuals. "Present-day American social science," he wrote, "is dedicated to the proposition that all men are endowed by the evolutionary process or by a mysterious fate with many kinds of urges and aspirations, but certainly no natural rights."[3] Strauss sketched a rough intellectual parallel between what was happening in America in his day (the mid-twentieth century) and what had occurred earlier in Germany, where by 1922 the idea of natural right no longer had any purchase. The initial result was a public mind dominated by relativism or "nihilism." The aftermath in Germany, in which liberal democracy was abandoned, was a story that needed no elaboration.

Strauss's words would no doubt have aroused the patriotic sentiments and spiritedness of the unbiased American. Let me now put myself in that American's shoes and "speak" for him. He or she would be angry, but at what, or at whom? German thought, to be sure. But this is an object too distant and impersonal to satisfy his indignation. Something or someone closer to home bears greater, or more immediate, responsibility. Strauss provides the answer. It is "American social science" together with a significant portion of the opinions of "the learned." These sources have been the purveyors of German thought, applying its basic concepts to America's tradition. They have replaced the foundations of the Declaration and Gettysburg Address with a new teaching based on the ideas of scientific evolution and historicism.

There is therefore a third moment in Strauss's account of American political development. It marks the transformation from the old to the contemporary America. This moment belongs to the Progressives and to their heirs, who specifically deny the original foundation of natural right. Their aim is to displace the original Founders and claim the status of being America's new Founders.

However ominous the tone, the opening pages of *Natural Right and History* must surely have given rise to expectations that "help is on the way." For what author would be so harsh as to begin a work so full of foreboding unless he somehow planned to offer relief—unless he had a blueprint for banishing corrosive German thought from these shores and restoring natural right to its proper place in America's intellectual firmament?[4] To discover whether or not this relief would actually be forthcoming, however, readers would need to face the daunting task of considering the whole history of the idea of natural right. To address their immediate discomfort, Strauss offers a piece of quick consolation in the form of flattery of national pride. Americans can at least take solace in thinking that, as citizens of "the most powerful and prosperous" of all nations, they are at the center of every major inquiry.[5] What happens here, what happens to America, affects the fate of everyone and everything in the modern world.

Early paperback editions of *Natural Right and History* only confirmed the "Americanness" of the book. For many years the University of Chicago Press offered a cover with a color scheme of red, white, and blue—not the colors of Athens or Sparta—with an offprint of the text of the Declaration of Independence in the background. More recent editions, however, as Strauss's own analysis might have foreseen, toned things down, switching the color to a postmodern *noir* and introducing the studied ambiguity of the uncompleted title of the Declaration of Independence in a faintly visible mauve lettering running from the back to the front cover. The title gets only as far as the "p," suggesting perhaps that America has lost its "endence" and that her cherished faith is slowly but inexorably ebbing away, destined to lose one letter for each subsequent edition. It is impossible, of course, to judge a book by its cover, and it may be that the University of Chicago Press adopted this design to move its merchandise. If so, this fact might redeem *Natural Right and History* as an American book by expressing faith in the old Lockean claim that "according to the natural law . . . man in civil society may acquire . . . as much money as he pleases."[6]

After these opening pages, so full of concern for America, the American reader comes in for a rude awakening. America is unceremoniously dropped from consideration, never directly to be spoken of again. American writers or themes appear only in passing or in footnotes.[7] Leo Strauss, it appears, had the effrontery to write a book that is not about America. America may be, as Hegel once said, the "land where the burden of the World's history shall reveal itself," but apparently this fact counts as next to nothing when set beside reflections about deeper themes of philosophy. In shifting focus from America to strange ideas like eternity and transcendence, Strauss challenges the core sensibility of modern thought, which "explicitly condemn[s] to oblivion the notion of eternity."[8] Our pride is wounded at being asked to consider looking up to something higher than ourselves.[9]

Worse still, the book begins to try our patience, mightily. America—Tocqueville said so—is the civilized country that cares least about philosophy. Americans take their philosophy, if they bother taking it at all, with a view to what our pragmatists later called "truth's cash value." What, then, is an American to make of an author who asks us to consider, as an important objection to historicism, that "if and when there are no human beings, there may be *entia* but there cannot be *esse*"?[10] We Americans will have our *entia* any way we can get them, with or without *esse*.

Finally, some readers might have begun to worry that Strauss had not only left America waiting in the lurch, but also had turned on her. While *Natural Right and History* appears to be friendly to the general idea of natural right, it is critical of some of its concrete historical manifestations. The idea of natural right, as Strauss explains, has appeared in different forms: in the "classic" types of Socratic-Platonic natural right, Aristotelian natural right, and Thomistic natural right, and in its dominant modern form of the doctrine of natural rights.[11] Strauss's discussion of the modern version leaves little doubt that he had certain reservations about it. Indeed, the earlier-identified villain—"historicism"—so far from being completely culpable for our modern predicament of nihilism, is partly excused by extenuating circumstances. It developed in reaction to certain flaws of modern natural rights philosophy, for which it tried to offer a correction. (In fact, however, it succeeded only in radicalizing matters further.) Historicism therefore cannot be blamed without also indicting modern natural rights philosophy as a co-conspirator. Modernity in Strauss's account has been driven by the cunning of a demonic process in which attempts to save the world from crisis seem only to have thrust it into a deeper crisis. If culpability for the modern situation must be assigned, a large portion of it would seem to belong to the founder (Thomas Hobbes) and the refounder (John Locke) of modern liberalism. Strauss made himself famous, or infamous, for his less-than-celebratory treatment of John Locke, which ends with his oft-quoted sentence: "Life is the joyless quest for joy."[12]

True, Strauss never directly assimilated the Declaration of Independence with John Locke's political philosophy. And he surely never equated the American Revolution with the French Revolution, the event that most clearly brought to light the dangers associated with modern theorizing about natural right. If we learn anything from Strauss's remarkable discussion of Edmund Burke in this book, it is that the same things (or things that on the surface look the same) have different meanings in different circumstances.[13] Theorizing and political action are, in large measure, distinct realms. Still, it is impossible to dissociate John Locke from the American Revolution, so important was Locke's influence on our Founders. Strauss's apparent reservations about Locke might therefore be taken as expressing certain reservations about America.

If *Natural Right and History* does not cause us to be dismayed, it at least leaves us unsettled. And yet, isn't this what a book of philosophy is supposed to do?[14]

SCHOOLS OF INTERPRETATION

Natural Right and History has a surface message. In contrast to the view of most of his contemporaries, Strauss introduces his reader to the idea that natural right is possible—indeed, not only possible but also likely; indeed, not only likely but also partly demonstrated. At the same time, he shows that modern natural rights philosophy is incomplete, perhaps flawed, and unstable as a doctrine. It is less comprehensive and less evident to common sense and experience than the classic version of natural right found in Aristotle. This surface message drives one toward a surface conclusion that addresses the problem or crisis in America: Americans should set about trying to restore the possibility of the idea of natural right, but they should do so in a way that takes into account the shortcomings of the modern doctrine of natural rights and that seeks to modify or correct it.[15]

This surface conclusion forms the core of "Straussianism" insofar as it has become a project of American political thought. Take political Straussianism in any of its three forms—East Coast, West Coast, or faith-based—and one sees that, however differently each school has chosen to present the matter, they all share in promoting this basic idea.[16] The East has followed one reading of Strauss in viewing the American founding as reflective of Locke and modern natural rights philosophy; the American founding thus stands in need of direct and visible "correction" from without. By contrast, the West argues that this "correction" already exists *inside* of the American founding, and in particular inside of the Declaration of Independence.[17] (It may even be inside the thought of Locke, properly read.) Two different dispositions emerge from these starting points. The East professes to have more critical distance from "our own," which Easterners claim is the posture that accords best with the philosophical spirit and the practice of sound political philosophy. Westerners respond that this critical distance has been purchased at the cost of promoting doubts that detach us from our origins. These doubts weaken America.[18] The West expresses greater certainty about its position, which enables Westerners to cherish their faith and avoid any hint of skepticism, be it dogmatic, erotic, or zetetic. Easterners reply that the West's certainty comes at the risk of denying or obscuring the limitations of the modern natural rights position; furthermore, if the West's stance is meant to be a public or exoteric pose based on a prudential judgment, it has been pursued with such single-mindedness that it has fooled its own adherents more than it has edified any of its doubters.

The two camps also differ in their understanding of the source of the current crisis and on the best practical strategy for coping with it. The East locates our problems not only in historicism but also in modern natural rights philosophy. While acknowledging the great difference between classical and modem times, the East, with its preference for the classics, adopts a less rights-based, and more republican or communitarian, outlook, which translates for many Easterners into a more welfare statist, or liberal, political orientation. The West locates the source of our problems in the doctrines of historicism (especially Progressivism) and relativism.

These are original sins having no necessary connection to modern natural rights doctrine, at least in the form in which that doctrine was articulated in America. Despite an appreciation for the classics, the West is more rights-oriented in outlook and more supportive of limited government.

The general tone of the discourse of the two camps reflects their respective dispositions. Easterners "explore" matters from many different angles, allowing conclusions to emerge at the end. Westerners "demonstrate" positions, writing to prove a position that is known in advance. In their views of natural right, Easterners lean more toward a view of a hierarchy of ends embodied in a regime; they are wary of formulae. Westerners identify natural right with modern natural law, that is, the doctrine of natural rights, which established the criteria of the best regime. The East has been a bit more partial to the Constitution, the West to the Declaration. For obvious reasons Easterners have been attracted to Tocqueville, who seems to have been providentially sent to represent their cause. Westerners have dared on occasion to criticize Tocqueville, who is said to have sinned by failing to praise the Declaration. For opposite reasons, the West is attracted to Jefferson (at least in his more sober moments) and to John Locke (properly understood). In their public posture, the East is more philosophic, the West more political. Some Westerners allege that the Far East, by which I do not mean China but Boston College, is not much interested in "the regime" at all, but only in philosophy. Philosophic politics is the highest form of political philosophy; political philosophy needs to be practiced in a way that defines the first goal to be to protect philosophy, which by accident finds its home in America today chiefly in political science departments. Easterners invite speakers to talk on political subjects, but then disparage them for deigning to be concerned with the real world. To all this Easterners respond by charging that the Far West has all but abandoned philosophy for the mad world of politics. Westerners, they continue, profess greater admiration for statesmen than they do for philosophers; they invite speakers to talk on philosophic subjects, but then express disappointment that more time is not spent parsing the Declaration or examining Lincoln's speeches.

Despite all these differences, these groups still read from the same book and pray for funding from the same foundations. Most important, when one sets aside all the names and labels and studies the substance of the matter, East and West agree on the need for a political foundation in America based on a regulating idea of natural right that combines the substance of modern rights with an appreciation of certain classical virtues. This common goal has meant that, over the years, some of the differences between them have blurred, along with much of the contentiousness. Even the original geographical bases of influence have lost much of their significance. Easterners have gone West, and Westerners

East. If members of these groups take a step back from their old quarrels and survey the situation (as some are now doing), they will be able to take some pride in what together they have accomplished.

A FOURTH MOMENT?

The greatest and most unexpected change in American political thought since the 1950s has been the revival of the concept of natural right. The revival is, of course, a long way from being fully realized and is challenged today by the philosophical school known as political nonfoundationalism, which openly dismisses the concept of nature and denies the need for a political foundation of any kind. It is nevertheless striking how far claims of natural right now go in the public arena and even in some academic circles. This change from the 1950s, which can be provisionally characterized as inaugurating a "fourth moment" in American political development, may be credited in large measure to the influence of the thought of Leo Strauss.

The revival of the concept of natural right occurred in a different manner than in the past. Previous instances took place when the concept had identifiable "work" to perform in relation to a specific problem or task, such as justifying the Revolution in 1770s and opposing slavery in the 1850s. The crisis of which Strauss spoke in 1950 was, by contrast, an intellectual or theoretical one—the emergence of relativism and nihilism. But in light of what he observed elsewhere, this crisis was no less real. As a thinker respectful of the practical situation, Strauss would never have mentioned a merely theoretical problem in the American context if he did not think it posed some genuine dangers. From a practical standpoint, the statesman has no reason to wade into controversies about foundational ideas unless they threaten something important in political life. As Burke once noted, "The bulk of mankind on their part are not excessively curious concerning any theories, whilst they are really happy; and one sure symptom of an ill-conducted state is the propensity of the people to resort to them."[19]

Strauss could not be sure of the exact effects of the theoretical crisis he identified. He doubted that Americans would follow the Germans in turning against democracy, so great in America is the instinct or prejudice in favor of democracy of some kind. (We are fortunate—"only God knows why"—that our social scientists and intellectuals prefer "generous liberalism" and democracy to consistency in their intellectual views.[20]) What was more likely to emerge was a loss of confidence in liberal democracy, resulting either in expressions of open doubt and defeatism, which in fact occurred with the arrival of the New Left in the 1960s, or in a certain kind of listlessness in defending American liberal democracy, which is the deepest aim of the modern ideology of anti-Americanism.[21] Strauss expressed his concern about this loss of confidence in many later writings, in which he openly worried about Americans' misunderstandings of the character of Communist tyranny. A foundation in natural right can serve as an antidote to listlessness, as indeed it has done over the past few decades.

Did the initiation of a project for the reintroduction of the idea of nature and natural right into the American mind constitute a proper use, or an abuse, of *Natural Right and History*? Strauss himself never explicitly called for such a project. A full answer to the question of his intention would require an examination of the relationship among the different types or modes of thought that he identifies: philosophy, political philosophy, and national political thought. Each mode has a different purpose, even if all of them might ultimately be connected at a higher level.[22] A perennial theoretical problem, which has never been fully solved, revolves around keeping discoveries that apply to one type of thought from being directly applied to another, for what holds true of things in one realm (e.g., philosophy) may be inadequate or likely to be misconstrued in another (e.g., American political thought). American political thought, while it occasionally deals with the question of the best regime, serves primarily to give expression to the nation's tradition and to suggest ways to maintain and improve it. It can be elaborated, for most purposes, without a full recourse to philosophy or political philosophy, although at its highest levels it will always require the guidance of political philosophy.

Natural Right and History, despite its opening passages, is not a book about American political thought. A judgment about its conclusions for America would have to engage in the complex process of working "down" from higher levels of thought (philosophy and political philosophy) to American political thought, and "up" from elements of American political thought to higher levels of thought. The results of such an inquiry would not likely produce simple formulae, though they would pay great dividends in our understanding of the relationship among the different modes of thought. Strauss left this kind of inquiry for others. It was a matter, too, for prudential judgment. How and when to present political doctrines will necessarily change with a change of circumstances.[23] Still, when all is said and done, Strauss chose to initiate his inquiry into the question of natural right by expressing his deep concern about America's loss of belief in its original foundation. A political project to inaugurate a fourth moment of American political development cannot be considered to be at odds with this concern.

STRAUSS AND DEWEY

It is necessary to undertake a second journey. Many of the readers who encountered *Natural Right and History* in the 1950s were not from the category described above as the "unbiased," but were in the thrall of social science and contemporary intellectual thought. These readers would have been those deeply influenced by Progressive thinkers such as John Dewey in the realm of philosophy, Charles Beard in the field of history, and John Burgess in the field of political science. All of these thinkers shared the goal of dethroning the doctrine of natural rights and the concept of nature. For Beard, this way of thinking was the product of a previous age that modern thought had now surpassed: "Efforts have been made to give force to rights by calling them natural [but] that was an eighteenth century custom."[24] Burgess was more blunt: "every student of political and legal science should divest himself, at the outset, of this pernicious doctrine of natural rights."[25]

This attack on the doctrine of natural rights was meant to have an immediate effect on both philosophy and politics. For American pragmatists, these two realms were directly connected. Philosophy was not meant to stand aloof and gaze on the eternal, which in any case does not exist, but to enter, in Dewey's words, "the social and moral strifes of [our] own day . . . and be an organ for dealing with these conflicts."[26] The Progressives assailed the doctrine of natural rights for two reasons: because it gave too much protection to the rights of property, which led to the injustices of the era of advanced capitalism; and because it underwrote the idea of the individual understood as an atom or a "ready made" unit apart from society, which denied sufficient power to the collectivity (the state). Progressive thinkers dismissed the "old individualism," with its roots in John Locke and the Declaration, while offering to replace it with a "new individualism," also referred to as "individuality," which vaguely called for the development of each person's aesthetic capacities.[27] The new individualism was said to be compatible with a collective understanding of man that would be realized in a future "Good Society," which was to be built and guided under the aegis of the social scientist.

John Dewey's influential *Reconstruction in Philosophy*, published in 1920, was the most important work of American political philosophy in the twentieth century prior to Strauss's *Natural Right and History*. Dewey treats philosophy from its origin, using a "genetic method" that begins by going back in human development to a time before the emergence of philosophy. Drawing on Auguste Comte's account, Dewey argues that man originally lived under a purely mythological account of the cosmos that was born of his experiences in hunting and of his overwrought imagination.[28] This account proved over time to be less efficient in directing the hunt or in organizing society than an account that incorporated positivist or scientific evidence. A more rational view of the cosmos was needed, and the Greek philosophers eventually provided one. Metaphysics (based on the notions of eternity, the ideas, and the separate realm of reality and fact) was designed to replace mythology. It was intended to stabilize society and provide support for the existing structure of rule of the political hierarchy.[29]

While the study of the origin of Greek philosophy can thus tell us a great deal about Greek society and culture, its importance extended far beyond its own locality and age. The language and concepts of philosophy came to exercise a vast structuring influence over all subsequent Western thought. The metaphysical concept of nature, according to Dewey, was the centerpiece of Greek philosophy. This concept is responsible for two major problems. First, it is inherently undemocratic. It underwrites an idea of permanent hierarchy in the world, depicting permanent forms or types that are static, hierarchic and feudal.[30] This view is transferred to the political realm, fulfilling philosophy's original conservative political and social purpose. Modern accounts of the concept of nature, as found, for example, in the thought of Francis Bacon, obviously modified this original understanding of nature. But the striking fact for Dewey is how much the moderns end up sharing with the ancients by the mere fact of continuing to use the concept of nature. Second, the concept does not recognize things in their individuality. It covers or subsumes things under patterns or categories (forms), thereby stifling or depreciating the unique qualities of all existing beings. Jettisoning the concept of nature, which is what Dewey proposes, would have a revolutionary impact on thought and politics. It would serve, in his view, both to democratize our view of the cosmos (and the political realm within it) and to clear the way for the primacy of individuality, which accords with the true character of things.

Dewey's use of the genetic method in *Reconstruction in Philosophy*, in which he tells the story of the emergence of the concept of nature, was designed to help free Americans from the lingering grip of the prejudices that classical philosophy had created. By going back to the pre-philosophic period, the reader can see how classical philosophy developed to serve the class interests of an elite. Its categories and concepts were never "neutral" or objective. The final step in our liberation from these categories is achieved not by going back behind philosophy to the thought of the mythological age, but by pushing forward to a new and higher stage of positivism in which man can at last deploy scientific knowledge of social and moral processes to create a better future. Only today, in the aftermath of Darwin, did Dewey think that we were in a position finally to throw off the yoke of metaphysical thought and begin to "reconstruct" philosophy in the moral and political realms. This project requires breaking from past faiths and making plans for a "Golden Age" in the future, a future that we would create.

Leo Strauss also uses the genetic method, going back before the emergence of philosophy to pre-philosophic thought. In contrast to John Dewey, whose account was intended to document an a priori idea of progress, Strauss's aim was to attempt to rediscover the meaning of the concept of nature in all its fullness and richness, which Strauss was convinced had been lost to modern thought. It is difficult for us today, in the wake of Strauss's contribution, to recall how thinkers of this period simplified and distorted classical thought, creating cartoon Platos and action figure Aristotles. Strauss rescued from near oblivion not only the "metaphysical" and cosmological understanding of the classical concept of nature, but also, and more importantly, its human and political aspects. He did so, moreover, in a practical or empirical way, showing in concrete terms what the concept of classical natural right meant and openly inviting a comparison between the classical account of nature and the more scientific modern versions.[31] His account of premodern nominalism, which begins from the particulars of the political and human situation as they appear to man's perception in the light of day, serves as a down-to-earth alternative to modern or pragmatic nominalism, which begins, ironically, once removed from the *pragmata* with a theoretical idea of what constitutes matter.[32]

A comparison between Leo Strauss and John Dewey seems almost unavoidable. After leaving the New School in New York in 1949, Leo Strauss went on to teach in the political science department at the University of Chicago from 1949 until 1967. John Dewey also taught at the University of Chicago, in the philosophy department, from 1894 to 1904, before going to Columbia University in New York. Leo Strauss had many students and disciples who have filled important positions in our universities and in higher echelons of government. John Dewey had an enormous number of students and disciples who have worked in many areas—above all in the field of education, where Dewey's teachings entirely transformed theory and practice. Strauss offered the most compelling articulation ever in America of classical political thought; Dewey became the most prominent American spokesman of pragmatism. Strauss wrote many books of political philosophy of great depth; Dewey wrote many books of philosophy.

Dewey's effort at "reconstruction" led him not just to criticize the Founders' foundation of natural right, but also to suggest that any kind of theoretical foundation was an impediment to democracy. He originally hoped to replace a theoretical foundation with the notion of the scientific method, to which he thought the public could subscribe. (Belief in the method of science was different, of course, than subscribing to some metaphysical truth.) Dewey is one of the patriarchs of the doctrine of nonfoundationalism. Strauss was in full accord with Dewey in his opposition to theoretical foundations that supported absolutisms of one form or another, but, for Strauss, it was not evident that nonfoundationalism was either viable or an inevitable ally of freedom. The better or more prudent response, he thought, was to consider a foundation that served as a check on absolutism and a defender of liberty. In his most direct discussion of Dewey, in a book review of Dewey's *German Philosophy and Politics,* Strauss concluded as follows:

> No one will deny "that philosophical absolutism may be politically as dangerous as matter of fact political absolutism" (p. 113). But is it not also true that the "frankly experimental" "method of success" (p. 142) has proved very dangerous in the hands of unscrupulous men, and that the belief in an "absolute" inspired the words "that all men are created equal, that they are endowed by their Creator with certain unalienable Rights"?[33]

STRAUSS AND LATTER-DAY PROGRESSIVISM

The Progressive heirs of John Dewey reacted to Strauss's book with a slight measure of satisfaction accompanied by a huge dose of resentment. The satisfaction derived from Strauss's recognition of the Progressives' achievement as, in effect, new Founders who nearly accomplished their goal of overthrowing the doctrine of natural right in America. The resentment, which is more complicated, resulted from Strauss's exposing of a decisive weakness in the Progressives' position. The weakness was one about which they were becoming increasingly aware, but which they struggled mightily to cover up.

The original questioning of natural right took place around the turn of the century, in the first flush of pragmatism's youth, when there was full confidence that the spread of liberalism was the order of the day. Progress, the root term of Progressivism, was to take the place of nature as the main foundation of American democracy. By the 1930s, however, the manifest failure of democracies in Europe and the rise of Hitler, and perhaps Stalin, had shaken to the core the confidence of many American intellectuals. It was no longer clear that progress was certain. Some of those who took part in the earlier crusade against natural right began openly to experience a case of buyers' regret.[34] Many came to see that it had not been so wise to dismiss the Founders and the tradition, with its affirmation of natural rights, which served as an important bulwark against threats to a democratic way of life.

Strauss addressed the pragmatists on their own grounds, beginning with their concern for "consequences," a term that runs like a refrain throughout the introduction to *Natural Right and History*. He observed that many of "the most vocal [original] opponents of natural right" were now among those most concerned with the result of that theoretical step for maintaining the democratic system they cherished. In fact, it was the "harsh experience of [certain] consequences" that Strauss believed was leading to a "renewed interest in natural right."

The situation in American intellectual life when *Natural Right and History* appeared thus bore scant relation to the one that prevailed when pragmatism came on the scene. Part of the progressive intelligentsia was now in search of a graceful exit that would allow them to maintain their theoretical relativism while somehow affirming the political doctrine of natural rights. Hence the expedient proposed by Charles Beard, to defend natural rights as a "myth," and even by John Dewey, to affirm them as an "ideal." As Strauss put it, "The majority among the learned who still adhere to the principles of the Declaration of Independence interpret these principles not as expressions of natural right but as an ideal, if not an ideology or a myth."[35] But these latter-day progressive "solutions," hardly worthy of the name, added up to little more than a notion of "let's pretend together." How could the American people, only yesterday told to respect no god but the scientific method, now suddenly be asked to embrace myth? How could a people instructed to consider consequences now be told to guide itself by (groundless) ideals?

Leo Strauss easily could have joined this flabby new consensus and become part of the burgeoning "let's pretend" club then spreading throughout academia. He steadfastly refused to do so. His great offense against the American academic establishment of his day was not his rejection of science, but, on the contrary, his insistence that any affirmation of the doctrine of natural rights be preceded by a genuinely scientific investigation into the possibility of the theoretical concepts of nature and of natural right. For this act of intellectual impertinence, some have never forgiven him. But it is for this reason that we continue to read his book today.

II

THE FOUNDERS, CONSTITUTIONAL DESIGN, AND THE ROLE OF POLITICAL SCIENCE

4

✛

Fame and *The Federalist*:
The American Founders
and the Recovery
of Political Science

Students of American politics owe a debt of gratitude to the late historian Douglass Adair for having raised the general theme of "Fame and the Founding Fathers," the title of one of his celebrated essays (and later a book). Adair wrote at a time when many historians embraced a simple, two-fold schema for describing the motives of political actors.[1] On the one hand, there was self-interested behavior, understood as the individual's desire for maximizing material gain, on the other, disinterested behavior, understood as selfless devotion to the public good. By this account, either America's Founders were motivated by "property consciousness" and "the dollar" (Vernon Parrington's description), or they were one of history's rarest collections of secular saints.[2]

Adair attempted to transcend this distinction by questioning the model of human psychology on which it was based. Drawing on the thought of Alexander Hamilton, who in turn had been influenced on this matter by David Hume, Adair argued that the category of self-interested behavior presented a cramped and inaccurate account of the motive of self-interest. This account needed to be expanded and refined. Beyond the search for profit, self-interest should be understood to include an ennobling form of self-regarding behavior known as the "love of fame," which Hamilton called "the ruling passion of the noblest minds."[3] This passion produces a completely different effect from that generated by the love of lucre, leading individuals to risk fortune and body to perform memorable deeds.

In spite of the efforts of many Progressive historians to debunk the Founders for their attachment to their property, the "fathers," as they are sometimes called, have managed to win their just measure of recognition. The nation's capital, Washington, D.C., so designated in honor of George Washington, contains many buildings and monuments that celebrate the Founders, from the Madison Library to the Jefferson Memorial. Almost every major city in America commemorates the Founders in some way, be it in the names of streets, shopping malls, or public schools. In our history textbooks, at least those that have not been hopelessly infected by Progressive dogma, schoolchildren can still read of the great exploits of the Founding generation. Although it seems redundant to say so, the Founders' fame rests ultimately on the act of the Founding—on the creation of a new nation in 1776 and on the establishment of a successful new national government a little over a decade later. These accomplishments, which are generally counted today as two "moments" of the same achievement, put America's Founders in the select club of history's great lawgivers.

There is, however, another source of fame for three of the Founders: the book known as *The Federalist.* Written by Alexander Hamilton, James Madison, and John Jay under the pen name of Publius, *The Federalist* is widely recognized today as a major work of political science and a classic text of liberal democratic theory. In some circles, and this may prove increasingly to be the case as time goes on, its authors are as likely to be remembered for writing this book as for their actions as political leaders. They stand as examples of those in a relatively small group of political thinkers who have won lasting fame for an *intellectual* achievement.

FAME AS A MOTIVE FOR POLITICAL AND THEORETICAL ACHIEVEMENTS

Most who seek fame never achieve it, while some who achieve it never seek it. The "love of fame" must therefore be kept distinct from the acquisition of fame, which sometimes results from other motives. The love of fame is nevertheless a constant spur to action, not only in the realm of politics, but also in other realms of human endeavor, from art to music, literature, and science. Think, for example, of the scientists and writers of today who covet the distinction of winning a Nobel Prize. Even philosophers, it seems, are not immune from the pull of this passion.[4]

Moralists often condemn the love of fame because it is an expression of self-interestedness and pride. Political analysts, however, have been more concerned with the practical question of whether this motive promotes or detracts from the public good. The love of fame has a double-edged quality. It can prompt men to undertake actions for the good of the community, but it can also lead them to sacrifice that good for their own benefit. Many judge the second result to be the more likely, because the love of fame may tempt one to alter or destroy what exists in order to surpass the reputation of those who built it. No one has made this point more forcefully than the young Abraham Lincoln:

> Many great and good men sufficiently qualified for any task that they should undertake, may ever be found, whose ambition would aspire to nothing beyond a seat in Congress, a gubernatorial or a presidential chair; *but such belong not to the family of the lion, or the tribe of the eagle.* What! think you these places would satisfy an Alexander, a Caesar, or a Napoleon? Never! Towering genius disdains a beaten path. It seeks regions hitherto unexplored. It sees *no distinction* in adding story to story, upon the monuments of fame, erected to the memory of others. It *denies* that it is glory enough to serve under *any* chief.[5]

The temptation to destroy in order to achieve fame is found not only in politics but also in the arts and even in philosophy. The effects are probably least harmful in the artistic realm, where there is a certain value in seeing things in a new and different light. (Nevertheless, the impulse to shock, which is characteristic of today's *avant garde*, has become a tedious pose that undermines the quality of art.) The matter is different in politics, where stability itself is an important value. Of course, there are times when change is needed; in these cases, the quest of certain individuals for fame can sometimes prove to be in harmony with promotion of the public good. But, as Lincoln suggests, the passion for fame is more often likely to promote harm. No invisible hand operates in political affairs, as it does in economics, to regulate matters for the public benefit. As for the realm of political theory, it is difficult to weigh the advantages and risks posed by the philosophers' love of fame. But the case seems to resemble politics more than it does the arts. Political theorists can play havoc with the health and foundations of societies in their effort to build monuments to their own originality and genius.

Alexander Hamilton is widely credited with providing the most profound treatment in American thought of the theme of "the love of fame" within the political realm. For Hamilton, the existence of powerful forms of self-regarding behavior (avarice, ambition, a love of fame) was a reality that any lawgiver had to recognize. To pretend otherwise and insist that men usually act for disinterested reasons was a fatal illusion. Applied to the construction of political institutions, this realistic starting point meant accepting that "the desire for reward is one of the strongest incentives of human conduct" and that, so far as possible, institutions should be "formed to make [men's] interests coincide with their duty." A love of fame could serve as a potential resource that, when properly harnessed and channeled, could "prompt a man to plan and undertake arduous enterprises for the public benefit."[6]

Hamilton was especially concerned with structuring the office of the presidency to attract persons who, so far as they were moved by self-regarding motives, would be swayed by the love of fame rather than by ambition or avarice. A love of fame is fundamentally an aristocratic passion. Under the correct institutional arrangements, it can help a president resist cultivating temporary popular favor and turn his attention instead to the rewards of posterity. It can induce a leader to be concerned, in Hume's word, with "the judgments which will be formed of his character a thousand years hence."[7] Fame can be won only by the accomplishment of great deeds.

But what of the problem that Lincoln raised? Hamilton went about as far as possible by institutional means to resolve the tension between the love of fame and the promotion of the pubic good. His idea was to endow the office of the presidency with sufficient authority and scope so that it might attract and satisfy those moved by the love of fame, allowing them the distinction not only of being president, but also, the occasion presenting itself, of being a "great" or "transformative" president. The quest for the love of fame could then be fulfilled by the most spirited without destroying the Constitution.[8] There is no need to speculate here about Abraham Lincoln's own motives in the 1850s, which do not necessarily fit the portrait he sketched above. The facts speak for themselves: Lincoln effectively refounded the American republic, giving it a new birth of freedom, from *within* the presidency. Whether he sought fame or not, he surely acquired it—in a measure at least equal to that achieved by the Founders.

THE FOUNDERS AND THEORETICAL FAME

Douglass Adair sought to reestablish the dignity of "the love of fame" as a motive of human action. He did so by showing that there are distinctions within the category of self-regarding behavior that are as morally and politically important as those between the categories of interested and disinterested behavior. His presentation, however, is not without flaws. It is possible that in his enthusiasm for his own discovery, and in his efforts to prove he was as tough-minded as the other psychologists of his day, he too quickly discounted the role played by the disinterested motives of concern for justice and patriotism. No shame should attach, even to an historian, for admitting to the existence of these higher motives, and in some cases these seem to provide the best description of the Founders' behavior. In addition, insofar as self-regarding concerns were paramount for the Founders, Adair may also be faulted for ignoring the role played by "negative" motives. The love of fame, which is an anticipated pleasure, has an obverse in the form of the fear of obloquy, which is an anticipated pain. By the middle of the 1780s, with the problems of the government of the Articles and the states mounting, there were no doubt some Founders who were worried that they would be remembered, if they were remembered at all, as abject failures—men who had led their country down the path to ruin.

The Founders' prospect for fame depended on the success of their political action in establishing the world's first viable liberal democratic government. What can be said, then, about any additional renown for the authors of *The Federalist* for their intellectual achievement? *The Federalist* is unique among the major works of political theory by virtue of its direct relationship to, and dependence on, a concrete political task. It is impossible to imagine the existence of *The Federalist* without the Constitution. The content of the work is fixed by the need to explain and justify the Constitution, and the authors' primary concern at the time was surely to help secure the passage of the Constitution, not to present a great work of theory. Still, *The Federalist* represents an achievement that is partly independent of the Constitution. The work pursued its immediate political aim by making a case on theoretical grounds, contributing enormously in the process to the development of political science.

Promoting the Constitution and making a theoretical contribution were thus largely, but not entirely, complementary objectives. Had the authors been writing a general treatise on liberal government, they no doubt would have treated more deeply certain issues that they largely ignore. It has often been noted, for example, that *The Federalist* hardly deals with the great question of the mores needed to support liberal democracy—and this, for the simple reason that this theme was not a direct concern of the Constitution. In addition, the authors might have presented a few of their arguments with less certainty and perhaps refrained from employing some of their famous "rhetorical" flourishes: "Hearken not to the voice which petulantly tells you that the form of government recommended for your adoption is a novelty in the political world; that it has never yet had a place in the theories of the wildest projectors; that it rashly attempts what it is impossible to accomplish. No, my countrymen, shut your ears against this unhallowed language. Shut your hearts against the poison which it convey[s]."[9] What is remarkable, however, is how much a work that is political in its objective nevertheless meets the rigorous standards of a theoretical essay.

But if the political purpose of the book imposed certain limitations from the standpoint of "pure" theory, it also demanded a special form of intellectual discipline that opened up new possibilities. A theoretical work is a construction under the control of its author, meaning that the material to be included rests with the author. While great authors seek to reveal the world in all its complexity, it is only natural that at certain points they may sacrifice the presentation of certain problems or difficulties for the sake of creating a more beautiful or powerful work. *The Federalist* is allowed no such luxury. It treats a real constitution offered in a real case and under real circumstances. There are certain difficult problems that it cannot avoid, such as how to handle a compromise on slavery, or when it is prudent to exceed a legal authorization and redo, rather than just amend, an existing government. And there is one theoretical question that *The Federalist* was, so to speak, compelled to address: the extent to which general theory and science can instruct opinion in particular situations. This theme is treated throughout the book, for the simple reason that the authors were conducting the real-life experiment of seeing how far political science can influence political life.

Some works of political theory gain in richness and complexity by being written in the form of a dialogue, as is the case explicitly in Plato's *Republic* and implicitly in Book III of Aristotle's *Politics* (in the famous exchanges between the democratic and oligarchic "speakers"). The dialogic form allows for objections, thus preventing any one side from limiting or monopolizing the arguments presented, which is arguably a flaw inherent to the form of the treatise or disquisition. Yet even in a dialogue written by a political theorist, it is still the author who creates the script and decides what is in it. *The Federalist* also frequently proceeds by a "dialogue" in which the chief interlocutors are the opponents of the Constitution and its defender—that is, the author "Publius." But this dialogue is closer than most to being a real one, not fully controlled by the author. Publius is constrained by the reality of the debate going on in the nation and cannot ignore or omit the most important criticisms of the Constitution, or these will be left unanswered. Less perhaps out of generosity than necessity, the voices of the opposition to the Constitution receive a remarkably full hearing.

Following the ratification of the Constitution, *The Federalist* won enough acclaim as a work of constitutional commentary and political science that its chief authors, Hamilton and Madison, became eager to be recognized *in posterity* for their contribution. (During their own day, however, both men often had reason to be reticent about publicly claiming authorship of specific papers, as their positions on some contemporary issues appeared to be at odds with views they had supported in *The Federalist*.) In one of the more interesting sidelights of American history, Hamilton and Madison sparred over the allotment of credit for the book. Hamilton, the organizer and moving force behind the project, left a message just before his fateful duel with Aaron Burr in which he claimed authorship of sixty-three of the eighty-five papers, against fourteen for Madison, five for Jay, and three jointly written with Madison. Madison subsequently disputed

Hamilton's version and insisted that he had written twenty-nine of the essays, offering even to take an oath to vouchsafe for his contention.

Resolving the conflict over authorship has not been as easy as one might think, largely because the authors succeeded so well in subordinating their individual styles to a single voice. So much does *The Federalist* read like the work of one mind that it is hard to believe that "Publius" never existed. Partisans of Hamilton and of Madison continued for years to defend the claims of their principals, and the exchanges were often highly spirited. Following numerous research efforts, including some that employed the earliest versions of software designed to detect authorial recognition—all, incidentally, to no avail—a consensus has emerged in support of Madison's account. Friends of Hamilton ascribe his exaggerated claim to the fallibility of memory, which is known to become more pronounced under the pressure of stressful circumstances, while those less charitably disposed to him tend to count his error as an instance of "the love of fame" getting the best of honesty. However this matter is judged, Alexander Hamilton must still be counted the main author of *The Federalist* in terms of the quantity of papers written. The debate over which man wrote the most notable essays will never be settled, as each took the occasion to display his own mark of genius.[10]

As for the authors' motives, to the extent that these men were concerned with fame in this period (1787–1789), it was for their political deeds, not for writing a book. (Whether *The Federalist* would ever have been considered a classic of political science if the Constitution had been rejected is difficult to say, but it is unlikely that the authors would have thought so when they wrote it.) The fact that they were not vying for fame as intellectuals undoubtedly improved the quality of the work, as they felt no need to make exaggerated claims of theoretical originality, nor to "reverse and undo what has been done by a predecessor" in order to establish their own intellectual merits.[11] They wrote to secure passage of the Constitution and develop political science, not to stake a bid to be recognized as great thinkers. Here was a rare case of achieving fame without really seeking it.

THE THEORETICAL ACHIEVEMENT OF *THE FEDERALIST*

The Federalist is acclaimed today for setting forth many of the ideas and principles that form the architecture of modern constitutional government. Some of these ideas were original to the authors (or nearly so), while others were reformulations and applications of insights of previous theorists. Among the main items the authors treated (the list is not complete) are the idea of a written constitution (*Federalist* no. 53), the doctrine of judicial review (nos. 78 and 81), the concept of federalism (nos. 37 and 45), the theory of pluralism and of the "extended republic" (nos. 10 and 51), the doctrine of the separation of powers and checks and balances (nos. 48–51), and the idea of the modern executive (nos. 70–76).

Important as these doctrines are, however, the work's most notable theoretical achievement lies in its recovery and application of the discipline of "political science," which is the body of knowledge that is the source of all of the specific ideas.[12] Political science was the great contribution of the Greeks, most notably of Aristotle, and it was renewed and strengthened in the seventeenth and eighteenth centuries, above all by Locke and Montesquieu. The American Founders nevertheless deserve much of the credit for refining this science and introducing it in a way that showed what it could contribute to the political world. The American Founding marked the high point up to that time—and in retrospect, it seems, of all time—for the application of political science to human affairs.

Various nations at different epochs have become famous for their intellectual achievements. Athens during the fifth century B.C. and Germany in the nineteenth century are known for their contributions to philosophy; Flanders in the fourteenth century and Italy in the fifteenth century are famed for their revolution in art; and imperial Rome left its great legacy for its development of jurisprudence. Given the technological breakthroughs that have taken place in the United States in mechanics, electricity, and medicine, it would be plausible to claim that this nation's singular intellectual achievement has been in applied physical sciences. But an equally strong case can be made for the restoration and development of political science, an achievement that solidifies the fame of those who wrote *The Federalist*. Their contribution appears all the more impressive when one considers that when they wrote, the discipline of political science was being challenged by two new disciplines, "natural history" and "Philosophy of History," that were meant to replace it as the principal science for understanding and guiding society.[13] Although *The Federalist* was not intended as a philosophical work, its authors discovered that in defending the Constitution and the cause of liberty, they also had to defend political science against these theoretical rivals.

NATURAL HISTORY

The science of natural history, which came into its own in the eighteenth century, was the first alternative that was proposed to supersede political science. Modeled on the natural sciences, it is the forerunner to biology and anthropology.[14] Its premise, insofar as it touched on human life and society, was that the factors that account for basic social outcomes, including the level of development and even the basic form of government, derive from certain pre-political causes. The two most important are: (a) the physical environment and climate, and (b) the characteristics of the "varieties" of man, meaning the different races.

Publius's treatment of this science is found in a discussion of one of its major findings, known as the degeneracy thesis, which had direct practical implications for how Europeans viewed America (and the rest of the world). Leading European natural historians held that the highest type of human being was the white race, particularly the white race living in the physical environment of Europe, and that the animals in America, human beings included, were inferior to their counterparts in Europe. The humans in question referred not only to the indigenous American population (the Indians), but also to Europeans who had come to America. Due to features in the physical environment in America, chiefly the high humidity, Europeans who immigrated to these shores began to lose their physical strength and intellectual capacity.

Alexander Hamilton presents this strange idea in a passage of *The Federalist* that has long been treated largely as a curiosity:

> Men admired as profound philosophers have in direct terms attributed to her [Europe's] inhabitants a physical superiority and have gravely asserted that all animals, and with them the human species, degenerate in America— that even dogs cease to bark after having breathed awhile in our atmosphere. Facts have too long supported these arrogant pretensions of the European. It belongs to us to vindicate the honor of the human race, and to teach that assuming brother moderation. Union will enable us to do it. Disunion will add another victim to his triumphs. Let Americans disdain to be the instruments of European greatness! Let the thirteen States, bound together in a strict and indissoluble Union, concur in erecting one great American system superior to the control of all transatlantic force or influence and able to dictate the terms of the connection between the old and the new world.[15]

This specific conclusion here is of less theoretical importance than the overall character of the new social science being proposed to replace political science. Natural history, according to its proponents, held an advantage over political science because it could go behind politics and explain the selection of the political regime without reference to the choices of leaders and citizens. As long as the outcomes of politics depended on choice, the results could never be fully predicted. Natural history was therefore more rigorous than political science. It elaborated causal models based on predictable pre-political factors. These factors could also be studied under controlled circumstances, which included analyses of the physiology and psychology of samples of humans from the different races. By contrast, there can be no controlled experiments for the political world.

The motives of the "men admired as profound philosophers" who founded this science are also of interest. Included in this group were the Count de Buffon, his disciple Thomas Raynal, and Cornelius De Pauw (whom Hamilton specifically cited in the passage quoted above).[16] Although these individuals are not so widely known today, they were prominent at the time, especially Buffon, whom the intellectual historian Ernst Cassirer credits with having "established a new type of natural science and . . . a companion-piece to Newton's *Mathematical Principals of Natural Philosophy.*"[17] From what we know of Buffon, he was moved, if not by a love of fame, then at any rate by a highly developed sense of vanity, nicely captured by David Hume: "it seemed as though the greater stature with which he himself had been endowed by nature made it difficult for him to lower himself to the study of smaller things."[18] As his five most revered authors, Buffon once listed "Newton, Bacon, Leibnitz, Montesquieu, and me."[19]

The Federalist rejected natural history's claim to serve as the science of political life, arguing instead that the major factor shaping human society is the character of its political constitution. The political constitution or regime, while it is influenced by various pre-political factors, is also partly a matter of choice made at the political level. A science of politics cannot start "beneath" politics. The debate over the ratification of the Constitution in which *The Federalist* is engaged proves this point. The fate of America and of liberal democratic government is being decided at this very moment.

It is also of interest to observe how *The Federalist* proceeds to judge the claim that America is inferior to Europe. Hamilton refuses to employ the methods of natural history of undertaking clinical "observations" to determine whether one variety of human beings is mentally superior to another. He proposes instead a political test. If America is degenerating, then this fact should be evident in the world in which people live and operate: America should be incapable of establishing good government. If, on the other hand, America should succeed in establishing a viable and just republican constitution powerful enough to defend itself, then it will have provided a refutation of the degeneracy thesis more convincing than anything offered in a speculative treatise on natural history. The outcome of the debate on the degeneracy thesis will be decided by the political choice that Americans now make.

In proposing this test, *The Federalist* does not turn from the study of facts or of "nature," but concentrates on the part of nature that is germane to understanding and explaining the political realm. Much of *The Federalist* focuses on analysis of human nature as it reveals itself in what people do when engaging in political activity and choosing regimes. What occurs in history—what is part of "that best oracle of wisdom, experience"—

provides the surest instruction about human nature and politics.[20] The science of natural history is premised on a theoretical assumption that *The Federalist* deems to be unwarranted or at least unproven. It defines nature as one substance (physical causes) and tries to explain all things, or at least all biological things, by the same model. This assumption of a unified science in turn seems to reflect the pride—and perhaps the desire for fame—of certain philosophers, who pretend by this notion of science to be able to replace the judgments of political actors in the political realm. *The Federalist* proceeds by dividing nature provisionally into different parts and by recognizing therefore that there may be different kinds of sciences, with different standards and methods, appropriate to different kinds of beings and activities. What is appropriate for studying animals is not appropriate for studying man and politics.

Along with their immediate goal of securing adoption of the Constitution, the authors of *The Federalist* spelled out some of the factors that would help to sustain constitutional government in the future. One factor of great significance is the science that society relies on as its guide for political life. For this reason, a defense of political science becomes important for the future of constitutional government. The ascendancy of natural history would have the consequence of undermining peoples' belief in their capacity to influence their destiny and of teaching that some peoples are genetically incapable, no matter what the circumstances, of adopting free government. Constitutional government rests on the premise that peoples, circumstances permitting, might be able to select their governments by "reflection and choice." *The Federalist* does not argue the dangerous thesis that power decides truth, but it is mindful of the influence that political success (or failure) can have on theoretical developments in the world. Just as ideas in political theory influence politics, so events in politics sometimes influence theory. The idea of European superiority, *The Federalist* argues, owed much to the long-standing political predominance of Europe: "Facts have too long supported these arrogant pretensions of the European." By the same token, the success of the American experiment would help to discredit the degeneracy thesis and lay the groundwork for an enhanced status for political science.

This last result depended on exactly what an American success was understood to have disproved. There are two possible interpretations. One is that success would show the superiority of one biological "variety" or tribe (the "American") over another (the "European"), which, while it would deny the specific claim of European superiority, would support the main theoretical premise of natural history. The other is that success would demonstrate the primacy of the *political* regime in shaping society. By this explanation, which is the one *The Federalist* adopts, the American "experiment" becomes "interesting to the world." All peoples can take heart in an American success, for it shows what can be accomplished through political action: "Happily for America, happily we trust *for the whole human race,* [the leaders of the Revolution] pursued a new and more noble course [and] . . . reared the fabrics of government that have no model on the face of the globe."[21]

Natural history and political science also pointed to different models for how knowledge is to be inserted into political life. Natural history, by assigning causality to physical or pre-political factors, minimizes the importance of ordinary political action. The pre-political causes can be affected, if at all, by methods of physical or social engineering. Political leaders must turn to scientists—ethnologists and climatologists—for their primary solutions, limiting the "political art" to deciding when and how to apply expert knowledge. The political advice that emerged from natural history illustrates the point. Advocates of the racialist position often encouraged policies that separated the races so as to avoid contamination of the higher race by the lower, while proponents of the climatic view advocated vast projects, such as deforestation, for altering the climate.[22] Political science, by contrast, works inside of or through political processes. Knowledge enters political life by the dissemination of the science and its conclusions. It advises political actors. *The Federalist* itself is the example par excellence of political science being inserted into political life. It executes in practice what it teaches in theory. Although political science contains some technical aspects that may be of interest mostly to specialists, it is knowledge that is intelligible to statesmen, legislators, and important parts of the citizenry. Its subject matter overlaps the horizon of those concerned with politics.

Natural history and political science seek knowledge for different purposes. Natural history, with its roots in natural science, is looking for a full explanation of how things have developed. This knowledge may ultimately be used to manipulate or control, but the science begins with the abstract goal of understanding for its own sake. Political science is less concerned with pure knowledge in this sense. It is oriented to inquiries that can assist legislators and citizens in the task of handling affairs. It is a "practical" science. Political science tries to establish certain probabilistic propositions of the type that indicate how certain arrangements—for example, a separation of powers—tend to promote certain outcomes—for example, nondespotic government—under some set of specifiable conditions. All of its propositions have to be applied by persons acting in specific circumstances. Because the circumstances may be more decisive in a specific case than any general rule, and because there can always be something new or unique in any case, the propositions are advisory only and can never be a substitute for political judgment.

PHILOSOPHY OF HISTORY

The other science that sought to replace political science as a guide to political life is known as "Philosophy of History," or what its most preeminent spokesman of the age, the Marquis de Condorcet, called the "new philosophy."[23] Its premise was that there is a source of inevitable movement operating inside history that shapes the politics of the future. The development of commerce and the emergence of rationalist philosophy were pushing developed nations along a path that would lead progressively to what *The Federalist* characterized as a "happy empire" of a peaceful universal world order. In the more optimistic versions, the world was said to be heading toward a "golden age" of "perpetual peace."[24]

Philosophy of History sought to replace political science by eliminating the political regime as an independent cause. While the regime was important, it was determined at each stage by the deeper cause of historical movement. Political science, by this account, had the reduced task of helping to work out how to proceed within the interstices created by this process. *The Federalist* rejected Philosophy of History as a false science offered by "visionary and designing men" and "political projectors" who constructed doctrines—we might say an ideology—that began from a preconceived political project.[25] Its speculations ran counter the "the history of mankind" and "experience."[26] By assuming an automatic movement toward peace and order, it tried to erase in one swoop all of the tensions of political life, such basic matters, for example, as the problem of mingling liberty and security "in their due proportions."[27] A pseudo-science of this sort might be easy to dismiss except for the fact that the structure of thinking at the time was susceptible to any set of ideas that could somehow present itself under the guise of science or philosophy. For much of the period, the conflict of ideas was defined by the distinction between the "new thinking" of science, which was opening the world progressively to a new and enlightened age, and the old forces that were based on superstition and prejudice. *The Federalist* was one of the early works to explode the simple science-superstition distinction and to warn that false doctrine in the modern age would most likely wear the face not of superstition but of science, the better to insinuate itself with peoples who took pride in being enlightened. It is one of the first books to expose what we today call "ideology."

The Federalist denies that there is any movement inside of history that has foreclosed decisive political choice. Of course, the authors recognized tremendous changes in historical circumstances that both created new possibilities and imposed new limits on human action.[28] The size and scope of political units were different than in ancient times, when the city-state prevailed. Now it was the nation that prevailed, and no people wishing for independence and power could do without a large territory and a commercial economy. There were many other respects in which modern man faced a new world confronted by a new set of issues and dilemmas. But this fact did not erase the political dimensions of life. The decisive political questions—whether men will live in free or despotic governments, whether they will live under a rational order or under new forms of ideology—remained matters to be decided at the political level. This point is woven into the very fabric of *The Federalist*, which begins and ends by expressing uncertainty about how the political "experiment" in constitutional government would turn out. Everything in 1789 hung in the balance, and it remained unknown "whether societies of men are really capable or not of establishing governments from reflection and choice, or whether they are forever destined to depend for their political constitutions on accident and force."[29]

One of the Founders' singular achievements was their contribution to a "science of politics" that could help sustain the new liberal democratic system they established. It is unfortunate that the discipline as practiced today has abandoned their focus of inquiring into the factors that support and undermine different political systems in favor of knowledge that aims to maximize the explanation of variance. Its models are the natural sciences and economics. The greatest monument to the Founders today would not be the construction of another edifice cast in brick, stone, or steel, but rather a project devoted to reviving their understanding of political science.

5

✦

Demagoguery, Statesmanship, and Presidential Politics

Presidents today generally expend a large amount of time and effort seeking to secure a direct connection to the American public and to manage and win over public opinion, an activity now known in the textbooks as the "public presidency," the "personal presidency," and, most often, the "rhetorical presidency."[1] Woodrow Wilson described the ideal of this relationship more than a century ago in his classic work *Constitutional Government*: "The nation as a whole has chosen him, and is conscious that it has no other political spokesman. . . . Let him once win the admiration and confidence of the country, and no other single force can withstand him."[2] Presidents and presidential candidates, according to this understanding, regularly engage in efforts at mass persuasion, seeking to elevate the public by appeals to high principle or to inspire it by the articulation of a great vision.

Who wills the end must also will the means. To achieve public support, presidents rely extensively on the art or science formerly known as "rhetoric" and today as "public relations." They have at their beck and call teams of speechwriters, communications specialists, and pollsters, all paid for from the public treasury. No serious candidate would think of running a national campaign without a full stable of media consultants and public relations experts.

These practices are fairly late developments in the history of the presidency. Although presidents have always valued public support, the use of many techniques of public relations was tightly circumscribed prior to the twentieth century. Political parties would employ all the popular techniques, but not presidents or presidential candidates. Presidents rarely took their case to the people in speeches that treated matters of public policy. This practice was considered unpresidential and, at the outer limit, a challenge to Congress's constitutional prerogatives.[3] One item in the Articles of Impeachment against President Andrew Johnson involved his going public, citing his "intemperate, inflammatory, and scandalous harangues" aimed at inciting disrespect of Congress, promoting the "cries, jeers and laughter of the multitudes then assembled in hearing."[4] Presidents had no special staff to assist them with speechwriting, and when they received help, as President Washington did in drafting his Farewell Address (from both Madison and Hamilton), it was done with discretion, a quality that has become more rare among modern speechwriters, who often make haste to claim credit for their lines. Presidential candidates likewise generally avoided canvassing for votes, discouraged in part by the norm that "the office should seek the man, not the man the office."[5] Although this norm was widely known to be more fiction than fact, it retained enough authority to command adherence to certain public forms of behavior.

By the beginning of the twentieth century, this kind of reserve of presidential candidates and presidents was being challenged. Powerful personalities such as William Jennings Bryan and Theodore Roosevelt refused to adhere to these restrictions and sought out direct links to the public. The older view, which regarded speechifying with suspicion, gave way to a new idea that, in Wilson's words, "it is [only] natural that orators should be the leaders of a self-governing people."[6] The 1912 presidential campaign, involving President Taft, Theodore Roosevelt, Woodrow Wilson, and Eugene Debs, was perhaps the greatest example of rhetorical competition in American history. The transformation from the more reserved idea of the presidency to the modern rhetorical presidency did not take place without opposition, as many worried that the new conception would undermine constitutional restraints and increase the risk of dangerous popular appeals and "demagoguery."[7] But the dominant thinkers of the Progressive movement dismissed these concerns as old-fashioned, insisting that a more enlightened public made such appeals obsolete. To succeed in modern politics, they argued, leaders would need to employ public, serious arguments and make high-minded, inspirational appeals.

Modern students of the presidency have not been as optimistic as the Progressives. They have instead warned of the dangers of "merchandizing" and "packaging" presidents and candidates and decried the advent of the "permanent campaign" and "negative advertising." The titles of some of the books tell the story: *The Selling of the President* (Joe McGiniss), *Dirty Politics: Deception, Distraction, and Democracy* (Kathleen Jamison), and *Politics Lost: How American Democracy Was Trivialized by People Who Think You're Stupid* (Joe Klein). Dubious aspects of public relations techniques have apparently developed hand in hand with the rise of the rhetorical presidency. For all these concerns, however, most commentators have been reluctant to invoke the "d" word (demagoguery), perhaps because it offends democratic scruples by suggesting that part of the problem lies with a defect in the people. The more usual approach is to suggest that the greatest dangers derive, somehow, from oligarchic threats, such as "big money" and the "interests." Nor does the word "demagoguery" often appear in the leadership studies of political scientists, where the dominant approaches feature theories based on the principle-agent model and political entrepreneurship. Traditional terms such as "demagoguery" and its frequent companion (and antithesis) "statesmanship" are considered too vague (or too normative) for scientific analysis. After all, one woman's statesman may be no more than another man's demagogue.[8]

No one can quarrel with the pursuit of rigor. But a science ultimately can only be as precise as its subject matter allows. Excluding traditional concepts does more harm than good if the effect is to limit consideration of important issues, even when the meanings of these concepts are difficult to pin down.[9] The aim of the current inquiry is accordingly to revisit the term "demagoguery" and, to a lesser extent, its companion concept, "statesmanship." The analysis begins from the top down, surveying how these terms have been applied in the past, and then proceeds from the bottom up, investigating noteworthy instances where there have been widespread accusations of demagoguery in presidential politics. Just as the notion of "greatness" in the presidency cannot be examined without discussing specific cases of great presidents, so it is impossible to "appreciate" demagoguery without considering—and even ranking—some of our most effective demagogues. They merit no less.

THE FOUNDERS AND THE PROBLEM OF DEMAGOGUERY

The office of the presidency that the Founders created in 1787 represented a new kind of political institution. Its originality rested on two main features: a mix of powers and functions designed to supply republican government with the energy it previously lacked, and the selection of the chief magistrate by a system that accorded great weight to popular preferences. If, as opponents to the Constitution charged, the president's powers resembled those of a king, they at least conceded that the new office was an *"elective* monarchy."[10] But while taking this democratic step, the Founders were concerned that popular competition could open the door to the "vicious arts by which elections are too often carried," enabling those adept at cultivating popular favor to win office and destroy the system.[11] The Founders used a number of terms to describe such persons, including "popular leaders," "favorites," and "orators," but the strongest word was "demagogue." Demagoguery frames *The Federalist*, figuring prominently in the first and the last of its eighty-five essays. Demagoguery for the Founders thrived in the political space of direct appeals to popular audiences. It was most likely to appear in elections, but it might easily extend beyond this phase to affect sitting presidents, who, in their wish "to be continued," might show a "servile pliancy" to public passions or who might attempt to manipulate public opinion to gain an advantage.[12] The qualities of firmness and energy that the presidential office was intended to embody could be placed in jeopardy.

Following classical political science, the Founders regarded demagoguery as a principal source of the instability of ancient republics. "History will teach us," *The Federalist* asserts, that "of those men who have overturned the liberties of republics, the greatest number have begun their career by paying an obsequious court to the people, commencing demagogues and ending tyrants."[13] According to James Madison, the problem was already in evidence in some of the states, where many representatives had become "the dupe to a favorite leader . . . varnishing his sophistical arguments with the glowing colours of popular eloquence."[14]

The Founders thought they had discovered new means to control the problem of demagoguery in the selection of the president. By transforming popular government from democracy in a limited territory, where orators addressed the public in open assemblies, into representative government covering a large expanse, where direct communication of national leaders with the public was more limited, the opportunities for practicing demagoguery would be diminished. The exclusion of the public from direct responsibility for making policy decisions was counted another mechanism of control, since demagoguery flourished in large meetings in which orators spoke on matters to be immediately decided. It is one of the "infirmities incident to collective meetings of the people," *The Federalist* contends, that "ignorance will be the dupe of cunning, and passion the slave of sophistry and declamation." The author (Madison in this case) continues: "the more numerous an assembly may be, of whatever characters composed, the greater is known to be the ascendancy of passion over reason. . . . In the ancient republics, where the whole body of the people assembled in person, a single orator, or an artful statesman, was generally seen to rule with as complete a sway as if a scepter had been placed in his single hand."[15]

Yet even with these new safeguards, the Founders remained wary. No institutional solution is foolproof. Inventive demagogues might find novel ways to break through whatever barriers were erected to thwart them. Demagogues could arise not only in electoral contests but also in political organizations or movements. Demagoguery was clearly at its most dangerous, however, when it was employed inside the governing process, serving as a technique to activate public opinion and transform it into a source of political influence. Rather than power deriving from the constituted authority of the offices, it would rest on a claim to speak for the public. Formal constitutional government might then devolve into "informal" demagogic governance. In modern terms, the presidency is characterized by the "permanent campaign" in which, according to Hugh Heclo, presidents and other leaders "engage people to tell them what they want to hear in ways that will promote one's cause against others."[16] Constitutional government stood in continual threat of a shadow demagogic regime that undermined it from within.

The Founders' analysis echoed the classical treatments of the same problem. In his life of Caius Gracchus, Plutarch explored the effects generated by this "greatest" of Roman demagogues. Caius subtly challenged the forms of existing constitutional practice: "Whereas other popular leaders had always hitherto, when speaking, turned their faces toward the senate house," Caius "was the first man that in his harangue to the people turned the other way." The result of this seemingly "insignificant movement and change of posture" was to "mark no small revolution in state affairs, the conversion, in a manner, of the whole government from an aristocracy to a democracy." Plutarch then expanded on this theme by detaching the practice of demagoguery from the person of the demagogue. To counter Caius's popular appeal, some of the leading senators persuaded the Senate to attempt to outbid him "by playing the demagogue in opposition to him and offering favors contrary to all good policy."[17] The Founders similarly worried about the general practice of raising public opinion to assault the formal prerogatives of an office.

In view of the danger of demagoguery, the Founders took further steps to curb it by giving the new government a constitutional tone. This tone would be enforced, if not always by the political leaders themselves, then by enlightened parts of the public. *The Federalist* is filled with warnings against flattery and against the "artful misrepresentations of interested men" who encourage the people to indulge "the tyranny of their own passions."[18] But norms by themselves were thought to be insufficient. In the case of the presidency, the Founders argued for a fairly lengthy term to allow presidents to pursue projects without the need to cater directly to public opinion. They also instituted formal mechanisms of public communication, obliging presidents to present to Congress "information on the state of the union" and to supply publicly the reasons for a veto. This system, according to Jeffrey Tulis, was meant to "constitutionalize" presidential communication by channeling it away from informal popular orations and toward more deliberative forms of rhetoric.[19]

For the presidential selection process, the Founders counted heavily on the "automatic" effects that derived not just from the size of the national constituency but also the multitude of interests found in a commercial republic. Candidates in this setting could not generally hope to win the presidency by playing to the intense passions of a single group. The same remedy the Founders relied on to block majority faction would discourage demagoguery. The two problems were connected, as demagogues were the usual agents of faction formation. Once again, however, the Founders sought "auxiliary precautions," since the extended geographical sphere could not always be counted on. The precaution was found in the presidential selection system.

The Constitution, contrary to what one reads in most textbooks, created not three but four national institutions: the presidency, the Congress, the Supreme Court, and the presidential selection system. The question of presidential selection was of fundamental importance to the Founders. They established a system that was meant to institutionalize the process from start to finish—from the gathering and winnowing of suitable individuals up to the final election. The institution was intended, on the "up" side, to secure a good president, but in any case, on the "down" side, to block the demagogue and suppress demagoguery. The system was meant to be popular. It provided for election of the president by specially chosen electors, a method that, given the insuperable practical obstacles at the time to conducting a national popular vote, made the use of electors the only practical means available to provide for public influence.[20] Yet once the device of electors was decided upon, the Founders added features that could operate as checks. The electors had formal discretion in their vote and, in one of the most important provisions, had *two* votes for the presidency.[21] While public opinion might constrain them on one of their votes, they would have much freer rein with their "second" vote, using it to select responsible leaders.

Taken as a whole, the system seemed to be designed to give great weight to public opinion, especially in the case of a public judgment of an incumbent's performance, where the public could be expected to have developed a real opinion. With no limitation on the terms, this element of the decision process would have been more often in play than is the case today after the passage of the Twenty-second Amendment, limiting a president to two terms. Beyond this, when it came to elevating an individual to the presidency, the system was meant to focus attention on judging the candidates' reputation and record of national service. The selection of individual would not turn on immediate candidate appeals made during an election campaign, and there was no indication that there would be a popular campaign directly involving the candidates. If ambitious men came to see that demagoguery ("talents for low intrigue, and the little arts of popularity") was not the means by which they could hope to be elected, they would turn their efforts to building a solid record of service; they would seek to win the "esteem and confidence" of large parts of the public to show that they were "characters pre-eminent for ability and virtue."[22] The selection system was meant to send signals that would structure the behavior of politicians throughout their careers.

CHANGES IN PRESIDENTIAL SELECTION AND IN THE FOUNDATION OF PRESIDENTIAL POWER

The Constitution's selection system did not survive intact beyond the two elections of George Washington. By the third election (1796), political parties emerged and managed to have the electors selected on the basis of their pledge to support the party nominees for president and for vice president. The electors lost their discretion on both of their votes, becoming bound (or at least pressured) delegates, not independent agents. In recognition of these changes (and of the related mischief stemming from a tie in electoral votes between Jefferson and Burr in 1800), the Constitution was amended to end the two-vote system.

Under the Twelfth Amendment (1804), electors were limited to a single vote for president and a separate single vote for vice president. The filtering function of the Constitution's electoral system was eliminated. Political parties now effectively took over the task, winnowing and selecting the candidates at the nominating stage.[23] Parties made their choice initially using the only practical mechanism that was readily at hand, which was a meeting of its members in Congress convened in a party caucus. The criteria of selection now included partisan commitment, but beyond that most of the "constitutional" considerations continued to operate. The final election, in which the public or state legislators chose bound electors, was between two candidates already vetted by the parties. The public, or legislatures reflecting public sentiment, made the final choice.

This change from a constitutional to a nonconstitutional instrument (the political party) might seem to have been a reasonable expedient for controlling demagoguery, certainly in the early stages of the process. Yet it suffered at the time from the grave problem that few regarded it as a permanent institutional solution. Early partisans generally conceived of political parties as temporary organizations. The aim of a party was to win power and eliminate the opposition once and for all, allowing for the subsequent reestablishment of nonpartisanship on its "true" foundation. When Jefferson in his first inaugural address declared, "We are all federalists; we are all republicans," he was stating the goal of most partisans. They wanted an end to parties, although each group of partisans on the basis of *its* party's principles. As long as the great question of which principles would be victorious remained up in the air, partisan competition continued. But it was not for very long.

With the arrival of the so-called era of good feeling, political party competition effectively came to an end. The Federalists were eliminated as a national party after 1816, and by 1824 enormous pressure had built within the one remaining party, the Democratic-Republicans, to eliminate its last vestige of party organization—the congressional caucus. It was difficult to justify a procedure of party nomination if all candidates were bona fide Republican-Democrats and if nonpartisanship was the official mantra of national leadership, which became the case under President Monroe. In addition, with only one party, nomination by the caucus appeared more and more undemocratic, earning that institution the fatal name of "King Caucus." Not only did this system, as John Quincy Adams noted, "place the President in a state of undue subserviency to the members of the legislature," but—since nomination with one party was now tantamount to election—it also deprived the public of any real role in the election of the president. The final election became a mere formality.

The caucus was abandoned in 1824. The result was that there was no national mechanism to nominate candidates and limit their number. There was only the final election, which, because of previous changes, took place by bound electors selected by voters or state legislatures. The presidential contest was now a (fairly) popular nonpartisan selection system, but with all the restraints and checks that the Founders intended eliminated. The potential for the appearance of demagoguery in the final election loomed much larger. Five candidates presented themselves for the final election in 1824, with popular appeals to the electorate made by or on behalf of each of them. With none of the candidates in the field appearing likely to attain an electoral majority, candidate strategies aimed at winning a smaller segment of the electorate, enough to finish among the top three electoral vote recipients, which is the threshold for inclusion for the final election vote in the House of Representatives.

Historians who look back on the 1824 election generally treat it as an aberration. With the exception of George Washington's two elections, it was the only fully nonpartisan election in American history. It is also the only election in which no candidate achieved the required minimum of electoral votes, which forced the final choice into the House of Representatives. But if 1824 is an aberration, it only became so because of deliberate steps that were taken after the election. At the time, the system of 1824 looked to most politicians to be the permanent new method of selecting the president. It was the method in accord with the reigning ideas of nonpartisanship and of popular election of the president. Most of its consequences seemed likely to continue.

Led by Martin Van Buren, the junior senator from New York, a group of politicians argued that this system was a disaster for the nation. Without a means for paring down the choice to two candidates, the most likely outcome would be elections in which there would be no majority at the electoral stage, forcing the decision to be made by the House. Many were unsatisfied with this system, with its awkward one-vote-per-state rule and with the old threat posed to the separation of powers by a legislative choice of the president. Without nomination, the final election became an open contest among individuals for the prize. More important, the system served as an open invitation to demagoguery. In the words of one of Van Buren's followers, it inevitably resulted in candidates' "traveling through the country, courting support . . . and assiduously practicing all the low arts of popularity."[24] Appeals to sectional divisions proved to be especially effective as a tool. As Van Buren wrote, "If the old ones [party feelings] are suppressed, geographical divisions founded on local interest or, what is worse, prejudices between free and slaveholding states will inevitably take their place."[25] With the presidential election being the focal point of national politics, Van Buren feared that the descent into demagogic politics would lead in short order to national disintegration.

Van Buren's remedy was the reestablishment of party competition as a permanent feature of the political system. Van Buren is the "father" in America of the idea of permanent party competition as a full institutional component of the American political system. As much as Van Buren wanted victory by his own party (the Democrats), he wanted even more the triumph of the system of party competition. His deepest "partisanship" was for this "constitutional" transformation. Two moderate national parties, each having a long-term principle and an interest in maintaining itself, would nominate responsible candidates. Each party would try to build a coalition to win a national majority, with the result that the presidential election would be decided at the stage of the vote by the electors (which in reality became a vote by the public); recourse to the undemocratic and problematic auxiliary system of selection by the House of Representatives, where each state has one vote, would be avoided. (In fact, no presidential election since 1824 has gone to the House.) Political parties would serve as the gateways through which all the major aspirants to the presidency would now have to pass, which restored a vital filtering mechanism to the selection process. Parties would stand "above" individual aspirants. Rather than advancing their own, temporary programs as the basis of their candidacies, which would be an invitation to demagoguery, candidates would have to embrace the long-term principles of a party.

Party nominations would also help resolve another difficulty now emerging with the passing from the scene of the generation of the Founders: the problem of stature. All presidents up through Monroe possessed a degree of stature by virtue of having played some role in the great enterprise of the Founding. The ordinary politicians of the next generation lacked this standing. Either this would lead to the selection of persons who had achieved a name by means that were irrelevant to their political competency—Van Buren originally viewed Jackson in this light—or it would tempt ordinary politicians into demagoguery as the basis to distinguish themselves and win popular favor. The political party, Van Buren argued, was the great instrument that could successfully bring the nation into the democratic age and supply responsible politicians, persons having no claim to being Founders or military heroes, with the needed credibility. Then as now the investiture of an individual with a party nomination transforms him overnight into a new person, higher in rank than before.

From early on, Van Buren concluded that the caucus system was finished and that a new system of party nomination was needed. This period became the Age of Jackson, in which people demanded a greater role in choosing their leaders. By 1828, all but two states selected their electors by popular vote, and almost no one was prepared to return to the rule of parties by a small group of Washington politicians. In the party system that was created in the 1830s, the task of nomination was assigned to a new institution of the party convention, a meeting of delegates, chosen by the state party organization, who were generally strongly attached to the party and who now had a stake in the whole process. Not only was the convention more democratic than the caucus, but it also allowed large numbers of politicians to meet face to face to work out the arrangements, including the choice of the nominee, that secured party harmony. As time went on, of course, the conventions also occasionally became the forums for revealing and intensifying factional differences.

In this new era of party dominance, the parties generally ran the campaign, with the candidates remaining on the sidelines. As one scholar described the system, "The parties, trusting their professionals, deemed candidates exploitable and interchangeable. The party did not want a candidate to interfere: Parties were enduring; candidacies were fads."[26] However much Van Buren and his group of party builders differed from the Founders in the means they employed, they shared with them the objective of discouraging individual demagogic appeals in presidential politics. The party system achieved this end in a new and arguably more democratic manner than the Founders had envisioned. Parties were not impermeable to popular movements or renewal from below, but such movements would have to achieve a fairly high threshold of support in order to become influential in the party. They would need to be something more than merely personal followings of a single individual.[27] Demagogic candidates were forced to the outer reaches of American politics in third parties.

Elements of the party system that was created in the 1830s remain in place today, but the differences are more notable than the similarities.

Parties still nominate, and the decision is still made (nominally) by party conventions. But beginning with a long and drawn-out process that commenced with the Progressives in 1912 and culminated in 1972, Van Buren's conception of party selection was dramatically altered. The effective nomination choice was removed from the party conventions (and the party-oriented delegates who controlled them) and given chiefly to the public by means of primary elections. The Progressive proponents of this change were explicit in their objectives. They sought to reduce the corporate influence of the party in the nomination decision on the grounds that the parties were corrupt and controlled by big interests; the system, they alleged, stifled the emergence of genuine popular statesmen. The remedy was to reverse the presumption contained in the party system founded by Van Buren and place the individual candidate "above" the party, with the party forming around the successful nominee's program as articulated in a popular contest. As chief orator and leader of public opinion, the presidential candidate, and eventually the president, would enjoy expanded power and influence. The new system would supply the conditions in which individual popular appeals live and thrive.

Without pronouncing final judgment on the overall merit of this change, it is necessary to note one of its consequences. The modern selection process, in which the long nomination phase is now open to a large number of aspirants making direct popular appeals, has clearly opened the door to the appearance of more oratorical campaigns. Call the style populist, charismatic, or demagogic, there is no question that this kind of popular leadership campaign is now at the center of the selection process. To date it is plausible to argue that the genuinely demagogic candidates running these campaigns have been screened out before the final election phase, although perhaps not without having influenced the tone of presidential campaigns and the character of the presidency.

THE EVOLUTION OF THE CONCEPT OF DEMAGOGUERY

The term *demagogue*, deriving from the Greek roots of *demos* (people) and *agogos* (leading), emerged in the fifth century B.C. In Athens, and in many other Greek city-states of the time, the political situation was characterized by a division between two parties vying for control: one comprised chiefly of the nobles or oligarchs, the other of the common people. Initially, the term "demagogue" referred descriptively to a "leader of the people" or of the popular party and carried no special opprobrium, or no more opprobrium than might have been assigned to any leader of this party. Thus, Themistocles and Pericles as well as Cleon were all referred to as demagogues.[28]

The normative dimension of the term appears to have developed from the contrasting portraits of Pericles and Cleon that were so vividly presented by Thucydides. Both were leaders of the popular party in Athens, but the difference between them was like day and night. Pericles appears as the great leader—educated, noble in vision, and accomplished as a memorable speaker (his funeral oration stands as the most famous public address of antiquity). Pericles was so substantial a figure that, after a time, he acquired sufficient stature to free himself from being beholden to the passions and prejudices of the multitude. Rather than follow the public, he could lead and instruct it, which is something that in America perhaps only George Washington had the full confidence to do. (Such was not always the case on his way up, when Pericles became known for indulging the public with generous payments for attending popular assemblies.) Under his leadership Athens was a democracy in name, but a "government by its first citizen" in fact.[29] His standing and independence enabled him to keep the public on an even keel: "Whenever he saw them [the people] unseasonably and insolently elated, he would with a word reduce them to alarm; and on the other hand, if they fell victims to a panic, he would at once restore them to confidence."[30]

Cleon, by contrast, lacked these attractive qualities and seemed to be concerned only with acquiring personal influence. This difference led to the distinction between the "demagogue," understood now in a pejorative sense, and the "statesman" (*politikos*), a term first used extensively by Plato.[31] The demagogue now came to be understood as a particular kind of leader of the people, one who leads by inflammatory appeals or by flattery and who proceeds to build personal popularity without concern for promoting the public good. The statesman, who may lead either the popular party or the party of the nobles, aims to serve the public good and has acquired knowledge of the art of doing so ("statesmanship"). Three hundred years later, Plutarch adopted and solidified this vocabulary in presenting his famous gallery of the leaders of Greece and Rome. He supplied the prototypes of demagogues and statesmen from which others drew, including, of course, William Shakespeare.

Political analysis since Plutarch has treated demagoguery and statesmanship as a dyad. But while the two terms offer a contrast, they are not perfect mirror opposites. The reason is that they emphasize different spheres of activities. Demagoguery always functions in the realm of appealing to a public; its distinguishing characteristic is the practice of enhancing popular standing. It tends to flourish in systems, or in parts of systems, in which public approval or standing can generate power. It is thus not usually found in the internal councils of government or in a senate, unless a senator is addressing (directly or indirectly) the crowd. Demagoguery is more at home in the mass assembly, or on the street before a crowd, as in Marc Antony's famous address following Caesar's assassination, or, in modern times, in election campaigns. The demagogue has accordingly been defined by the Oxford English Dictionary as "a popular leader or orator who espoused the cause of the people against any other party in the state."[32]

Demagoguery is not directly concerned with handling political affairs, but with boosting popular support. Many classical demagogues preferred to limit their role to promoting positions in the assembly without ever taking an actual office, a stratagem that allowed them to avoid assuming direct responsibility for even their own proposals. Demagoguery applies to decision-making or governing only incidentally, insofar as certain kinds of stock demagogic policies, such as schemes for the redistribution of wealth, contribute to enhancing approval. Demagoguery in its pure sense is indifferent to the goodness of the policies it promotes, which is not to deny that some demagogues sincerely believe in at least some of their proposals. Yet because achieving the public good in politics is often difficult, and because it often requires measures that are not immediately popular, demagoguery will frequently miss the mark and support measures that would do more harm than good. Walter Lippmann expressed this point well when he observed that demagoguery "stops at relieving the tension by expressing the feeling. But the statesman knows that such relief is temporary, and if indulged too often, unsanitary. He therefore sees to it that he arouses no feeling which he cannot sluice into a program that deals with the facts to which the feelings give rise."[33]

Statesmanship, following Lippmann, is concerned chiefly with handling political affairs. It is the art of directing matters to promote the public interest and, to add a "classical" touch, of educating or ennobling the public. Statesmanship often refers to activities where winning popular approval is not at issue, as in instances of conducting diplomacy and negotiations. Statesmanship can therefore describe leadership in nondemocratic systems, as when Henry Kissinger refers to the statesmanship of the Austrian diplomat Metternich, who represented the Hapsburg Empire. In popular systems, however, statesmanship must deal with the democratic components of politics. The achievement of good policies involves winning sufficient votes to be elected and securing popular support. In these activities, the popular statesman, no less than the demagogue, must be adept in the art of persuasion. Even so, the statesman's rhetoric will ordinarily be different from the demagogue's. It will seek, as a rule, to calm rather than excite, to conciliate rather than divide, and to instruct rather than flatter. The statesman is willing to speak sternly to the people, in the fashion of Pericles or Publius; his characteristic posture is to say what the people *need* to hear rather than what they *wish* to hear. The statesman's way is not to "flatter [the people's] prejudice to betray their interests";

he is not an "adulator."[34] The demagogue's art, by contrast, is meant to satisfy the public's appetite; Socrates nicely compares it in the *Gorgias* to that of "the pastry chef."

Maintaining a restrained and elevated tone is not, however, always possible. As a system becomes more democratic, with continual demands for communications between politicians and people, the kind of sternness just depicted may appear too forbidding or arrogant, if not simply boring. At some point in the democratization of a political system, greater familiarity—a dose of the "little arts of popularity"—is almost a requirement for a normal politician to survive. Nor is a restrained tone always advisable. Situations arise in which something different is required for the public good. The problem presented by trying to thwart an able and dangerous demagogue is an example; the statesman under some circumstances might have no choice but to resort to something like demagoguery. Fire can sometimes only be fought with fire.

These regrettable exceptions, in which the statesman needs to avail himself of something akin to a "rhetorical prerogative," pose an obvious complication. Simple definitions break down or cannot do justice to the phenomena. The analyst must look "behind" the external character of leadership appeals and make judgments about the intentions and the likely effects of actions. Insofar as definitions are helpful, it makes sense to separate the demagogue from demagoguery. The demagogue is one who consistently practices demagoguery, doing so without restraint. The demagogue will not sacrifice his own interest for the public good.[35] The statesman will always wish to avoid demagoguery and will make use of it only where needed to avert greater harm to the city or nation.

TYPES OF DEMAGOGUES

Classical political science distinguished between at least two types of demagogues. The first was modeled on Cleon, a person whose profile fits the likes of a George Wallace, a Jean-Marie Le Pen, or a Patrick Buchanan. The demagogue in this case presents himself as not only for the people, but also conspicuously of the people. He has no family name or elite status, nor has he performed a notable service or heroic deed that has earned him personal stature. (Cleon was the owner of a tannery[36]; neither Le Pen nor Buchanan held important public office, while Wallace, as governor of Alabama, never obtained real distinction, as opposed to notoriety.) The demagogue wins political influence through oratory and position-taking. He searches for a wave of opinion, hoping to ride the swell as far as it will carry him. Where necessary, he produces his own wave by fomenting or exploiting latent divisions, finding a convenient target to assault, or introducing what are today called "wedges." The demagogue may pit the "people against the powerful," rural folk against city dwellers, or the "little guy" against the "pointy-headed intellectual."

Because the demagogue lacks personal stature, his appeal is the basis of his standing with the public. It follows that he will feel vulnerable to being outflanked or "out-demagogued."[37] His insecurity in relation to potential rivals pushes him to compete in the extremity of his positions or in the flamboyance of his actions. As Aristotle said of Cleon, "He was the first who shouted on the public platform, who used abusive language and who spoke with his cloak girt about him, while all the others used to speak in proper dress and manner."[38] Demagogues often attract attention to themselves by breaking existing norms or "forms" that protect propriety or the constitutional dimension of power.

One way this kind of demagogue (referred to here as "Type I") can obtain a measure of personal standing independent of his opinions is to show bravado in defying the elite. The demagogue will sometimes invite the contempt of the better sorts, which he then wears as a badge of honor. His barely concealed, or even openly avowed, appeals to envy fortify this image; he "stands up" for the "little guy." Yet, because he lacks genuine stature, the public does not look up to or respect him. If he is not continually rising in his bid to win greater influence, the public may turn on him, as they did with Cleon. The demagogue pulls the people down in ways that they sometimes half sense. From this fact derives one of the backhanded compliments of democracy, which is that the people are invariably better than their worst demagogues.

The Type I demagogue will also appeal to the closed elements and prejudices of the community—the things that protect its traditions and way of life. The demagogue is the intolerant defender of the community's mores, orthodoxies, and creed against the persons or forces depicted as undermining them. Such a stance accounts for this type of demagogue's reliance on fear and anger, which are the passions most easily aroused among those who feel that their way of life is under threat. Joe McCarthy practiced this form of demagoguery in his attacks on alleged Communists in the early 1950s. The demagogue in such instances targets those who are different or alien (foreigners or religious minorities), or those who are said to be cosmopolitan (free thinkers and philosophers). Rhetoric of this kind enables the demagogue to expand his appeal well beyond the poor to a much broader audience, which can include portions of the elite class. Plato depicts a notable example in the *Apology*, where the accusers of Socrates try to win support by charging him with corrupting the youth by questioning the gods.

Many in the upper classes treat Type I demagogues with contempt, disparaging them for being "mere" demagogues who stir things up, but who lack the real ability to rule, which is found only among aristocrats. Some aristocrats try to use these demagogues for their own purposes, allowing them to do their dirty work before casting them aside when the time is right, a strategy that sometimes works. According to V. O. Key, this tactic was employed by elites in some of the Southern states in the early twentieth century, when they tolerated local demagogues to handle the "Negro problem." But those in the upper class, in their arrogance, just as often make the mistake of underestimating lower-class demagogues, whose crudeness and lack of breeding does not necessarily mean that they lack the desire to rule or cunning to do so. Many German intellectuals and aristocrats in the 1930s believed that that they could control Adolf Hitler, a hope nicely captured by the German phrase, *den Führer führen* ("to lead the Leader"); it was too late before they realized their error.

While the likes of Cleon served as the initial model for the demagogue, classical thinkers identified a second type, one more dangerous because less obvious. If flattery is most artful when it is least noticed, the "better" demagogue is the one who escapes ready labeling. This form of demagoguery (Type II) is usually exercised by a figure from the patrician class or by someone who has achieved stature from military exploits. Plato sketches this second type of demagogue in his account of Pericles, whom he viewed quite critically. Another example was the young and attractive Alcibiades, whom Plutarch labeled "the greatest of the demagogues."[39] Probably the most famous example, however, is Julius Caesar, who, according to Tim Duff, fit perfectly the model of "a popular leader who comes to power through demagogic means and uses that power to install himself as a tyrant."[40]

"Caesarism" now serves as a label for absolutist rule established initially by popular means, and it applies to more modern figures like Napoleon. These leaders may initially appear easygoing or enlightened, at least until they secure their position; afterward, finding popular support to be too unreliable a foundation on which to rest their authority, they subvert republican government. Caesar serves as the frequent anti-model for many of the Founders. The *Federalist* reminded Americans of this point when it observed that most of "those men who have overturned the liberties of republics . . . [began] their career by paying an obsequious court to the people, commencing demagogues and ending tyrants."[41]

THE APPEALS OF DEMAGOGUERY

The "raw material" for demagoguery is found in the opinion and sentiment that the artful leader can create and exploit in a particular place and time. The possibilities are almost limitless. The options can range from the perennial standby of stimulating class hatred, to fomenting racial or religious prejudice, to manipulating a dislike of politicians or "insiders" (a technique perfected by Ross Perot in 1992). The "good" demagogue will have a fine ear for appeals that generate divisions and lift his standing among the public.

Two early classics of American politics illustrate some of the options. In *The Federalist*, Publius warned how the sentiment of "jealousy" toward authority (especially of executive authority) was serving as a demagogic ploy in the campaign opposing the Constitution. Fear of a "tyrannical" king had, of course, served the nation well in the revolutionary struggle, when it was directed against a foreign government (Great Britain) that had a nonrepublican government. Now, however, it was being used to "stigmatize" the concern for "energy and efficiency in government" as "the offspring of a temper fond of despotic power and hostile to the principles of liberty."[42] The appeal to "jealousy" was all the more effective for claiming to be a friend to the cause of liberty.

In *Democracy in America*, Alexis de Tocqueville similarly identified "the *decentralizing* passions" found in America in the 1830s as a rich source of demagogic appeals. The manipulation of these passions, he argued, was the core of Andrew Jackson's leadership as president. Even if Tocqueville's charge against Jackson was off the mark (as many have argued), his description of demagoguery can hardly be improved on: "He maintains himself and prospers by flattering these passions daily. General Jackson is the slave of the majority: he follows it in its wishes, its desires, its half-uncovered instincts, or rather he divines it and runs to place himself at its head."[43]

Despite the variegated content of demagogic appeals, it has been argued that they evoke one of three root passions: envy, fear, or hope. Envy, a kind of "pain [felt] at the good fortune of other," is the staple of class-based demagoguery.[44] The demagogue calls attention to something that the many lack—be it wealth or position or honors—and tells his listeners that they are entitled to the object of their wishes—"every man a king," in the motto of Huey Long—or that those who possess these things should be dispossessed of them. Envy is elevated to the status of a principle by being confounded with arguments of democratic justice. This is the great populist cause of "the people versus the powerful," which will only be made right when the powerful are humbled.

The cultivation of the other two general passions—fear and hope— allows the demagogue to appeal well beyond the confines of the poor. Plutarch referred to these two passions as the chief "rudders" that govern men's political actions, and a number of philosophers have identified them as the "natural" or psychological source of the religious impulse.[45] As such, they can have a deep, almost primal effect that brings into politics powerful nonpolitical feelings. Demagogues often indulge or inflame such fears and hopes as a way of building personal support. Since so much political rhetoric addresses fear and hope, by no means can it be said that these passions are the exclusive preoccupation of the demagogue. It is rather how they are employed. The statesman tries to make constructive use of these sentiments to promote the public good, sometimes instilling hope when people are in despair or reminding people of danger when they are too confident. The statesman, as a rule, appeals to these passions to moderate the public. One of Franklin Roosevelt's most memorable phrases, that "the only thing to fear is fear itself," was meant to buoy Americans' spirit in the depth of the Depression.

Because the term "demagoguery" is of Greek origin, most discussions of the phenomenon draw heavily, at least when referring to its early history, on persons and events from Greek and Roman history. Some analysts, however, have broadened the study to include another great source of antiquity: ancient Israel. The phenomenon, if not the word, is treated in the Old Testament, in particular in the books of Samuel and Kings. David, who wins and consolidates his kingship with the help of cultivation of the popular element, is a person who instinctively understood the art of public relations. Who can forget his whirling and jumping before the ark in full view of the public and his slave servants, an act that earned him a stiff rebuke from his aristocratic-minded wife, Michal, who was ashamed of his popular pandering? Yet David was not bothered in the least by such scruples: "I shall be even more lightly esteemed than this . . . and I shall be humiliated in my own eyes, but among the female slaves of whom you speak, by them I shall be honored." David even declared that he would welcome further opportunities to bolster his public standing: "I will become even more undignified than this" (2 Samuel 6:22).

David, who used his skill in the popular arts to be a responsible king acting for the public good, had a son, Absalom, who carried his appeal to the people a step further. Absalom was known for his beauty and for a bountiful head of hair that would have been the envy of a former vice-presidential nominee and two-time candidate for his party's nomination, John Edwards. (Edwards became known for his fastidiousness for his hair, which he primped with the help of some very expensive cuts.) Absalom sought his father's overthrow, which he initiated by hanging around outside the gate of Jerusalem and telling each petitioner who arrived that "were I made judge [leader] in the land . . . everyone who has any suit or cause would come to me, and I would give him justice" (2 Samuel 15:6). And when the petitioners would approach him, Absalom would go further and kiss each of them, and "so he stole the hearts" of the people. "Kissing the people to steal their hearts" is not a bad start for a simple definition of demagoguery.

Popular speech remained important in the ancient polity of Israel, even after the monarchy became institutionalized. A singular form of this public speech often came in the pronouncements of those claiming the "office" of prophet. In his work *The Statesman's Manual*, Samuel Taylor Coleridge offered the Bible as the best source for understanding "the elements of *public* prudence, instructing us in causes, the surest preventatives, and the only cures, of public evils," and he proceeded to focus much of his attention on the problem of demagoguery.[46] In a most original translation, he reads *mat'im* (Isaiah 9:16), usually rendered "those who lead the people astray," as "demagogues." The "demagogues" are found among the "false prophets" who "fill you with vain hopes," telling you "it shall be well with you," and that "no evil shall come upon you."[47] False prophets often managed to rise in influence—"the people love to have it so"—by fostering dangerous illusions; they are the manipulators of hopes and fears.[48] By exposing these techniques, the biblical narrator (and Coleridge) sought to unmask the demagogue's art, enabling others to appreciate the danger.

Coleridge's discussion serves as a bridge to considering modifications of the original "natural" passions under the influence of religion. Revealed religion (Christianity) eventually provided the demagogue with new resources with which to influence popular audiences; the tools consisted of making claims to speak for God along with rhetorical appeals to sin and damnation (fear) and to redemption (hope). The message of the Gospels in the first centuries gave evidence of the power of popular rhetoric that went beyond anything that the Greek and Roman theorists of rhetoric had imagined. When Christianity had won the day in the Roman Empire by the fourth century, transforming the Church into an established institution, religious doctrine and rhetoric were deployed to support established authority, tamping down for the moment further popular appeals. But it was almost inevitable at some point that popular leaders, operating from below, would embrace and exploit a religious rhetoric in order to build a personal base of power. One of the most spectacular cases occurred in the Florentine republic in the late fifteenth century. Amid a people that, as Machiavelli notes, was "far from considering [itself] ignorant and benighted . . . Brother Girolamo Savonarola succeeded in persuading them that he held converse with God." Deploying a rhetoric that emphasized damnation and worked mostly on the passion of fear, Savonarola managed to dominate the political life of Florence for over a decade.[49]

The rise of Puritanism in England in the seventeenth century brought new challenges to established authority. The appeals of religious dissenters to hopes and fears figured prominently in creating the dissatisfaction that led to the English Civil War. Reflecting on these events, Thomas Hobbes condemned the recourse to religious rhetoric in public life, decrying the

Church's appeals to superstitious beliefs and the "Kingdom of Darkness," and the dissenters' new popular appeal to "conscience," which became a novel source of demagoguery.[50] David Hume later categorized these two forms of religious appeal into terms that were common in early America: "superstition" and "enthusiasm." Superstition or "terrified credulity" referred (usually) to a defense of authority that played on "weakness, fear and melancholy." Enthusiasm was characterized by a "warm imagination," appealing sometimes to hope and sometimes to fear, that had an unsettling effect on political authority.[51] The popular rhetoric of the Puritan republics of New England displayed elements of enthusiasm—of both damnation and of messianic hope—as well as, on occasion, superstition.

The Enlightenment created its own overlay on the basic human passions. It established a binary theoretical distinction between "prejudice," associated with horror of the past ("monkish ignorance and superstition"), and "enlightenment," associated with hope for the times to come.[52] In this account, a theoretical distinction was developed to categorize a priori bad and good discourse. Any appeal to the past became backward and demagogic, while an appeal to the future, freeing people of prejudice, was in the public's interest. This distinction was intended to immunize anyone in the Enlightenment's inner circle from the charge of demagoguery, no matter how extreme the position. American Progressives adopted a variation on this theme by safeguarding appeals to progress. If a leader, Woodrow Wilson noted, perceives "the next move in the progress of politics [and] fairly hit[s] the popular thought . . . are we to say that he is a demagogue?"[53] A progressive cannot be demagogic. In reaction to such arguments, conservatives in the aftermath of the French Revolution elaborated an opposite distinction: any appeal to abstract principle or speculative reason was Jacobin or demagogic, intended to upset tradition and authority. For both Left and Right, demagoguery now became a category of ideology. Both conceptions were applied in America during the party conflict of the 1790s. Jeffersonians accused Federalists of whipping up superstition and xenophobia to blind public opinion to a plot to institute monarchism, while Federalists charged Jeffersonians with playing on abstract hopes and utopian sentiments to promote the cause of Jacobinism.

The theory of classical liberalism and the regimes established on its principles would seem to offer little place for demagogic politics. Indeed, liberal regimes seem almost to have been constructed to dampen any and all demagogic appeals. The dominant "passion" (if this is the proper term) of liberalism has been identified as the desire for "comfortable self-preservation," which by its very ordinariness and sobriety discourages emotional appeals. This passion could nevertheless be used to support demagoguery in the form of appeals made *against* what threatens comfortable self-preservation. Playing on a fear of instability and change has been identified as the basis of a kind of liberal ("petit bourgeois") demagoguery, as found in such movements as *poujadisme* in France, which enlisted shopkeepers and small businessmen against alleged movements of social disruption.

For the most part, however, the sentiment of comfortable self-preservation has served as a resource for demagoguery inside of liberal societies by reason of the reaction against it and against liberalism more generally. Labeled by Romantic thinkers in the early nineteenth century as the "bourgeois" (or middle-class) sentiment, the concern for comfortable self-preservation became the target of a campaign in both art and politics that appealed to contempt and disgust for everything middle class. Initially, in the nineteenth century, the cultivation of these anti-bourgeois passions was confined to disgruntled portions of the aristocratic classes and to a small "bohemian" element, who railed against the mediocrity and insensitivity of bourgeois society. (A poem by D. H. Lawrence titled "How Beastly the Bourgeois Is" nicely captures the artistic contempt at the time for the ethos of the middle-class.) By the middle of the twentieth century, disgust for the bourgeois found a much larger audience among artists, mainstream intellectuals, and "alienated" youth, expanding into the culture of university life and joining with various movements for peace and social justice. The New Left, as the general movement became known, was a huge force in the American politics of the 1960s, with parallel movements in Germany and France, all of which spawned a new breed of demagogues who rose in part by playing on the passions of anti-bourgeois contempt.

Probably the most pervasive sentiment of recent times, however, is a milder passion that has accompanied that of comfortable self-preservation among the middle classes: compassion or pity. It is now the core public sentiment of advanced liberal societies, attached to a vague system sometimes known as the "religion of humanity." Compassion has an attractive, moralizing aspect to it, which is absent in the passion for comfortable self-preservation. It is considered "good" and "hopeful" and is very much in tune with contemporary democratic instincts. It elicits a strong response not only with the middle class, but also with large parts of its formerly "alienated" critics, who have found in it a respectable public substitute for their former anger. Compassion unites the middle class and its critics along a common front. Demagoguery in this case consists of the artful cultivation of compassion that evokes sympathetic moral indignation against "those who do not care." It undermines, where it does not reject outright, the appeal of some of the sterner virtues.[54]

THE RHETORICAL SITUATION

Popular political communication takes place in a general context, referred to here as the "rhetorical situation." It consists of six formal components: (1) the source of the speech act, (2) the medium of communication, (3) the prevailing "science" of communication, (4) the audience, (5) the time horizon of the communication act, and (6) the objective. To illustrate, these components, in the case of Periclean Athens, are (1) an individual speaker (e.g., Cleon) (2) delivering a speech (3) influenced by the sophists' rhetorical theory (4) addressing the assembly of citizens (the ecclesia) (5) on an imminent vote (6) arguing for a specific policy or course of action.

Changes in the rhetorical situation affect the likelihood of the appearance of demagoguery as well as the form it may assume. The main factors that produce shifts in the rhetorical situation are the prevailing science of communication, the size and legal character of political regimes, and the state of communication technology. A few comments can be made about these factors and the changing rhetorical situations.

Popular oratory in Athens was the object of a science, with teachers, institutes, and theoretical and practical treatises. The most important body of theory derived from a school now known as "sophistry," which specialized in the study of the art of mass persuasion (rhetoric), both for politics and for the courts. Its most renowned teachers traveled among different cities of Greece, selling their services to interested clients. Sophistry taught individuals how to succeed and, like the modern science of public relations, was unconcerned with the well-being of the city. The sophists, not unlike the modern campaign consultants—people like Pat Cawdell, Lee Atwater, Dick Morris, Joe Trippe, and David Axelrod—were eager to win a reputation for cleverness, which served their financial interest while also feeding their often legendary egos. Leading sophists were well remunerated. Plato reports that Evenus of Paros received a fee of five hundred drachmae for a single job, a rate competitive to that charged by the best consultants today.[55]

Beginning with Socrates, the philosophers sought to change the rhetorical situation by gaining control of the science of communication and making it more responsible to the political community. This effort culminated in Aristotle's *Rhetoric*, still considered one of the best practical manuals on persuasion ever written. Aristotle discussed the techniques of rhetoric, doing so with a depth and precision that apparently exceeded anything previously accomplished by the sophists. Unlike the sophists, however, Aristotle refused to treat rhetoric as an independent or stand-alone discipline; he placed it under the aegis of political science, demanding that issues of persuasion be considered in part with a view to their impact on the quality and stability of political regimes. Aristotle also gave much

greater weight than the sophists to the deliberative component of rhetoric, arguing that a form of rational demonstration (the enthymeme) was
more effective at persuasion than emotional appeals and various kinds of
gimmickry. His emphasis on rationality also seems to have been intended
to make the science of rhetoric safer for political life by creating a new
set of norms for the oratorical community (the teachers of oratory, the
orators, and the commentators on rhetoric). The aim, according to Bryan
Garsten, was "to respond to the dangers of demagogy" by "attempting to
reform the rhetoricians' own understanding of what it takes to successfully master the art of rhetoric."[56]

Turning to prevailing views of communication in America, it is no sur-
prise to learn that the Progressive thinkers who fashioned the idea of the
rhetorical presidency had extremely high expectations for public rhetoric.
These expectations, which Progressives believed were fully supported by
a growing enlightenment of the citizenry and advances in modern communication, justified their call for institutional change. There was now
much less need to fear demagoguery in presidential election campaigns
or to worry about possible rhetorical excesses in the presidency. As long
as there was discussion and debate, Woodrow Wilson contended, demagoguery could not succeed: "Thorough debate can unmask the plausible
pretender . . . charlatans cannot long play statesmen successfully when
the whole country is sitting as critic."[57] Along with this confidence in oratory came the conviction of the salutary effect of "publicity." Where there
was publicity, there could be no demagoguery. Progressive reformers,
writes Adam Sheingate, "followed Kant in seeing publicity as a path to
rational and enlightened deliberation."[58]

Yet at the very moment that the rhetorical presidency was being advanced, a new science of public opinion and public persuasion was reaching the very opposite conclusion. Reflecting the influence of the discovery
of the subconscious in psychology and of the spread of cinematic images,
social scientists argued that mass public opinion was governed mostly by
irrational impulses and dominated by appeals to "symbols." Experience
with the widespread use of mass propaganda techniques during World
War I only served to support this view.[59] A chasm opened between the
Progressives' expectations and the dominant findings of social science.
The modern profession of public relations and its political counterpart
(campaign consultancy), which were established in this period, largely
embraced social science's general view of an irrational public. An irrational public was one that could be controlled. With an understanding
of the processes that shaped public opinion, it was possible now to master and tame it. As Walter Lippmann wrote, "Persuasion has become a
self-conscious art. . . . The knowledge of how to create consent will alter
every political calculation and modify every political premise."[60] Like the

sophists, modern consultants sold their product (the techniques of mass persuasion) with no formal concern for the public good.

Since the 1960s, a reaction to this understanding has taken place that has emphasized the more rational aspects of the formation of public opinion. Leaders of this reaction have sought to alter the rhetorical situation by changing the prevailing theory of communication. The effort was inaugurated in a work titled *Essays on the Scientific Studies of Politics* (1962), which challenged many of the prevailing premises of political behavior and pointed out the dangers that these views posed for maintaining liberal democracy.[61] It was necessary also, however, to demonstrate empirically that public opinion was not as irrational as had been claimed. V. O. Key took up this task in *The Responsible Electorate*, which began with a simple but explosive statement: "Voters are not fools." Key went on to argue that existing theories of political communications not only purported to explain how persuasion took place, but also bore partial responsibility for *influencing* the character of public discourse, which placed too great a stress on irrational appeals. Social scientists had an obligation to broaden their studies and consider the norms that support democratic government. Joseph Bessette later added breadth and depth to this argument in his book *The Mild Voice of Reason*, which reintroduced the category of "deliberation" into political science. Bessette showed that, under suitable conditions, reasoning "based on the merits" exercised an influence on democratic decision-making.[62]

The science of political communications, including its possibilities and limits, was revived in its classical form, as part of political science, in the Rhetoric Project at the University of Virginia in the 1970s, from which Jeffrey Tulis's *The Rhetorical Presidency* emerged. The Rhetoric Project was greatly indebted to the thought of Aristotle and the American Founders; it urged inquiry into the institutional arrangements and types of communication that promoted statesmanship and curbed demagoguery, terms it did not flinch from using. A parallel line of thought in normative political theory in this period, drawing from the thought of Jürgen Habermas, has raised in a more abstract and idealistic fashion the question of how to promote "deliberative" or "discursive" democracy.[63] Taken together, these developments have influenced the modern oratorical community, helping to create an academic study of communication whose work now more closely considers the impact of rhetoric on the quality of public debate.

The greatest changes in the rhetorical situation over the ages, however, have probably owed more to shifts in the size and nature of political regimes and to revolutions in communications technology than to deliberate efforts to redefine the science of rhetoric. By virtue of the great political transformation in antiquity from the city-state to the empire, speakers could no longer reach the relevant mass public through the medium of an ordinary public address in an assembly. With the demise of the republican form, the popular assembly as the sovereign ruling body ceased to exist. (The Roman Senate continued for a time, but it lost its power.) Oratory continued to be practiced in local venues, but the chief means of communication was by the circulation of written texts. The substance of these texts was sometimes disseminated to various local speakers, who aided in molding public opinion by oral disquisition. The spreading of the Gospel by the early Christians became a model for capturing and influencing the public mind. The Acts of the Apostles can be read in many ways, but surely one of them is that of a practical manual of how to conduct a vast multimedia campaign of persuasion across three continents. Machiavelli later took the dissemination of Christianity as his model for how to spread a new secular "gospel" of modern philosophy throughout Europe. The aim of these communication acts was not to influence policies of the day, but to address a longer-term project or to alter or support the character of the political order. Given the mode of communication and the length of time needed to have an impact, no other choice was possible.

With the formation of the larger nation states of Europe in early modern times, the most important source in the rhetorical act was no longer the individual speaker, but the writer. The advent of the printing press meant that written tracts could be disseminated more quickly and easily than in medieval times. Although many works had a theoretical character meant to reach only a small group, some were clearly designed for broader audiences, as was the case with Locke's *Second Treatise*, Hume's *Essays*, and Edmund Burke's *Reflections on the Revolution in France*. Where these works proved too difficult, second-tier writers or "publicists" would simplify and spread the messages.[64]

The rhetorical situation in America in the period leading up to the Revolution is highly indicative of the age. Because republican institutions existed from early on in the colonies, the forms of popular communication were more varied here than elsewhere. There were influential popular speeches pronounced before live audiences, the most notable of which was James Otis's speech against the Writs of Assistance at the Old State House in Boston (1761), when, according to John Adams, "the child of the Revolution was born," and Patrick Henry's speech at St. John's Church in Richmond (1775), where he aroused all present with his plea to "Give me liberty or give me death."[65] Hundreds of sermons, many political in content, also stirred the public mind. Some addresses and sermons were disseminated quickly as written tracts, thus having a double influence as a speech and a pamphlet. Finally, there were the popular political writings of the period, never given as speeches. These included John Dickinson's "Letters from a Farmer in Pennsylvania," Thomas Jefferson's *A Summary*

View of the Rights of British America, and Thomas Paine's extraordinary *Common Sense.* All "spoke" in a popular style that aimed to move a nation.

The medium of the written word altered the nature of popular appeals. It did so first by removing the physical presence of the person, and thus personal qualities, from the act of persuasion. The character of the writer was surely not irrelevant, but it carried less weight and influence than is the case when the speaker stands directly before the audience. Written communication also diminished the importance of certain kinds of pathetic or emotive appeals that depend on a live setting and on the kinds of *collective* reactions that emerge only in crowds. (David Hume, in defending the liberty of the press, noted that it would not have the same "ill consequences as followed from the harangues of the popular demagogues of Athens and tribunes of Rome [because] a man reads a book or pamphlet alone and coolly."[66]) Indeed, if the demagogue is defined as an orator, then, strictly speaking, demagoguery no longer operates where the medium is the written word. But if the meaning of demagoguery is expanded, one can speak not just of certain demagogic attributes of the written medium, but of its *distinctive* demagogic attributes. The written word gives more weight to rational and abstract argumentation, creating the possibility of theoretical or doctrinal demagoguery (or ideology) that appeals to ideas that strangely combine to excite intellect and passion.

Hume, Burke, Tocqueville, and the authors of *The Federalist* were among the most effective writers to identify doctrinal demagoguery, seeking in the process to expose it and weaken its influence. They created a kind of anti-ideological rhetoric meant to put their readers on guard against being sucked in by dangerous theories. *The Federalist* attacked "projectors," "visionary and designing men," and "utopian speculators" who promoted theories that appealed to hope without any restraint or a sense of limits. Unlike the traditional demagogue, these thinkers were not usually looking to win popular approval for their own political careers. Either they were sincere devotees of their doctrines, or they sought intellectual acclaim, whether in their own day or for posterity. Whatever their personal motives, their writings could be used for demagogic purposes. In the late eighteenth century, as Tocqueville argued, men of letters endowed with a "literary spirit" spun out theories that enflamed the intellectuals' minds and contributed to the extremism of the French Revolution.[67] Ideological thinking became more pronounced in the late nineteenth and early twentieth centuries, when supporters of socialism and fascism disseminated written tracts ("propaganda") designed to foment mass opinion.

In America, with its democratic system, the speech remained an important part of politics. The speech was featured in legislative chambers, where forms evolved to encourage deliberative speech (not always successfully), and speechmaking remained important in political campaigns and popular meetings. But when it came to reaching the nation at large, the speech of any given individual could not be "heard" firsthand. For a political leader to contact the public at large, he had to rely on the medium of writing, even if it was just to publish the text of a speech or message. The political party (or faction within the party) was the organization that had the greatest interest in disseminating messages to the public, and the parties accordingly took on the responsibility in the early nineteenth century for establishing and subsidizing many of the nation's newspapers. Newspapers reflected the line of the party (or faction) and would sometimes directly publish speeches or statements of its leaders.

Over time, newspapers became the "sources for the speech act" in their own right, as some editors developed their own line within the general party fold. By mid-century, many newspapers became increasingly independent of the parties, as technological advances in printing and organizational innovations enabled them to survive on the revenues of their sales, eliminating the need for party subsidies.[68] Editors and reporters, sometimes closely guided by the owners, became powerful voices in the communication system, far more important than most politicians. Men such as Horace Greeley or William Randolph Hearst considered themselves capable of molding or leading public opinion through the power of the written word. Newspapers could now engage in something akin to demagoguery, one form of which (known as "yellow journalism") involved crude and sensational efforts to stir up the public (and sell newspapers).

By the middle of the twentieth century, the attempts by editors and owners to indulge and manipulate public opinion fell into disrepute, at least in the upper echelons of the press. Journalism began to develop into a profession, with standards that called for objectivity in the interpretation of events. This claim, together with the increased status of major journalists in the leading newspapers, weeklies, and electronic media, led top members of the national press to think of themselves as occupying a rank above the parties and politicians. Parties and politicians saw the world in a merely partisan way, whereas the press interpreted things in a nonpartisan and objective light. The press's assertion of power and right was captured in a pompous title that members of the press assigned to themselves: the Fourth Estate. Journalists were able to increase their influence relative to political institutions and political actors. Following a series of events in the 1960s and 1970s that created widespread suspicion toward government, in particular the Vietnam War and the Watergate scandal, journalists also became adept at cultivating distrust toward political actors, usually in ways that served to boost their own authority. The elevated role of the top journalists—a Walter Cronkite of *CBS News* or an R. W. Apple of *The New York Times*—was widely acknowledged. Still, many critics began to call this system into question. Some charged journalism with a soft kind of demagoguery that played up the importance of the immediate news events at the expense of a longer-term perspective (thereby boosting their own importance), while others argued that beneath the façade of objectivity the journalistic community was strongly hostile to the views of modern conservatism.

Over the past two decades, the power and status of the cadre of top journalists has declined dramatically. The change has been due in part to technological and legal changes that have dramatically opened up points of access in the communications system. Cable television, talk radio, and the Internet have given citizens more to choose from than in the days when there were only three television networks. At the same time, a series of blatant instances of journalistic bias by leading newspapers and networks shattered their claims of journalistic objectivity. No news source today commands the confidence of citizens across the board, and the very notion of the objective delivery of news seems now to have passed from the scene. While the overall importance of the entire "system" of the media remains, the power of any single cadre or element within it has greatly diminished. The system is now fragmented into hundreds of smaller pieces. The practice of petty demagoguery by journalists and commentators has now become more widespread, but the variety of views and the absence of a softer journalistic manipulation that often hid under the veil of objectivity make it less dangerous to the public than during the period of the Fourth Estate.

The other factor influencing the rhetorical situation has been changes in communications technology. The early twentieth century saw the rise of the cinema and newsreel, which downplayed the spoken word and reason in favor of the large pictorial image. The sheer power of these new media and the ways in which they were frequently employed contributed to the idea that public opinion was shaped by irrational forces. This technological change was surpassed and overshadowed a few decades later by the advent of the electronic mass media, first radio and then television. The ultimate effect of both has been to allow the individual political leader to speak directly and simultaneously to the whole of the public. Never since the gathering of the assemblies in small city-states has it been possible for individual leaders to address the entire community "in person." The contemporary rhetorical situation therefore more closely resembles that of classical republics than anything that has existed in the past twenty-five centuries. Differences there are between the two cases, but this overwhelming similarity in many respects brings the story full circle. Suddenly, all that was written about politics in the city-states of antiquity strikes a chord with politics today. Subsequent technological changes, such as the development of the Internet, are important, but they pale in comparison to the change that has brought leaders into direct contact with the sovereign body of the full populace.

Consider briefly the status today in high-visibility politics, such as presidential campaigns and presidential governance, of the six components of the rhetorical situation: the speaker, the speech, the prevailing science of communication, the audience, the span of the rhetorical event, and the objective of the speaker.

1. The main source in modern communication is the individual leader operating with a substantial degree of personal discretion. The leader is fully visible to the public; he or she is judged in part on positions and arguments but also on the basis of qualities and character as known from past activities and as shown in public appearances. Displaying one's person is an important factor in modern persuasion; a performance that shows or confirms a character flaw, such as a disastrous performance in a television debate (Al Gore in 2000), can break a political career.[69] Competing sources exist that "speak" to the public (newspapers, news networks, bloggers, parties, etc.), but they are less important today, relative to the self-presentation of individual leaders, than they were a century ago.

2. The "speech," not the written word, has returned as a major medium of communication. (A speech is defined here as largely unmediated communication between the individual and public; this includes personal interviews and performances in debates.) Individual leaders have other ways of communicating with the public—ads, written messages, grassroots contacts by their organization—but these are less important than the speech. Two of the most important moments of the modern presidential campaign revolve around speech events: the nomination acceptance address and the presidential debates.

3. There is today, as there was in Periclean Athens, a powerful profession of political consultants with expertise in techniques that aim at persuasion. These include creating organizations and communication networking, managing the news cycle, polling, speechwriting, campaign advertising, and fundraising. The techniques are in full view during presidential campaigns; most of them continue in some form (and sometimes more discreetly) in the presidency, often with key figures from the campaign playing leading roles in the White House. At the same time, in an analogous way to how philosophy engaged sophistry, the purely instrumental foundations of the public relations profession have come under much greater scrutiny from outside, in part from renewed studies of rhetoric and communication that have supplied a broader understanding of the role of political communications and of

the dangers to the public good that come from a discipline that makes persuasion alone its goal.

4. The modern audience, at least for certain key events like a presidential debate, consists of a substantial portion of the public which views and assesses the speaker in "real time" (or on tape shown shortly afterward).[70] The mode of "assembling" the public differs from the classical situation. It is not a physical and collective gathering, but an "assembly" in which most people view an electronic image independently and in private. A television speech (even one that is seen being delivered to a live audience) alters the character of the event in comparison to a speech delivered in person. The effectiveness of certain kinds of appeals—in particular, it seems, the angrier and more fear-provoking "harangue"—seems to diminish, while gentler and more insinuating appeals may flourish. Television has been called a "cool" medium, which seems to disadvantage the pure Type I demagogue.

5. The time horizon of communication events in America varies greatly with the context. A presidential speech can be aimed at educating or persuading the public in preparation for a policy decision that may take place shortly. By contrast, speeches in presidential campaigns usually involve no actual policy decision; they are components in a campaign to persuade the public to select someone for office. The events of selection (primary elections or the final election) may be months away from the moment a speech is delivered. From the perspective of rhetorical theory, the campaign consists of one great speech act. The character of demagogic appeals for a campaign, which must be designed to work over a great length of time, will undoubtedly differ from those employed when an action is to be taken by the public assembly immediately after hearing a speech.

6. The objective of the speech today likewise varies with the context. A president in many cases may aim his speech at trying to influence public opinion on an important policy matter, where the question at hand may be deliberative (deciding on the merits of a course of action). The presidential campaign has a different aim: to persuade people to support and vote for a candidate. Matters of "ordinary deliberation" may contribute to that objective—candidates give policy speeches—but they are only pieces of a larger whole, subordinate to the primary goal of winning support for the person in question.

SOME CASES OF DEMAGOGUERY

Demagoguery is (or was once) a concept of political science, but it has also become a highly charged political epithet, a fact which threatens to destroy its worth as an analytic concept. Still, if the purely political aspects can be filtered out, a neutral core remains. Demagoguery, while a term of derogation, is never treated as a synonym for ineffective or bad leadership. However poorly some judged a Gerald Ford or a Michael Dukakis, no one ever accused either of them of being demagogues. Demagoguery is restricted to certain kinds of behavior—namely, using popular methods to foment divisions by appeals to certain passions or theoretical categories and subverting by popular means the letter or spirit of constitutional government. Based on these criteria, the number of cases in American presidential politics of widespread accusation of demagoguery is not very large. These cases need to be examined to consider why the charges were made and if they were warranted. The inquiry should lead to a successive refinement of the general concept.

In the early republic, charges of demagoguery were leveled most frequently at Thomas Jefferson and Aaron Burr. Jefferson's case is the most important. The criticism was greatest during the 1790s, in the lead-up to the elections of 1796 and 1800. To many Federalists, Jefferson's support for the French Revolution after 1791 indicated that he fit squarely into the new category of the radical ideological demagogue. In addition, as a self-proclaimed leader of the popular element against the few, Jefferson was accused of crossing the line and violating the forms of constitutional government by involving himself (secretly) with establishing a newspaper, where his message could reach the public, and by creating a political party, which was then regarded as an anti-constitutional instrument. Jefferson was most sensitive to this last charge, which he justified chiefly as an emergency measure to save the nation from a worse fate: the subversion of republican government. He also suggested that party competition was inevitable in a democracy and would become an accepted part of constitutional government. His foresight on this point attenuates retrospectively the main charge of demagoguery. Furthermore, once Jefferson was elected to the presidency, the accusations of demagogic behavior diminished, even as opposition to many of his policies grew.[71] There was nothing demagogic in Jefferson's style of presidential leadership.

Andrew Jackson probably endured the most sustained onslaught of accusations for demagoguery of any sitting president. The charges began well before he assumed office, in the campaign of 1824, when it looked as if he might become the first leader of conspicuously popular origins and tastes to be elected president. A rough-cut Westerner known for his rashness, Jackson was of a different "class" than the nation's first six presidents, lacking their education and refinement. His military background only added to the concerns about demagoguery, as many suspected him of capitalizing on the popularity deriving from his battlefield exploits to win a political office for which he, unlike George Washington, bore no special fitness. The campaign waged on Jackson's behalf after the 1824 campaign, charging that the election had been stolen, further increased concerns of Jackson's lawlessness.

This controversy took place inside of a new electoral system that functioned without political parties and that turned on pure "personalism." Jackson's future ally and confidant, Martin Van Buren, worried about just this point: "His election as the result of his military services without reference to party, and so far as he alone is concerned, scarcely to principle, would be one thing."[72] When Jackson was elected with the support of a "personal faction" in 1828, charges of demagoguery inevitably carried over into his presidency; and when Jackson decided not merely to sit back and preside, but to pursue a course of action contrary at times to the congressional majority, his opponents upped the ante, accusing him of seeking to subvert the Constitution and establish a popular tyranny. Opponents despised Jackson's policies, but the crux of their public case against "King Andrew" was his use of presidential powers, which he employed in new and controversial ways, appealing to the public for vindication.

The verdict on the most serious charge of Jackson's demagoguery accordingly rests on an assessment of the actual character of presidential powers under the Constitution. On this count, Jackson's overall position had much support at the time, and it has been largely vindicated by subsequent practice. The paradox of Jackson's presidency is that the deep concern over his demagoguery helped to supply the political energy, under Martin Van Buren's artful maneuvering, for transforming the political system. It changed from a regime focused on personalism to one that became beholden to political parties.

The next instance of serious allegations of demagoguery came not in reference to an individual, but to an event: the Whig Party's presidential campaign of 1840. John Quincy Adams described this campaign as marking "a revolution in the habits and manners of the people."[73] The Whigs invented the idea of the campaign as a mass spectacle, mobilizing the people as the medium to carry the message. The party organized its followers to hold rallies, sing songs, and enact dramatic skits, all to celebrate the down-home virtues of their candidate, William Henry Harrison ("Old Tip"); his simple ways were captured in the campaign's symbols of the log cabin and hard cider. The Whigs sought to out-Jackson Jacksonianism. Harrison's popular qualities were set in stark contrast to the aristocratic and sybaritic tastes of President Van Buren, who was accused of turning the White House into a palace of luxury. This campaign was all the more striking for coming from a party that, only four years earlier, had rejected the instrumentality of the party organization itself as being too popular and demagogic and that had prided itself on representing the more respectable elements of society that were too proud to truckle after votes. All this changed when, as one Whig observer remarked at the time, "men of the highest culture did not disdain at times to 'go down to the people.'"[74] The vulgarity of the campaign, which abandoned all pretense of high-mindedness and deliberation, astonished even some of its own architects.

The judgment of the day that this campaign was demagogic has partly dissipated in light of the subsequent acceptance of its practices as folkloric and as making up part of the fun and ritual of democracy. Americans have adjusted to a more "populist" tone, using this term not in its darker sense, but in a more benign sense to refer to the celebration (or flattery) of popular tastes against any hint of pretense or snobbishness. The Whig campaign of 1840 confirmed for both parties the abstract idea of the sovereignty of public opinion as well as the sovereignty of popular tastes. But while "populist" in this respect, the campaign avoided deeply divisive issues. It may even have been the case that the appeals to these milder popular passions served as a sop to avoid recourse to more dangerous ones. Even though the campaign broke all precedent by bringing out the candidate, William Henry Harrison, to engage in open speechifying—a step that some evaluated as being demagogic—no one ever charged Harrison's inoffensive rhetoric with being in the least bit inflammatory. Its effect, it seems, was somnolescent. Whig populism was so superficial that it was never intended to continue past the campaign. Once elected, Harrison, who died after little more than a month of service, showed no inclination to be a populist, much less a demagogic, president. This was true of Tyler, too.

The next set of campaigns to witness frequent charges of demagoguery came, predictably, with the breakup of the old parties in the 1850s. The Whigs were the first to go in 1856. Into this void stepped first the American or Know-Nothing Party, which targeted foreigners and Catholics as the source of the nation's problems. The party's nativist message, which appealed openly to popular fears, fits into one of the classic categories of demagoguery. All that was lacking was a real demagogue. The American party's candidate in 1856, the former Whig President Millard Fillmore, was hardly a very compelling figure. The movement soon collapsed, in part because more respectable conservative forces, which initially toyed with using the movement as a vehicle for riding to power, had second thoughts and abandoned the effort.[75]

Next to enter the fray was the Republican Party. Proponents of slavery in the South saw the new party as an extension of abolitionism and, in the case of its political leaders, an organization "gotten up" by ambitious demagogues seeking power. Similar complaints also came, however, from opponents of slavery, including the leader of the rump of the New England Whigs, Rufus Choate, who charged the Republican Party with theoretical demagoguery (taking too seriously the "glittering generalities" of the Declaration of Independence) and religiously inspired enthusiasm ("moralism"). For Choate, neither abstract ideas nor fervor had a place in democratic politics. Choate concluded by 1856 that only the Democrats, with their amorphous formulae, could hold the nation together and save it from the demagoguery of the "geographical party." In this view, Abraham Lincoln was the demagogue and Stephen Douglas the statesman; the divisiveness of the Republican appeal, epitomized in Lincoln's statement "A House divided against itself cannot stand," was certainly confirmed in the secession of southern states following Lincoln's election in 1860.[76]

This case obviously raises a basic issue about the concept of demagoguery. While the most serious instances of demagoguery involve dangerous and divisive popular appeals, does it follow that all appeals that are dangerous and divisive are demagogic? Lincoln's position shows that a public appeal to genuine principle, perhaps necessary for the public good, can also lead to divisiveness. Statesmanship, which ordinarily aims at a calming effect and seeks room for compromise, cannot at times avoid confronting, perhaps even provoking, division. Lincoln appears "statesmanlike" (in the usual sense) in relation to his efforts to moderate the abolitionists, but he would not back down from a position that polarized the public. No simple, external criterion such as promoting polarization would seem to be sufficient to distinguish statesmanship from demagoguery. The nature of the appeal itself—in this case the principle of natural rights that Lincoln invoked—must also be examined, as well as the political context in which it is used.

Lincoln nevertheless sought to refine, as far as possible, the "objective" distinctions used to apply to the concept. First, he argued against the all-too-facile "conservative" conception of demagoguery, embraced by Rufus Choate, which alleged that the introduction of any abstract or theoretical principle into politics was demagogic. Lincoln insisted that a modern nation, if it were to remain unified and be capable of resolve, must possess a common "philosophical public opinion."[77] From the standpoint of practical statesmanship, the question is not whether there is a core theoretical proposition that underpins "public sentiment," but rather which one it is.

Second, on the issue of divisiveness, Lincoln responded that there are some great issues—slavery, of course, being the great example—that are of such a fundamental nature that they cannot, at least in an enlightened era, be ignored or finessed. Slavery had always been "an apple of discord and an element of division" in America, and this division would never go away on its own until the question was resolved in one way or another.[78] The Republican Party was at once the expression of this truism and the instrument that highlighted (and promoted) the moral division.

Finally, on the level of the rhetorical tactics employed, the Lincoln-Douglas debates make another point clear. Not only was Lincoln's message more principled, but his rhetoric also relied far less on appeals to raw passion. Stephen Douglas pulled continually on the strings of fear, in the form of raising the prospect of contamination of the white race by amalgamation, and of hope, in the form of his appeals to progress through democratic expansion, or Manifest Destiny. Lincoln on occasion, usually in response to Douglas, used appeals that spoke to emotion. (He certainly appealed frequently to the moral sense.) But the distinguishing characteristic of his rhetoric in this period was its reliance on "logic" and rational argument. Lincoln's speeches also displayed a remarkable sobriety, which often contrasted sharply with the enthusiasm of many spokesmen from his own party.

Lincoln's conduct as president was scrupulous in its reserve, which ended all talk of demagoguery. His stature steadily grew, and by the time of his assassination he had earned the reputation of being a statesman of the highest rank. His rhetoric alternated between speeches of almost clinical rationality (like his first inaugural address) and addresses that are unequaled in their poetic grandeur (like the Gettysburg Address and second inaugural). The second inaugural address stands out as the greatest of all American speeches. It is also singular in its mysterious tone, with no speech before serving as an obvious model. The speech is notable not only in expressing a firm and unbending resolve to complete the harsh task at hand, but also in seeking to lay a foundation for reconciliation between the North and South.

By the time of his reelection in 1864, Lincoln emerged as a new "model" of the great democratic leader: a man of the people in origin and appearance, without any hint of elitism or outward aristocratic pretense (surpassing in this respect even "Old Tip" or "Old Hickory"), but one who nevertheless possessed virtue and intelligence in the highest degree and who had mastered like no other the art of democratic statesmanship. This model has intrigued, yet also bedeviled, American politics ever since. It represents an ideal that is always sought and hoped for, but that has not yet again been achieved. It may come at the expense of putting at a disadvantage persons of quality from a privileged background.

The next significant charge of demagoguery appeared in the case of William Jennings Bryan, who burst onto the national scene in 1896. Bryan's fit with some of the main features associated with the demagogue makes the appearance of these charges seem in retrospect to be almost inevitable. Bryan was a self-proclaimed champion of the "people," who early on earned the title of "the Great Commoner"; he was a leader of the Populist movement inside the Democratic Party; he was a religious advocate, an evangelical, who brought all the fervor of "enthusiasm" into political life; and last, but certainly not least, he was widely known in 1896 for being an "orator." At just thirty-six years of age, and with scant national political experience, Bryan seized on his opportunity to address the Democratic Convention, managing to catapult himself from a convention delegate to the nominee of his party. His remarkable "Cross of Gold" speech, delivered on July 9, 1896, left his audience spellbound, and the delegates rallied to him the next day to select him as their new leader. Probably no single speech in American political history has had a greater immediate impact. It derived much of its power from its generation of divisiveness, pitting a virtuous agrarian and democratic vision against a wicked capitalist conspiracy to destroy the people: "Burn down your cities and leave our farms, and your cities will spring up again as if by magic. But destroy our farms and the grass will grow in the streets of every city in the country."

Following the convention, Bryan campaigned openly for the presidency, following in the footsteps of Harrison, Douglas, and Greeley, traveling across the country and delivering hundreds of speeches. More than anyone else, he can be credited with establishing the modern role for the presidential candidate as a campaigner and speech giver. At the time, Bryan was taken to task in many quarters for demeaning the election by engaging so extensively in the practice of personally soliciting support. His response was classic: "I would rather have it said that I lacked dignity than that I lacked backbone to meet the enemies of the government who work against its welfare from Wall Street."

The presidential campaign of 1912 led to many of the most conspicuous charges of demagoguery in American history. The campaign was the first in which the new system of selecting convention delegates by primary elections was in effect, and the first therefore in which candidates openly campaigned for their party's nominations. They did so on the basis of their "personal" programs, thus replicating at an earlier stage (nomination) the kind of candidate-centered politics that prevailed in 1824 at the final election stage. By the terms of Woodrow Wilson's analysis, the new system opened a space for popular statesmanship; by Martin Van Buren's analysis, it opened a space for demagogic appeals.

Theodore Roosevelt's candidacy immediately put this question to the test. For Roosevelt and his followers, the nomination race was a great opportunity both to overthrow a sitting president who had veered from a progressive line and to renew the Republican Party. Others viewed Roosevelt's return to politics as motivated by personal opportunism. His appeals to the working class against the business interests and his attacks on the courts led President Taft to take the extraordinary step of publicly branding him "a dangerous demagogue."[79] The Socialist candidate Eugene Debs, who was trying to maintain control of the Left in the general election, followed up later on this theme, calling Roosevelt "a charlatan, mountebank, and an . . . utterly unprincipled self seeker and demagogue."

The new nomination system, which concentrated so much on the individual leader, also contributed to the "personalist" kind of "third-party" presidential candidacy that came to characterize such efforts in the twentieth century, most notably in the candidacies of George Wallace (in 1968) and Ross Perot (in 1992 and 1996). Roosevelt initiated the model for this development as well, bolting from the Republican Party after being denied the nomination to head the Progressive ticket, which relied heavily on Roosevelt's personal appeal.

Of the twentieth-century presidents, Franklin Delano Roosevelt was probably the one most frequently accused of practicing demagoguery. The charges surfaced after he was elected, as his campaign in 1932 proceeded in a fairly low-keyed manner. The accusations fit FDR into a new pattern, at least by American standards, that had been pioneered by his cousin Theodore: a "patrician" by birth who sided conspicuously with the popular party and claiming to represent the "common people" and the "little man." FDR's rhetorical skills were legendary and included the ability to create a feeling of personal closeness between himself and his audience. Roosevelt exploited a new medium of communication (radio), using it to develop a more familiar kind of rapport with the American people than had been tried by his two predecessors. The talks became known as "fireside chats," with the word "chat" bespeaking this new informality. Roosevelt often began by addressing his audience as "my friends," seeking to reduce distance between the president and the public and to establish a direct psychological link. Many found this intimate approach to be a threat to the tone of a constitutional office. It established a "personal" presidency.

These issues of tone only set the stage for the more substantive charges of demagoguery, which concerned the content of FDR's message. He was accused of fomenting class division, typified by his rhetorical castigating of the "tyranny" of "economic royalists," and then for attacking the Supreme Court. Controversy about Roosevelt's leadership appeals raged at the time and has continued ever since among his biographers. Many have lauded him for being the supreme popular leader, a piece of praise that seems to concede that he at least flirted with the demagogic arts. His defenders, however, insist that he stopped short of ever crossing the line.

Roosevelt's success as president, though it cannot completely exonerate him of these charges, has shifted historical judgments in his favor. He has profited in this regard most from his role as war leader, which enabled him to rise above heated internal divisions and become a unifying national figure. On the specific charges, the following responses have been offered in FDR's defense.

First, regarding his close personal relation to the public, the Great Depression was a period of such acute distress that the public needed someone to minister to the mood of despair and to provide reassurance and hope. As Saul Bellow remarked of his performance during the first one hundred days of his administration, "The secret of his political genius was that he knew exactly what people needed to hear, a personal declaration by the president that took account of the feelings of the people."[80] According to this view, FDR's informality was justified because it helped the American people get through a supreme crisis.

Second, on the question of class division, FDR's defenders argue that his rhetoric, however extreme, served to undercut similar, but more radical appeals, by Father Charles Coughlin and Huey Long, whom Roosevelt considered to be the real demagogues. By giving vent to the existing anger against the wealthy, but not ultimately threatening the capitalist system, FDR saved it. According to Morton Frisch, "the rhetoric of the class struggle was one of the facts of political life that had to be accepted or approved or stolen in order to be moderated."[81] Defenders add that many of Roosevelt's most provocative appeals to class division occurred during the presidential campaign of 1936. Although a campaign does not free a president from all restraints, it has generally come to be accepted that for the period of the campaign a president who is competing should be granted more leeway than usual, allowing him to "step down" and assume the role of a candidate. FDR played no small part in promoting this role for the president when he surprised the nation in 1936 by becoming the first party nominee (and thus the first president) to deliver a convention acceptance address. In another indication of the personalism of modern leadership, this address has now replaced the party platform as the central statement of the "party's" position.

Two charges of presidential demagoguery stand out in modern times, one involving Richard Nixon, the other Bill Clinton. The accusations rest on the claim that these presidencies took advantage of the prestige of the presidency to stimulate a division in order to pursue a political aim, unrelated to any pending policy matter. Nixon's case centered on a plan to take on the "Fourth Estate." The president sought to avoid direct, personal involvement by making use of his vice president, Spiro Agnew, who unleashed a series of attacks in 1970 targeting the media elite's (and the intellectuals') opposition to the administration. The speeches castigated an "effete corps of impudent snobs," the "nattering nabobs of negativism," and the "radiclibs." No one, of course, had the slightest doubt that Agnew's "campaign," which resembled an electoral-style series of speeches, was orchestrated by President Nixon. The demagogic tactic of dividing, combined with the use of unpresidential language, was consistent with a certain "history" by Richard Nixon, who was known for running tough and polarizing campaigns in the past. Furthermore, even the most casual observer could see in Nixon a personality who was struggling to prevent himself from giving vent to emotional appeals based on anger and fear. Nixon employed the mask of a practiced and inflated "statesmanlike" demeanor to assist him in this task of containing his demons, but on occasion the mask would fall and the "Old Nixon," always lurking just beneath the surface, would reappear. No one can deny that Richard Nixon was often severely provoked by his critics—even paranoids have real enemies—but this excuse changes nothing in judging the use of demagoguery.

In Bill Clinton's case, there is a strong temptation when thinking of the charges of demagoguery to concentrate on his unusual uses of popular rhetoric following his acquittal in the Senate impeachment trial. At this time he spoke plaintively of his "journey," of his "spirit [having been] broken," and of "the rock bottom truth of where I am," before making known that he had repented and was asking forgiveness. But his pleading here was of a "personal" kind, involving the use of "forensic" rhetoric reminiscent of the pleas made in ancient Athens in trials decided by the popular assembly. This strange kind of presidential rhetoric, which had never been heard before and may never be heard again, lies outside the category of political demagoguery. On this score, the charges of demagoguery are properly focused on the instances where Clinton engaged in veiled or direct attacks against strong conservatives. These occurred first in the aftermath of the Oklahoma City bombing, when he decried certain "loud and angry voices . . . spread[ing] hate . . . over the airwaves," which was clearly directed at hosts of talk radio; then in his oblique charges that there was a "national conspiracy" based on "racial hostility" in a spate of fires of black churches; and finally, during the Lewinsky controversy, via the declaration by his wife, Hillary Clinton, of the existence of a "vast right wing conspiracy" devoted to bringing down her husband. (Like Nixon, Bill Clinton was constantly maligned and provoked by a group of inveterate Clinton-haters.)

With Clinton, as with Nixon, there was a prehistory in his rhetoric that almost guaranteed charges of demagoguery once he became president. In Clinton's case, this had to do with matters of style or tone rather than substance. Bill Clinton relished the experience of giving speeches before live audiences, a task at which he excelled. He had a famed capacity, and evidently a felt urge, to "connect" with people in an empathetic mode, a trait that was often satirized in his supposed wish to "feel your pain." Clinton was also in tune with modern sensibilities in his appeal to compassion, which he could also quickly turn into an effective polarizing theme by striking at the target group of the "haters" and the uncompassionate. Finally, Clinton had few reservations in breaking with forms. As a candidate, he appeared on a youth entertainment network (MTV), which some considered undignified, and he subsequently appeared on a late-night TV show playing the saxophone—"jamming"—while wearing sunglasses. His legendary ability to connect with people spread to his mastery of the medium of television, where he was especially adept at the technique of creating a feeling of intimacy. He famously brought this familiarity to a new level during the first ever "town hall"–style presidential debate in 1992, when he stepped out from behind the podium, literally reducing the distance between himself and the audience, and directly engaged in a personal dialogue with a citizen who was asking him a question. President George H. W. Bush remained glued behind his podium.

ASSESSING DEMAGOGUERY IN AMERICAN POLITICS

In light of this brief survey, no president appears to merit the dubious honor of being unequivocally labeled a demagogue. Some have engaged in acts of demagoguery, but none has consistently followed this line. (This assessment grants a modest license for presidents to go further than usual during the campaign season.) One reason for the relative immunity is that the presidential office has had built into it, almost like a genetic code, a norm of "dignity" that demands that occupants act "presidentially." This norm is found in the understanding of constitutional forms articulated in *The Federalist*, but it was given flesh and life by George Washington, who as president consciously sought to establish precedents that would shape the future character of the office. Finding the right tone of democratic dignity, somewhere between formality and openness, was one of his great concerns and one of his greatest accomplishments.

Successors occasionally took steps to alter the tone of the office, usually in the direction of making it more popular. Some of these movements toward greater familiarity have come over time to be accepted, such as viewing photos of the president in more casual settings on vacation or engaged in recreation. Americans expect their presidents, at least on some occasions, to show a common touch—an attribute, incidentally, that Washington appreciated when he took his popular "tours" through the country. But there seems to be a limit to this popular image. Some attempts at change have run afoul of concerns of dignity, from Andrew Jackson's rowdy inaugural party at the White House in 1828 to Jimmy Carter's populist gesture of carrying his own luggage. It was Bill Clinton's lackadaisical attitude toward the dignity of the presidency—which was not limited to the Monica Lewinsky affair—that, to many, was his most troubling legacy. Deriving from the example of Washington, certain actions and words, overt demagoguery being the leading example, are considered unpresidential.

The story is different when one turns from the presidency to presidential campaigns. Instances of demagoguery have been frequent and are on the rise in modern times. The terminology of leadership appeals is notable for its imprecision, but the late increase of candidates proclaiming a "populist" or outsider style and message, one that makes a point of disdaining anything that might smack of high-brow, is notable. Simple populism need not be accompanied by demagoguery, but it is fertile soil for its development. The institutional form of current nomination campaigns, which sets the tone for campaigns in general, encourages a personalist politics that opens the door to demagogic candidates. The case of one of the better-known demagogues, George Wallace, illustrates this vulnerability. His quest for the presidency began when he was an insurgency candidate in the 1964 Democratic Party primaries, where he tested with success some of his backlash themes. He brought many of these appeals to the 1968 presidential race, when he ran a personalist third-party campaign that ended by capturing more than 13 percent of the popular vote. Wallace returned to the Democratic Party in 1972, showing a greater following with voters outside the South before being crippled in an assassination attempt during the primary campaign in Maryland. How far Wallace might have gotten in this race is unknown, although nomination by his party seemed to have been beyond his reach.

It is tempting, though perhaps too hopeful, to consider Wallace the last of the breed of the pure, traditional (Type I) demagogue. In his harshness, Wallace seems almost out of place in the softer-style politics of the TV age. Yet a more updated and polished version appeared in the personage of the self-proclaimed "populist" candidate John Edwards, who ran as a Democrat for the presidency in 2004, finishing second to John Kerry (and being rewarded with the vice-presidential nomination), and in 2008, when he finished third. Edwards, who had served one term in the Senate without notable accomplishment before his first bid, was an excellent orator who could mesmerize his audiences. He based his campaigns on the theme of two Americas, one rich and the other poor. It was a "classic" tactic of class division, with strongly empathetic and emotional appeals. Edwards went so far as to use his father, a retired textile worker, as a human prop at campaign rallies to represent the harsh reality of working people. As a result of a personal scandal involving an affair and the fathering of a child out of wedlock, both of which he first steadfastly and brazenly denied, Americans found out much more about Edwards than about most other politicians. The picture that emerged proved shocking, even to many hard-boiled Washington observers, in what it showed about Edwards's willingness to put his own ambition above the best interests of his party and country. There was also the amusing and instructive piece of hypocrisy of the self-styled man of the people balking at attending county fairs in order to avoid "fat rednecks trying to shove food down my face."[82]

A different sort of demagogic candidacy appeared in 1992, in the singular person of Ross Perot. Unlike Wallace, Perot seemed positioned for a time not just to make a decent showing but also to offer a real prospect for capturing the presidency. The mild division he fomented was not between different parts of the populace, but rather between the whole body of the citizenry untainted by involvement in a corrupted system ("outsiders") and the class of politicians and influence peddlers currently operating it ("insiders"). In one sense this division only echoed typical cleansing and purging reform appeals seen in the past, with Ross Perot serving as the outsider-in-chief and promising, in a slightly updated mechanical metaphor, to "open up the hood and fix it." But Perot carried to new lengths his tone of flattery and the ideal of leader's nominal subjugation to the public, summed up in the pithy five-word populist slogan: "I'm Ross, you're the boss." The anti-constitutional overtones of this appeal became more evident as Perot spoke vaguely of new forms of consultation between the leader and public by means of Internet polls, a suggestion redolent of some of the "Caesarist" acts of European leaders to hold plebiscites to support their positions. The technique of "official" consultation by an Internet vote did not end with Ross Perot, but was picked up later by Howard Dean in the 2004 nomination campaign, when he sought—and received—the permission of his supporters to break a pledge to accept public funding for his campaign and instead raise money from private contributions.

Perot's third-party campaigns were notable, but they only followed and developed the style of many nomination campaigns, which have served as the true nursery of candidacies by modern-day "orators." Among the more notable of these orators, besides John Edwards, have been Jesse Jackson, Pat Robertson, Patrick Buchanan, Alan Keyes, Al Sharpton, and Howard Dean. These candidates sought to raise an issue or cause within their party by spirited and sometimes provocatively divisive appeals. Reversing the previous notion that candidates should be judged in large part on the basis of their reputation for significant service in a public career, these candidates sought to build their reputation during the campaign, making use of the presidential selection system process to help boost or restart a career.

The most extraordinary recent case of the candidate as orator, however, was the successful 2008 Democratic Party campaign of Senator Barack Obama. A person with almost no experience in national politics when he launched his presidential bid, Obama gained favor with the American people in and through running for the presidency, relying to a substantial degree on eloquence and oratory. The Obama campaign fulfilled a possibility of the modern nomination system, as defended by Woodrow Wilson, of being elevated to the presidency on the basis of one's talents as "a popular orator." Obama's effect on his followers during the campaign was powerful, and their belief in him *personally* often appeared to have a religious-like devotion. The word many used to describe this appeal was "charismatic," a term that Max Weber first employed to describe the extraordinary personal hold of a leader over his following. Charisma is a vague word that nevertheless has—or can have—a more positive connotation than demagoguery. As for Obama, his nomination campaign was directed largely at overcoming, not creating, divisiveness, and the most "rhetorical" aspects of his appeal were based on kindling "hope" and promising "change." His candidacy could only have emerged under the institutional arrangements that have opened the door to rhetorical politics.

From the time of the founding, the defenders of constitutionalism have sought to build and maintain a series of concentric walls around the presidency to protect it from demagoguery. The innermost wall consists of structural features of the office designed to fortify a president against the immediate pressures of public opinion; next are attendant norms that prescribe a code of "presidential" conduct and a certain dignity in comportment; beyond this are the moderating effects supplied by an election in a large territory with a multiplicity of interests; finally, occupying the outer ring, are the restraining institutional devices of the electoral system, which for a long time rested on the mighty bulwark of traditional political parties.

This last barrier has been breached by a new party nomination process that allows a point of entrance for demagoguery, adding stress to the other parts of the network of defense. Some argue that whatever happens to this outer wall, the inner walls provide more than an adequate defense. This view is too hopeful. The office of the presidency is more "friendly" to the use of demagoguery today than it was in the past, as the norms and practices of campaigns increasingly shape ideas of leadership and bleed over into the style and conduct of the presidency. Current means of communication facilitate the exercise of rhetorical leadership. In facing a danger of this magnitude, there can be no such thing as too much vigilance. Given the lower institutional barriers to demagoguery today, greater responsibility for checking it must fall to other means. A better understanding of demagoguery is an essential element in erecting new lines of defense against it.

6

✛

Doctrines of Presidential-Congressional Relations

During the first decade of this century, a major controversy erupted over the nature and extent of the president's power. It centered on a claim of broad discretionary authority for the president in the conduct of foreign policy and security affairs. Known generally by the name of the theory of the "unitary executive," this position was advocated most force-fully by former vice president Dick Cheney and Professor John Yoo, who served in the Office of Legal Counsel in the Justice Department during the presidency of George W. Bush. As with most disputes about institutional powers, the conflict was bound up with the conduct of a specific policy—in this case, the Bush administration's measures during the War on Terror-ism for the detention and treatment of enemy combatants and suspected terrorists and for the gathering and handling of intelligence. These mea-sures were subject to legal challenges and became the target of a wave of public criticism, with opponents of President Bush resurrecting the old charge that his administration had created an "imperial presidency."[1]

This controversy had a partisan dimension, with many—though by no means all—Republicans defending the claim of the "unitary executive" and most Democrats roundly condemning it. But since taking control of the presidency in 2009, Democrats have lowered the temperature of their criticisms. President Obama, while often pursuing different policies than George Bush, has ended up defending the same legal prerogatives for the presidency, although without speaking of any general theory such as the unitary executive. The result of this détente is that despite the controversy of the last decade, there is today no clear and distinct difference between the parties in their *doctrine* of presidential and congressional powers.

("Doctrine" here means a public statement, articulated by a significant political force—a political party or movement—that seeks to establish a settled constitutional opinion within the populace about the proper workings of the institutions.)

Perhaps the differences that produced the recent controversy will once again come to the surface. For now, however, the only certain consequence of the dispute—and it is not an insignificant one—is that both sides claimed to take their bearings from the Constitution and from the intent of the Founders. No one in this matter was a proponent of the "living constitution." Those who favored the unitary executive found their position to be anchored in the vesting clause that opens Article II of the Constitution ("The Executive Power shall be vested in a President of the United States of America") and in the thought of Alexander Hamilton; those who opposed it spoke of the theory of separation of powers and looked frequently to James Madison's critique of Hamilton in the Pacificus-Helvidius debates of 1793. If the Constitution and the thought that generated is to serve as the guide, it is important to revisit the original debate of the Founders and to consider the four previous doctrines—of the Jeffersonians, the Jacksonians, the Whigs, and the Progressives—that sought to interpret the Constitution and determine the institutional relations between the president and Congress.

THE CONSTITUTIONAL DEBATE AND THE THEORY
OF THE SEPARATION OF POWERS

All who have spoken of the allocation of powers inside the federal government agree that the theory of the separation of powers is the starting point of the analysis and one of the keys to understanding the constitutional framework. The great problem, however, is that from the outset there has been a fundamental disagreement on the meaning of the theory and of how exactly it informs the Constitution. The authors of the Constitution (referred to here as the Founders) had one view of it, while the opponents of the Constitution (the Anti-Federalists) had another. The Anti-Federalists lost the struggle over the Constitution, but their understanding of the theory of the separation of powers not only survived, but also arguably has prevailed for most of our history. It deeply influenced the Jeffersonian and Whig doctrines and was in turn read back by them into the original document as the true and proper understanding of its meaning.

The Founders made use of the theory of the separation of powers, which they also developed and refined, to help them decide how to allocate power inside the federal government. The theory, which *The Federalist* referred to as an "invaluable precept in the science of politics," supplied the basic concept for the design of the government.[2] Yet—and this became a critical point in the debate—it did not exhaust the question of how to divide and assign powers.[3] For the Founders, other considerations were needed to complete the constitutional framework.

The theory of the separation of powers derived from the writings of Locke and Montesquieu and had been applied (or misapplied) in the constitutional design of the state constitutions in the 1770s and 1780s. As the Founders explain the theory in *The Federalist*, it had two major elements. First, it held that the exercise of authority or power by government falls naturally into three fairly distinct categories that are defined according to a general function to be performed. This abstract conceptualization of power is what *The Federalist* refers to as the determination "in theory [of] the several classes of power, as they may in their nature be legislative, executive, or judiciary."[4] (As in all schemes of categorization, boundaries are never perfectly clear, and some disputes are normal.[5]) By the time the theory came to America, it was accepted on all sides, working from Montesquieu's design, that there were three basic powers: a legislative power, meaning a power to make laws and determine taxing and spending; a judicial power, meaning a power to apply penalties (criminal or civil)[6]; and an executive power, meaning in a strict sense a power to execute or carry out laws and, more broadly, a discretionary power to act in behalf of the nation, especially in crisis or foreign affairs, where law either could not apply or where, if applied in a certain case, might conflict with the national interest.

The character of the executive power was the least well understood of the three, and it quickly became the subject of greatest controversy. Some of the disputes about the general theory of the separation of powers turn out on closer examination to be differences about the nature and character of the executive power. Many opponents of the Constitution defined the executive power as consisting only of the ministerial power to carry out the law. The executive is an errand-performing function, subordinate to the legislative function. By contrast, the Founders understood the executive power in a much broader sense. It included both the limited function of carrying out the will of the legislature *and* the exercise of a general discretionary power. Since statutory law cannot in its nature provide adequately for the direction of certain affairs, such as the conducting of foreign policy, or handle many crises that escape or defy legal definitions, a broad discretionary power is needed in government. The dispute over whether to recognize the executive power in this fuller sense and to make provisions for its inclusion in the government was one of the central questions in the debate over the Constitution.

The definition of the three powers describes their character in the abstract. But it says nothing whatsoever about where these powers should be lodged or how they should be distributed inside of a real government. The second element of the theory of the separation of powers, according to the Founders, addressed this question. The theory, they argued, holds that there are important advantages in housing the main part, or the bulk, of each power in a separate institution that possesses a substantial degree of independence and a capacity to proceed, in some measure, on its own. This element of the theory is reflected in the opening phrase of the first sentence of the first three articles of the Constitution: "All legislative Powers herein granted shall be vested in a Congress" (Article 1); "The executive Power shall be vested in a President" (Article 2); "The judicial Power of the United States, shall be vested in one supreme Court, and in such inferior Courts as the Congress may from time to time ordain and establish" (Article 3).

Notice that the names of the three institutions—Congress, President, Supreme Court—are different from the powers. This simple fact is a reminder of the partial autonomy of each institution from an abstract idea of a power; the institutions are not synonymous with the natural "classes of powers." At the same time, their close connection to these powers—the fact that each institution has been assigned primary responsibility for a power—results in the common use of the terms "the legislative branch" (to refer to Congress), "the executive branch" (to refer to the president), and "the judicial branch" (to refer to the Supreme Court).

What, in the Founders' view, were the advantages of placing the bulk of each power in a separate institution? First, dividing power among different institutions was thought to be essential for ensuring safety for liberty by avoiding a concentration of power in the hands of any one institution. In what may be the single best-known statement of *The Federalist*, the Founders argue, "The accumulation of all powers, legislative, executive, and judiciary, in the same hands, whether of one, a few, or many, and whether hereditary, self appointed, or elective, may justly be pronounced the very definition of tyranny."[7] Admittedly, this objective might have been achieved by a division of power among the institutions on some basis other than that of placing the bulk of each power into a different institutions; the three powers could have been dispersed broadly among three (or more) institutions so that no institution could dominate the others, giving us what one scholar described as "a government of separated institutions sharing power."[8] According to the Founders, however, recognizing an underlying principle for the division would assure that office holders (and the public) can know what the core function of each institution is and thus have a firm ground for protecting its independence over the long run. It was easy enough, as the Founders stated, to draw up "parchment barriers" to disperse power; the greater challenge was to assure that these barriers remained in place and did not fall victim to the encroaching designs of one institution over the others.[9]

A second advantage of allocating power according to the principle of the separation of powers is that it promotes efficiency, at least in one respect. Because the three functions are different in character, different qualities are required for their effective exercise. Each institution can be structured in such a way as to carry out its own function most effectively. The executive power can be housed in an institution headed by one individual in order to allow rapid and secret action, the legislative power in an institution that provides for broad representation and encourages deliberation, and the judicial power in an institution that assures knowledge of the law and detachment.

The Founders considered the theory of separation of powers to be helpful for understanding the character of the powers and for supplying the starting point for the basic architecture of the government. But, as noted, they did not think that the theory was meant to be exhaustive in determining the allocation of powers. This view of the theory stood in sharp contrast to the understanding of many of the Anti-Federalists, who insisted that the theory of separation of powers demanded a pure and complete separation. All of each power, and only each power, had to be placed in a distinct "home" institution. This understanding completed the deal and provided the full answer for how the powers should be allocated. It was all one knew and all one needed to know.

The Founders directly rejected this view in *The Federalist*, where James Madison points out that the main source for the theory, Montesquieu, had never argued for such a complete separation. Nor did the theory ever require it. Its demands were much less exacting: "where the *whole* power of one department is exercised by the same hands which possess the *whole* power of another department, the fundamental principles of a free constitution are subverted."[10]

Given this latitude to place powers according to considerations other than strict separation, the Founders then turned to the difficult question of deciding which specific elements of each power should be shared, to what degree, and for what reasons. Drawing on their experience, they advanced four grounds for a mixing or sharing of powers:

1. Powers can be shared with a view to assuring that each branch is better able to maintain its independence over time. A case in point is the veto, which gives the president a part of the legislative power and enables him to protect his powers from the designs of a legislature bent on encroachment.
2. Powers can be shared to assure a standard of republican legitimacy. For example, placing a portion of the war power—which is part of the executive power—in the legislature, in the form of the provision to declare war, is wise and almost necessary in a popular government.

Leaving the decision to launch a major war to one individual is too dangerous.

3. Powers may be shared to promote better governmental decisions (or avoid worse ones). For example, in the selection of cabinet officers and other high administrative officials, which is an executive function, the president nominates but the Senate must confirm the appointments (Article 2, Section 2). One reason for this division of power is to reduce the number of incompetent appointments and prevent cronyism. Another example is the president's veto power, seen in another aspect from the example above; this power enables the president to block ill-conceived legislation passed by the Congress.

4. Powers can be shared in order to promote efficiency or energy in governing. The president is given a role in the initiation of legislation by the powers of reporting on the state of the union, recommending measures to Congress, and convening Congress. The sharing in this case seems designed to promote a measure of what we call today "leadership" or "agenda setting," which comes from the hand of the president.

Some scholars have grouped these four criteria for the sharing of powers into what they call the theory of "checks and balances." Add this idea, they continue, to the theory of separation of powers and the combination accounts for the whole plan for the allocation of powers among the branches of the government. Even this formulation, however, is misleading. Not all checking and balancing derives from sharing powers, and not all sharing of powers produces checks and balances. Examining briefly each of these points shows the complexity of the constitutional design.

Checks and balances on power in the constitutional system do not derive only from the sharing of a power. The separating of power also produces checks, but in a different way. The accomplishment of many significant objectives requires the concurrence of more than one institution. For example, the completion of a president's strategic or diplomatic strategy often requires congressional legislation. The president may wish to continue a war or a policy—Gerald Ford sought to continue aid to the South Vietnamese in 1775, and Ronald Reagan wished to provide aid to the Contras in Nicaragua in the early 1980s—but Congress in these cases either failed to provide or specifically cut off the funding. The check here derives from each institution employing its own "independent" or separate power to thwart the objective of the other institution or to impose its will on it. Checks of this kind can be difficult and protracted, involving on occasion a good deal of brinksmanship. This understanding of a check goes all the way back to the earliest practices in England. The monarch, exercising his executive power, could commit the nation to war, but waging a significant war might require expenditures beyond what the king had at his disposal, necessitating at some point the support of Parliament to raise revenues. Parliament could then refuse or impose conditions on its support.

Turning now to the other point, the mixing or sharing of powers was not always intended to produce additional checks. Assigning the president a share in the legislative process, both at the back end (the veto) and at the front end (the state of the union and the power to recommend measures), was meant in one way to endow the government as a whole with a greater capacity for coherent movement. It adds the possibility of a dimension of initiative or "leadership" that otherwise would not exist. Beyond the specific powers of legislating, executing, and judging, the Founders recognized a need for "administration" in the broadest sense, meaning a capacity within government to set out a general direction and assemble sufficient support to put related policy into effect. Although the powers granted to the presidency come nowhere near providing it a monopoly in performing this leadership function—no institution could be granted that much power without risking despotism—the president is given certain instruments for playing this role. The Founders realized that the leadership function is too informal and too dependent on specific persons and events for it to be completely institutionalized; it might shift from place to place at different times. But as a rule, no institution was as well situated as the presidency to play this role, or to play it responsibly.[11]

The dimension of leadership or initiative was insufficiently studied in the separation of powers theory, either because positive legislation in domestic politics was infrequent or because this function was taken for granted as being inherent in the role of the king. The Founders now added this dimension to the analysis of government, as just noted, under the category of "administration," which *The Federalist* treats at some length. (Significantly, when observers refer today to the active part of the government that seeks to assemble power and make coherent policy, they speak of "the Administration.") In the nineteenth century, as part of their efforts to deny or discredit this aspect of the presidency, Jeffersonians and Whigs tried to characterize this concern with administration as the preoccupation of one man—Alexander Hamilton—and not of the Founders as a whole. But while Hamilton was the most eloquent in giving expression to this view, he was joined at the Constitutional Convention by Gouverneur Morris, James Wilson, George Washington, and Rufus King. This group of Founders wanted government power to be limited and its exercise of power to be checked, but they also were devoted to reversing the weakness of the government of the Articles and with constructing a government that could act: "the true test of a good government is its aptitude and tendency to produce a good administration."[12] To emphasize administration (or "leadership") as part of the constitutional design is accordingly not to read something alien back into the Founding, but to call attention to a quality that was sought from the outset. Proof of this fact is found in the objections made to the Constitution at the time, which claimed that the new government had created in the presidency an office modeled on monarchy. And sure enough, when President Washington proceeded to put the full leadership potential of the presidency into effect, Jefferson and his new party complained that America was on a clear path to "monarchism."

THE ANTI-FEDERALISTS ON THE ALLOCATION OF CONSTITUTIONAL POWERS

The Anti-Federalists also relied on the theory of the separation of powers, invoking it to oppose the Constitution. Their understanding of the theory, as noted, served as the inspiration for the institutional doctrines of the Jeffersonians and the Whigs. The connection among these three parties may be seen in their common use of the term "Whig," meaning for them a suspicion of kingly and later of executive power. "Whig" was the preferred label of many of the Anti-Federalists and became the name of a major faction of the Jeffersonian Party (the "old Whigs," headed by John Randolph) before finally being adopted as the title of a major party.

The Anti-Federalist position had four basic elements. First, the Anti-Federalists sought to limit the executive power, denying that it included any idea of discretionary powers. From the fear that the executive officer might use a standing army to establish a despotic state, they proposed to regulate the overall size of the armed forces by constitutional provision, keeping this power from the hands of any governmental institution. To the extent that powers of national security were granted to the government, the Anti-Federalists thought that they should be placed largely under the control of the legislative branch.

Second, the Anti-Federalists argued that the legislative branch was the supreme and only true representative of the people. More generally, they argued that the source of initiative or "motion" in government should derive from the legislature. Any discretionary power that the president might exercise must come either from explicit and narrowly drawn constitutional provisions or from specific grants accorded by statute, which of course could be revocable. The executive power itself was narrowly conceived as a ministerial power to carry out the legislature's will.

Third, the institution in which the executive power was housed—the presidency—should possess only this narrow ministerial power and should have no role in the legislative process. If the president was to be given a veto of some kind, it should be for the sole purpose of protecting the presidential office, not influencing government policy. Endowing the president with general responsibilities as a "leader" was out of the question.

Finally, the Anti-Federalists argued that certain structural provisions internal to the executive branch should be adopted to guard against the president's becoming too energetic and independent. Some Anti-Federalists favored a plural executive, and many preferred the selection of the president by Congress, in part to eliminate any presidential claim to a direct connection to the people. Under the Constitution, Anti-Federalists argued, the president had the powers of a king, and, as one writer put it, "a king of the worst kind: an elective king."[13] Far from being seen as a check on the president, a strong popular role in selection (which the Electoral College system contemplated) added new dangers to the office.

The Anti-Federalists presented themselves as the real champions of the theory of the separation of powers, which they interpreted as requiring a pure separation. If separation was good, then, by their reasoning, stricter separation must be better. The Anti-Federalists thought that the Founders had misunderstood the theory, with the result that the Constitution seriously violated its strictures. Yet perhaps more important for the Anti-Federalists than the criterion of strictness of separation was their restrictive view of the executive power. In defending their idea of the separation of powers, the Anti-Federalists were also promoting a weak executive and legislative supremacy.

The Anti-Federalist position thus fused a particular understanding of the separation of powers theory (one requiring a strict separation of powers) with a commitment to restrict executive power. This conflation, whether a result of an analytic confusion or of a deliberate rhetorical strategy, proved highly effective in debate and put the Founders on the defensive. Since the Anti-Federalist position on the separation of powers was simple and clear, while the Founders' position was complex and difficult, the Anti-Federalist understanding on this point often proved more convincing. And since all agreed that the separation of powers theory was somehow authoritative and behind the Constitution, the ability to control the interpretation of the theory was potentially a powerful weapon that could enable an appeal to the "true" logic of the Constitution even, so to speak, against its letter. The consequence of this approach would be to put the discretionary power of the presidency in greater jeopardy.

THE JEFFERSONIANS

The Jeffersonian doctrine on the allocation of powers emerged in the 1790s in reaction to the alleged "monarchism" of the administrations of George Washington and John Adams. The doctrine sought to rein in presidential power and establish the Congress as the central institution of leadership and policy. Jeffersonians presented their position as a return to the original Constitution—or to the true spirit that lay behind it. The Constitution, in their view, had been subverted by the Federalist Party under Washington and Adams, endangering the cause of republican government.

There were some differences among Jeffersonian Republicans. A faction known as the "old Whigs" defended the idea of full legislative supremacy, at times against the practices of the party's mainstream, which operated under the guidance of Thomas Jefferson. But when it came to articulating public doctrine, these internal disputes were usually muted. Jefferson usually supported the old Whigs' views of the Constitution, often redoubling his verbal concessions at just the moments when he acted contrary to their principles. Jeffersonian doctrine began by renouncing a good part of the president's executive or discretionary powers in foreign affairs and diplomacy. Jefferson denied to the presidency defensive war powers (even as he took bold action without congressional approval against the Barbary pirates), and he followed suit by acquiring the Louisiana territory (even as he denied that the president had the powers to do so).[14] With respect to the president's role in the legislative process, Jeffersonians regarded the idea of presidential leadership or agenda-setting as an encroachment on Congress's prerogatives. Jefferson ended the practice of delivering the state of the union address in person, and he let others proclaim congressional dominance in policy-making. Meanwhile, Jefferson exercised enormous personal influence over the legislative process by means of meetings with congressional members of his party. John Marshall famously foresaw the use of this tactic. Jefferson, he wrote, would "embody himself in the House of Representatives" and by "weakening the office of the President, he will increase his personal power. He will diminish his responsibility, [and] sap the fundamental principles of government."[15]

There was one point on which Jefferson deviated more openly from the "old Whig" position. This involved the president's relationship to the public. The Whig view, as noted, was opposed to creating a popular base for the presidency because doing so might strengthen its authority. Jefferson approached this issue from a different angle. In his early writings, he proposed a unique solution to the problem of how a separation of powers system could be maintained in practice in the face of inevitable attempts of one branch to dominate the others. This solution called for obligatory constitutional conventions every generation (about eighteen years), at which representatives of the people could redo the Constitution and seek to correct any imbalances that had grown up in the interim. The Founders rejected this solution, arguing that the practice of rewriting the Constitution would undermine the whole idea of a stable constitution and risk reopening all the great divisions in the nation. In order to maintain the separation of powers, they thought it sufficient to endow each branch with the motive, and to give it the means, to protect its own powers: "Ambition must be made to counteract ambition. The interest of the man must be connected with the constitutional rights of the place."[16] Jefferson thought that this solution had failed, as shown by the slide into "monarchism" in the 1790s. The election of 1800, he now conceived, might serve as the functional equivalent of a constitutional convention. By serving as a kind of indirect popular referendum, it could settle the question of the proper relationship among the branches of the government. As the president-elect and head of the party that waged the battle for this "second revolution," Jefferson asserted a degree of popular authority deriving from his election.

Jefferson's break from old-Whig doctrine, if such it really was, was limited in that it was meant to further the Whig objective of curtailing presidential authority. It is not clear, moreover, whether Jefferson considered the idea of a popular base for the presidency to be a desirable *permanent* aspect of constitutional design or a one-time exception (part of "a revolution") to put things straight.[17] Whatever Jefferson's own views, Jeffersonian Republicans did not afterward assert this position as part of their constitutional doctrine. Furthermore, by embracing the congressional party caucus as the institution for nominating presidential candidates, Republicans sought to ensure a large degree of congressional influence over the choice of the president. The idea of the popular-based presidency was more a Jacksonian than a Jeffersonian innovation.

The effects of Jeffersonian doctrine on the presidency only became evident in the administrations of James Madison and James Monroe. Both of these presidents were conspicuous for their modesty in policy leadership. One student of Madison's presidency concluded that "Madison could hardly have played a less important part during those eight uncomfortable years if he had remained in Virginia."[18] Henry Clay is reported to have said of James Monroe that he "has just been re-elected with apparent unanimity, but he has not the slightest influence on Congress. . . . Henceforth there was and would not be a man in the United States possessing less *personal* influence over them than the President."[19] Perhaps the most telling fact about the effect of Jeffersonian doctrine was that Monroe was in no way disturbed by his limited leadership role; he believed he was only doing what his party's doctrine demanded.

A connection exists in Jeffersonian Republican thought between the party's position on the institutional allocation of power and its position on limiting the overall powers of the national government. Jeffersonians favored a strict construction of national powers as a way of restricting the role of the federal government. While they advocated this position for its own sake, they also found it to be a helpful way to limit the president's power.[20] A national government that had little to do had no need of a strong leader. According to Ralph Ketcham, Madison woke up to the danger of monarchism in the 1790s and, in an effort to halt it, "stepped back from his ardent nationalism of the 1780s to favor both limited federal power in general *vis-à-vis* the states and a stricter interpretation of the powers of Congress and the executive."[21]

Jeffersonian doctrine was influenced by Anti-Federalist thought on the nature of separation of powers and on the role of the president. But Jeffersonians did not favor going back and introducing constitutional amendments to change the basic allocation of powers among the institutions of the national government. They sought instead to take control of how the Constitution was interpreted. Nothing in retrospect is more important for the establishment of constitutionalism in America than the Jeffersonian acceptance of the basic legal design of the Constitution. It meant that the Constitution was left intact, to be called on at a later day to support a different understanding than that found in Jeffersonian doctrine. Even James Madison broke with strict Jeffersonian institutional doctrine when he vetoed a bill providing for nationally financed improvements of canals and roads. Madison could do so because whatever Jeffersonian doctrine might have said, he had the clear constitutional power to veto in his hands.

Jeffersonian doctrine left an important question unanswered. From their reading of Locke and Montesquieu, Jefferson and Madison acknowledged the need for certain discretionary powers in government. They would therefore have known that their doctrine obscured this truth. All subsequent doctrinal thought, insofar as it has embraced the basic Jeffersonian position, has perpetuated this original deception. Jefferson and Madison might nevertheless have justified their doctrine by starting with the proposition that all doctrines are imperfect and that the choice among them must turn on which does the most good. For Jefferson and Madison, the original constitutional view, which implicitly sanctioned executive discretion (or was so interpreted by Hamilton and Washington), had already shown itself to be a grave threat to republican government. Jeffersonian doctrine was an improvement.

Yet, even if this was the case, Jeffersonian doctrine left the problem of how to deal with a "deficit" in executive power, defined as the gap between the power that a president needs to operate for the national interest and the more limited power that Jeffersonian doctrine assigned to the president. The efforts by Jeffersonian presidents to manage this deficit during the twenty-four years of their reign (1801–1825) show the difficulties and contradictions in their doctrine. Four points stand out.

First, Jefferson himself sought to reduce the need for discretionary executive power by trying to accomplish a change in the basic character of
political life. The Founders justified executive discretion in large measure
by appealing to the harsh nature of international affairs and the resulting
need for speed, secrecy, and the use of force. In pursuing his embargo
policy during his term, Jefferson hoped that he could alter permanently
how international affairs were conducted and reduce the need in the future for the use of secrecy and force. The paradox contained in Jefferson's
experiment was that to carry it out required the exercise of an extraordinary degree of presidential power that arguably exceeded anything that
had been attempted by Washington or Adams.

Second, the deficit of power could be dealt with by deception: by doing
one thing while saying something different. Jefferson followed this course,
but with the result, as noted, of leaving a legacy of examples of the bold
use of presidential power accompanied by disclaimers about whether the
president ever had such powers in the first place. The problem with this
solution is less its hypocrisy than the fact that it makes future exercises of
the same kind of hypocrisy more difficult. The disclaimers end up carrying more weight than the examples.

Third, to the extent Jefferson developed a coherent theoretical answer
about how to deal with this deficit, it was based on the idea of claiming
an executive prerogative *outside and beyond* the Constitution, rather than
a discretionary power *inside* of it. In the words of the presidential scholar
Gary Schmitt, "Jefferson presumably believed that if one could revise and
scale down the formal, constitutional powers of the president while at the
same time granting him, as circumstances warranted, the right to exercise
extra-constitutional powers, one would make the use of such powers less
likely."[22] Jefferson no doubt calculated that this policy represented the
best solution, on the grounds that it would restrain presidential power
most of the time, while allowing for the use of discretionary authority
when absolutely necessary. But others have argued that its effect is to create a precedent for jumping outside the law altogether and operating with
no restraint. A frequent recourse to extra-legal prerogative has the added
danger of jeopardizing the very idea of the rule of law.

Finally, the deficit of executive power could be "dealt with" by
accepting it and yielding to its consequences. According to Ralph
Ketcham, this seems to have been the conclusion that James Madison
reached. He preferred in the War of 1812 to put the nation at risk of los-
ing a war and seeing Washington, D.C., sacked and burned than to do
anything that might compromise the principles of Jeffersonian doctrine
on presidential power.[23] It is doubtful that many would find this solution satisfactory.

THE JACKSONIANS AND THE WHIGS

Jeffersonian doctrine reined supreme in the early part of the nineteenth century. A few voices here and there were heard to grumble about the dangers of a weak presidency, but the opposition was never sufficient to mount a full-blown challenge. Jefferson's statement in his first inaugural address, "we are all Republicans, we are all Federalists," meant, in terms of institutional doctrine, that all were now Republicans.

The defense of a strong presidency in the first half of the nineteenth century—to the extent one existed—fell to presidents Andrew Jackson and James K. Polk and to the Democratic Party of that period. This defense emerged in a reaction to the effort to apply pure Jeffersonian institutional doctrine against President Jackson. There is an irony here. The Democratic Party considered itself to be the heir of the Jeffersonian Republicans. This claim was undoubtedly true for both the personnel and voters of the party and for its constitutional view of the limited power of the federal government in relation to the states. But in regard to institutional doctrine, the Whig party seized the Jeffersonian mantle and pushed its principles even further. Whigs thought that Congress possessed a near plenary power to dictate public policy and that any presidential attempt to deny or interfere with this right constituted a violation of the Constitution.

Jackson, and later Polk, rejected this view and defended the prerogatives of the office by using the manifest legal powers granted by the Constitution. Neither president said very much about abstract theories, except occasionally to remind Americans that the theory of the separation of powers had been adopted to assure a strong and independent executive officer. They made their case largely on legal (constitutional) grounds, appealing to the language and plain meaning of the Constitution. Following a Senate resolution attacking Jackson for allegedly going beyond his constitutional powers, he responded, "Knowing [the constitutional rights] of the Executive, I shall at all times endeavor to maintain them agreeably to the provisions of the Constitution and the oath I have taken to support and defend it."[24] The nation was thus presented with a solid defense of the Constitution, but there was little effort made to restate the theoretical case for executive power and discretion in the way that had been done in *The Federalist*.

Some scholars claim that Andrew Jackson saved the American presidency, for at this moment it had no other defenders. Certainly, there was no support for the institution coming from old Jeffersonian doctrine, nor obviously from the position being developed by the Whigs. It is also true, however, that if Jackson saved the Constitution, the Constitution saved Andrew Jackson. Jackson was able to prevail because he had on his side broad powers contained in the document. Whatever Jeffersonian or Whig doctrine might declare, there was still the brute fact of the law itself—and of course the "ambition" of a president whose interest was "connected with the constitutional rights of the place."

Jackson's defense of the constitutional powers of the office stressed three main points. First, he asserted the president's authority to control the executive branch. Against the Whigs' theory that Congress could devolve a power on a cabinet minister (or at least the secretary of the treasury) and then by law prevent a president from exercising administrative discretion, Jackson argued that the president could press his views on a cabinet officer and, if need be, proceed to the extreme of dismissal in order to obtain compliance. As he noted, "Upon [the president] has been devolved by the Constitution and the suffrages of the American people the duty of superintending the operation of the Executive Departments of the government and seeing that the laws are faithfully executed."[25]

Second, against the Whigs' claim that the veto could not be used to thwart the will of Congress, Jackson asserted the president's authority to avail himself of this constitutionally sanctioned power. In his veto of the Bank Bill in 1832, he took his case to the American public to garner support, using the constitutional instrument of the veto message to communicate with the people. Without going so far as to claim a presidential power to use the veto as a policy tool—that was not necessary—Jackson argued for the legitimacy of the veto as an instrument to protect the Constitution as interpreted by the president (and not just to defend the presidency from encroachments by Congress).[26] His defense of the veto proved so compelling that it laid the groundwork for the later and broader claim that the veto was a normal instrument of presidential power to be used to serve the president's policy goals.

Jackson's leadership was, by and large, quite limited. As an heir to Jeffersonian Republican thought about the power of the federal government, Jackson sought mostly to *deny* the use of further legislative powers by the national government. As in the case of his opposition to the national bank, Jackson was using presidential power to restrict the scope of the federal government. The only nineteenth-century president before Lincoln who sought openly to assemble power to pursue a positive policy agenda was the masterful James Polk.

Third, Jackson affirmed the president's popular base of support, both in the conduct of his office and in his claim of the meaning of presidential elections. Polk built on this idea and argued that the president's claim to the representation of the American people was no less than that of Congress: "The President represents in the executive department the whole people of the United States, as each member of the legislative department represents portions of them."[27] For the Whigs, this assertion marked the supreme heresy. It confirmed the Anti-Federalist fear of an "elective

monarch" and challenged one of the main principles that supported legislative supremacy, which is that the legislature is the supreme embodiment of the public will. The Jacksonian claim of a popular foundation
for the presidency should also be understood as a reaction against the
Jeffersonian practice of keeping the president under the shackles of the
congressional caucus, which after 1808 had deprived the presidency of
the limited popular base that the Founders contemplated. While the Jacksonian claim of a full popular base for the presidency was new and went
beyond what the Founders had sought, it did serve to help restore some
of the institution's original power.[28]

Whig doctrine was accepted not only by the Whig party itself, but
later on by leaders of the Republican Party. (President Lincoln's exercise
of presidential power clearly violated most of his party's doctrinal orthodoxies, but Lincoln and others tried not to offend those orthodoxies
too greatly by arguing the exceptional character of the deviations.) Whig
doctrine claimed its roots in Jeffersonian Republican doctrine, and it purported to be based on the Constitution. Yet with the collapse of the caucus
as a way of controlling the presidency, Whigs found it impossible to stand
by the simple letter of the Constitution, even if it were interpreted "cor-
rectly" according to their doctrine. To save the Constitution, they insisted
that it needed to be changed. By proposed statutes and amendments,
the Whigs, and later some of the Republicans, assaulted the very core of
the president's powers. The Whigs challenged the president's executive
power to run his own administration through proposals to make the secretary of treasury dependent on Congress; they passed a Tenure of Office
Act that prevented presidents from dismissing executive officers; and
they tried, when in control of the presidency, to establish the precedent of
making executive decisions by a vote of the cabinet. They also sought to
reduce dramatically the president's legislative and policy-making powers
by a narrow interpretation of the legitimate use of the presidential veto,
by a proposed amendment that would allow a veto to be overturned
by a mere majority in each house of the Congress, and by presidential
pronouncements proclaiming a doctrine of noninterference in legislative
affairs. Whigs were content in theory to leave the presidency alone and
intact in its weakness and misery, provided presidents renounced the
Jacksonian heresy of claiming to represent the people. But in fact, they
twice sought to divest the president of his office. The first attempt was
a scheme to force John Tyler to resign by denying confirmation of any
cabinet officers to run the government; the other, by Republicans, was the
impeachment of President Andrew Johnson.

During the nineteenth century, it was the Democratic Party that came
closest to defending the Founders' view of the executive. Still, what is
striking in retrospect is the weakness of that defense. As the party of

states' rights, the Democratic Party had—except under President Polk and later under President Cleveland—no agenda other than to oppose proposals for national action. (The party's *de facto* pro-slavery program was often pursued by indirection.) The party that had no positive legislative program was the only defender of the presidency, while the parties (the Whigs and Republicans) that had a legislative agenda, and a view of federal power to support such a program, opposed a strong president. Furthermore, the Democratic Party grew weaker in its defense of a strong presidency after Polk, and during the Civil War it gained traction for a time by attacking the "dictatorship" of President Lincoln. But in any case, the content of Democratic Party doctrine after 1860 was of little direct consequence, since between Buchanan and Wilson, only one Democrat, Grover Cleveland, was elected president.

During the nineteenth century, no party really kept alive the "original" constitutional view. It was first obscured, perhaps deliberately, then appropriated, and finally lost sight of. For the brief time that the Democratic Party came to the defense of the constitutional prerogatives of the president, it did so largely on legal grounds, without ever restating the ideas and theory of executive power, in part because these were the products of discredited "monarchists" like Alexander Hamilton. The dominant view was based on Jeffersonian and Whig doctrine. Most remarkable of all, this view was widely considered to be the one on which the Constitution was based (or that represented its true understanding).

The practical consequences of this doctrinal confusion about the Founders' intent during this period were not always as severe as the preceding point might lead one to think. The reason is that political actors often ignored these doctrines, relying instead on concrete legal powers granted to them under the Constitution and on incentives that the constitutional structure created. This was true of Lincoln, who viewed his exercise of powers to be legal but exceptional, and of others, such as Cleveland and McKinley. A series of legal precedents and court decisions, which developed independently of these party doctrines, also influenced the behavior of presidents. The result was that the Constitution managed to survive its own doctrinal misinterpretations.

THE PROGRESSIVE DOCTRINE

Progressive doctrine was unique in that it was the only doctrine to advertise itself, at least initially, as being at odds with the original design, either in letter or spirit. Progressives maintained that the Constitution itself was fatally flawed—in particular, the theory of the separation of powers on which it was based. It was the Constitution, therefore, that needed to be changed. The Progressive doctrine, known also as the "idea of the modern presidency," became the dominant institutional theory for much of the twentieth century before the Vietnam War, at least among scholars and journalists. It was embraced by liberals within the Democratic Party and received the backing of many professional political scientists, including the near-official endorsement of the American Political Science Profession in 1950 in its report "Toward a More Responsible Two-Party System: A Report of the Committee on Political Parties."[29] Its central premise was that American government needed strong political leadership, vested in the president, in order to meet the challenges posed by the new industrial era. These challenges required a capacity for coherent and efficient policy-making, especially in domestic affairs. The leadership capacity should therefore be unchecked, except by democratic elections. America's Constitution was unfortunately constructed on an opposite theory of the separation of powers. According to Woodrow Wilson, the most famous spokesperson for the modern presidency, the Founding was Whig in its inspiration: "The government of the United States was constructed upon the Whig theory of political dynamics, which was sort of an unconscious copy of the Newtonian theory of the Universe."[30]

What then should be done? If a place of genuine leadership were to be constructed in the American system, it would have to be in opposition to the spirit of the Constitution. One way to accomplish this, which seems to be the frankest and most open approach, would be to alter the Constitution and build a new legal system on correct principles. Wilson proposed such a plan early on, and the idea of a full-scale transformation to a parliamentary form of government, or to something that approached it, remained the favored proposal of many reformers until well into the last century. But the idea of a formal overhaul of the Constitution proved to be utterly impractical, as Americans were unwilling to embark on such a dramatic path. The alternative, which is the one that Wilson and the Progressives adopted in the end, was to proceed by indirection, grafting the doctrine of the modern presidency onto the Constitution without any formal amendments. This strategy entailed building up presidential leadership by constructing extra-constitutional sources of presidential authority, which would include a new nomination system based on primaries, a party system that formed around the presidential candidates, and the promulgation of a new idea or concept of popular leadership. The idea was to eliminate *de facto* the system of separation of powers by providing the president with a disciplined party that would do his bidding in Congress. Wilson was hopeful that such a transformation could take place. Despite the "Whig theory" on which the Founding had been based, the Constitution, like all laws and charters, was ultimately a "vehicle of life" and "no mere lawyer's document."[31] Everyone, so to speak, could agree to wink together and interpret the Constitution in a new way that would now include what it was meant to exclude.

The Progressive accounts of the original Constitution design were flawed, perhaps deliberately so. The Constitution in its original form and conception allowed for considerable strength in the presidency and included tools to enable some degree of presidential leadership. The impressive record of the Washington administration, both in domestic and foreign affairs, shows what the original presidency was capable of accomplishing.[32] But instead of embracing this strength as part of the proper understanding of an original constitutional design to which they might return, the Progressives largely denied it. Wilson and others sometimes acknowledged that Hamilton and a few others had a more dynamic understanding of presidential leadership, but their view had not prevailed—whether in the Constitution itself or in dominant nineteenth-century doctrine did not seem to matter. The likely reason for the Progressives' unwillingness to pursue this historical point is that the Founders' view of the presidency still fell far short of the unchecked presidency they hoped to establish. In fact, the Founders' view represented a greater threat to the Progressive position, precisely because it allowed for some degree of presidential leadership, but not, the Progressives believed, nearly enough. The Founders' view was almost reasonable. Far better, then, to accept the weakness of the presidency by adopting the Whig characterization of the Founding; there was then more reason to agree on the need for a full-scale transformation of the system.

The Progressive strategy for change sought to create an institution—the modern or rhetorical presidency—that Progressive theorists acknowledged was manifestly non- or anti-constitutional. Placing this institution within the existing legal framework of the Constitution has proven to be most difficult. Lacking a firm legal basis, the modern presidency has rested on sand. True, expectations and demands on the presidency have increased, and the role of the president in both domestic and foreign affairs has grown, although perhaps only in part because of Progressive doctrine. The other cause is simply the greater demands placed on the federal government and the new role that the United States came to play in international relations. In any case, while the power of the modern presidency has expanded, it has never achieved anything like the unchecked status that Progressives wished for. The creation of higher expectations for the office in the face of its actual legal power has led inevitably to a gap that has sometimes created frustration and disappointment. The president may summon spirits from the deep, but they do not always come.

The story of the second half of the twentieth century, however, has been the abandonment of Progressive doctrine. The critical turning point came during the Vietnam War, when the policies pursued by a liberal president no longer accorded with the direction of what came to be defined as liberal policy. When liberals turned on that policy, they did so with a special vengeance, branding the institution that supported it an "imperial presidency," the modern name for "monarchism." Liberals suddenly became ardent supporters of what they once vilified: the written text or legal document of the Constitution, which they interpreted, at least in foreign affairs, to be more of a Whig document. Paradoxically, then, the heirs of Progressive doctrine, consisting of congressional Democrats and liberal intellectuals, promoted a new Whigism in foreign affairs and national security policy, which they dusted off temporarily to attack George W. Bush. In domestic affairs, liberals have been only slightly more faithful to Progressive doctrine: they have been for a strong presidency when a liberal is in office, but have been strong proponents of the written text of the Constitution (strictly interpreted) when Republicans are in office.

For nearly a century and a half, from roughly 1800 until 1950, the dominant understanding of the Constitution's allocation of powers was based on a flawed interpretation of the original design. The Constitution was never the Whig document that most either thought it was or found it expedient to say that it was. The achievement of the last half-century of scholarship has been the revival of a serious analysis of the Founders' thought on the presidency and on the separation of powers.[33] The new scholarship has not resolved all the issues or come to a common position, but the disputes and disagreements based on it are more deeply informed by a knowledge of the Founders' thought and of separation of powers theory than was previously the case. This scholarship has shown that if Americans wish to develop a sound doctrine to defend a strong, but still limited, presidency, there is no better place to begin than with a study of the Constitution. The theoretical understanding on which it rests offers the fullest account in American political thought of the character of the powers of government and the best guide for determining a healthy division of authority between the president and Congress.

III

MODERN CONSERVATISM

7

✛

Four Heads and One Heart: The Modern Conservative Movement

It has been said in jest that the conservative movement in America today is held together today by two self-evident truths: Barack Obama and Nancy Pelosi. Like many such comments, this one contains a kernel of truth. Much of the unity that exists among conservatives stems from their shared antipathy to liberalism. It serves as the common heart that beats in the breast of the conservative movement's diverse and often fractious components. If by some strange dispensation liberalism were to cease to exist tomorrow, conservatism would begin to break apart on the next day.

No shame attaches in politics to relying on the adhesive properties supplied by a common antagonist. America is a vast country in which it is only by coalition that a movement can hope to win a majority. Conservatism is such a coalition. In its theoretical composition, it is made up of four heads that draw their lifeblood from the same heart: traditionalism, neoconservatism, libertarianism, and the religious right. Conservatism is a movement characterized by what was once known—before multiculturalists took the term hostage—as diversity.

Liberalism, too, is a kind of coalition. It has today its more militant core that has adopted the name of "Progressive," and a smaller and more moderate wing of "blue dogs." Dislike of the opposition has also been vital to liberals in sustaining their movement, as shown by their healing antipathy to George W. Bush and Sarah Palin. But there is an important difference in the two coalitions. Conservatism is intellectually more heterogeneous than liberalism. Conservatism's heads or parts came into existence at different times and under different circumstances, and they have never claimed to be guided by the same principles. Liberals, by contrast, prefer at least to think that they are inspired by the same set of ideals. To the extent that "blue dogs" deviate from Progressives, it is not because they articulate a different theory but because they are responding to a different set of political pressures.

One consequence of this difference between the two coalitions appears in how they handle disagreement. When conflicts spring up among liberals, the Progressives regard deviation as heresy, since there is only one true liberal path. Conservatives are not schismatic in the same way, and this for the simple reason that they have never operated under the illusion of ultimate agreement. Older parts of the conservative movement accuse newer ones of trying to usurp the movement, or of not being genuinely conservative. But they rarely charge them with heresy or breaking faith: their sin is never to have possessed the right principles in the first place.

Critics of conservatism often depict its heterogeneity as a grave weakness. How often today does one hear liberal commentators, particularly those of a certain intellectual pretentiousness, trotting out a classic conservative source from one of its camps in order to try to embarrass the position taken by conservatives from another camp? This ploy invariably follows the same smug formula: "I should have thought that conservatives, above all, would follow their own great thinker X (Burke or Hayek, etc.) and be especially mindful of Y," where Y could be either a scrupulous protection of civil liberties and privacy (as if safety and national security were not also a concern of conservatives), or abjuring any kind of foreign occupation or exercise in nation building (as if a need to battle new kinds of challenges by new responses had never been recommended by any school of conservatism).[1] In the view of its liberal critics, the four heads of conservatism make it into an obvious monster.

But conservatives, when they are able to step back a moment from their internecine quarrels and reflect on the matter, see the creature in a different light. The ongoing debate among the talking heads sharpens thinking and avoids intellectual complacency, which is the death knell of any party. Better four heads than none!

FOUR HEADS AND FOUNDATIONAL PRINCIPLES

Each head of the conservative intellectual coalition favors its own first principle or foundational concept. Its foundation serves as the standard by which it judges what is right or good. For traditionalism, that concept is History or culture, meaning the heritage that has come down to us and is our own. Count it our great fortune, too, that this culture happens to be good. As Samuel Huntington lately observed in a book titled *Who Are We?*, which has been much lauded by traditionalists, the core of America's identity can be traced to its original culture. That culture was in existence long before the Revolution in the practices and beliefs of our colonial settlers, especially in New England.[2] Huntington labels this culture "Anglo-Protestantism," and he argues that it is to this source that Americans should look to find their basic moorings. Traditionalists today are defenders of the culture—for some, gently and urbanely, armed only with their bow ties; for others, more militantly and boisterously, menacing with their pitchforks.

The traditionalists' defense of culture sometimes turns out under examination to be rather vague and amorphous. Tradition, once characterized as "a certain assemblage of beliefs, convictions, rules, usages, traditions, proverbs, and principles," can be less important for what it affirms than for what it opposes.[3] Traditionalists mistrust efforts at full-scale rational structuring in politics, deploring the introduction of theory or general ideas. Beginning with one of the best-known of traditionalists, Russell Kirk, many have even expressed reservations about the opening paragraph of the Declaration of Independence, with its talk about "Laws of Nature." Traditionalists maintain that such abstract thinking inevitably leads to errors and excesses. Culture or tradition is good in large part because no one ever had to think it up or make it. It is just there, having evolved in a specific place or context. Traditionalists prefer what grows in politics—hence "culture," originally an agricultural term—to what is made.

For the neoconservative today, the foundational concept is natural right, which is a theoretical way of saying that the standard of right or good, so far as political or social action is concerned, is ascertainable by human reason, even if it may also have been established by divine law. An idea of right derived from reason would apply in principle to all, or would be universally valid, no matter to what extent distinct cultural influences might impede its recognition or make impracticable its acceptance. Universal validity does not require universal adoption. It follows as well for the neoconservative that human thought or reason, though vastly constrained by circumstances, can be an instrument to help alter or structure the environment.

Neoconservatives, in line with traditionalists, concede that much of what has been offered politically under the name of reason in recent times—say the last couple of centuries or so—has been dangerous abstraction and ideology. Many if not most plans of "social engineering" are mistaken. But some big plans, such as the Founding itself, are not. For neoconservatives, the American Founding is a decisive event because of its wholesale framing of a system; for traditionalists, the Founding is better viewed as a piece of evolution in the development of Anglo-Protestant cultural values. Where the traditionalist equates prudence with caution, the neoconservative sees that it can sometimes mean boldness. Neocon-servatives, in contrast to traditionalists, hold that the wisdom of different courses of action must be guided by reason, not its renunciation, which can lead to excesses of its own. It will not do to throw the baby out with the bathwater.

For the libertarian, the foundational concept is "spontaneous order," the postulate that there is a tendency operative in human affairs, and most likely in the whole cosmos, for things to work out for themselves and to cohere, provided no deliberate effort is made to impose an overall order.[4] In the classic formulation of Adam Ferguson, order is the result of human action but not human design. Even the choice of our morals and the basic rules of society had nothing to do with a choice or plan. Accord-ing to Friedrich Hayek, "We do not owe our morals to our intelligence, [but] to the fact that some groups uncomprehendingly accepted certain rules of conduct. . . . It was a process of cultural selection, analogous to a process of biological selection."[5] The only "order" that is good is one that is set up to ensure the free play of spontaneous processes, what has been called the "system of natural liberty."[6]

Most today are familiar with an application of the idea of spontaneous order to the analysis of economic affairs, where it goes under an assumed name of "the invisible hand." The invisible hand works behind our backs to ensure that while each person or unit pursues its own particular inter-est, unconcerned with the whole, the result will be to the benefit of all. For libertarians, economics, far from being a dismal science, is an illustration of beauty. Economics is queen of the sciences and architectonic for all other forms of knowledge. Its principles apply not only to economic mat-ters strictly considered, but also to the realms of social and cultural behav-ior, which can be analyzed by economic modes of thinking. The principle of spontaneous order also governs international relations, where many libertarians favor isolationist policies on the premise that order does not need to be enforced or guaranteed by a great power (America), but tends to emerge on its own.

For those in the religious right, the foundational concept is biblical faith. Different from the other foundational concepts, faith is not con-cerned in the first instance with politics, but with another realm: man's relation to the transcendent. It is therefore not surprising that many who took their bearings from faith were for much of the last century apoliti-cal, refusing to organize collectively in politics to promote any religious concerns. Involvement in politics for reasons relating to faith was spo-radic and arose only on specific issues. But sometime in the 1970s, many in the community of faith began to assert that there was a new situation in the nation characterized by a growing political and cultural threat to religion. The conviction grew that the two realms—the political-cultural and the religious—intersect, not just sporadically on particular issues, but systematically and on an ongoing basis. Some of faith therefore chose to organize and engage more directly in political and culture affairs. This decision was the basis for what shortly became known as the religious right, which by the 1980s became an integral part of the modern conservative movement.

Faith as a foundational concept in the political realm does not aim to supply a complete standard of political right for all issues. It supports a more limited political-cultural project related to the interests or concerns of faith. Stated defensively, that project includes collective action designed to protect havens conducive to fostering a life committed to faith, which in practice has often meant undertaking efforts to counterbalance forces working in politics and culture that are indifferent or hostile to religion. But the project is misunderstood if only its defensive aspect is considered. There is a positive element as well, captured in an older idea originally of Puritan roots, that America has a role to play as an instrument in the service of the transcendent. Speaking at almost the same time as the issuance of the Declaration of Independence, Samuel Sherwood reminded Americans, "The providences of God in first planting his church in this, then howling wilderness, and in delivering and preserving it to this day . . . are reckoned among the most glorious events that are to be found in history, in these later ages of the world. And there are yet more glorious events in the womb of providence."[7]

For those of faith, the adoption of the legal Constitution in no way abrogated the understanding of America having a special place in serving a higher cause. For many of the faithful, it has always been thought that there is a second and unwritten constitution meant to operate alongside of the legal one. The second constitution carried forward the cause of faith while the first dealt with matters of politics. Because these two constitutions were concerned with largely distinct matters, there was no need to combine them into a single document—indeed, it would be harmful to the purposes of both realms ever to merge them. The two constitutions existed together in the hearts and thoughts of many Americans and proved complementary in practice. For those of this view, America is not fully America—and cannot be fully loved and cherished—if the unwritten constitution is renounced and if faith survives here, at best, as merely one belief among many. Would it be too strong to say that an America without faith is "unconstitutional"?

A major concern of the religious right has been the reformulation of this project in a form that speaks to our times. Conditions have changed, and the specific character of the positive project must change as well. Once conceived as a mission of the "reformed" church only, it is today being reconceived—leaving aside the fine points of theology—as a common enterprise among those devoted to biblical faith to cope with a culture that increasingly conceives itself as "post-religious." The religious right has been notable for its building of alliances and coalitions among the faithful of different traditional religions—Protestant, Catholic, and Jewish—to promote its objectives.

OBJECTIONS TO LIBERALISM

These four foundational concepts—culture, natural right, spontaneous order, and faith—supply the basis for much of what conservatives find objectionable in liberalism. Conservatives agree with each other on many, though not all, of these objections, but each part of the movement, on the basis of its foundational concept, has assumed a special role in criticizing a different facet of liberalism.

For the traditionalist, liberalism's most objectionable feature is a casual Progressivism that disdains America's heritage and the concept or idea of the nation altogether. Liberals shop for the new, the trendy, and (metaphorically speaking) the "European" against the traditional and the American. Liberals are by preference multicultural, cosmopolitan, or "transnational"; they are more anxious to assume someone else's perspective than America's and increasingly view the political form of the nation as an anachronism, as the world is in transition to globalization. This liberal posture is diametrically opposed to the traditionalist's view, which is proud of our own culture—in part just because it is our own.

Neoconservatives object to liberalism's relativism, its claim that human thought leads to the conclusion that there is no standard of right. Liberals may know what is right by following the dictates of the heart—they speak constantly of humanitarianism and compassion—and they sometimes seek, without coherence, to derive from relativism itself an absolute standard of tolerance. But when it comes to the test, they back away from proclaiming any grounds for a rational standard of right, preferring instead the label of "pragmatism." For liberalism, the promulgation of such a standard smacks of arrogance and intolerance that ends in extremism. Leading liberal intellectuals favor the theoretical position known as "neopragmatism" (or political nonfoundationalism), which holds that advanced democracies are best served by foreswearing a foundational concept of any kind, political or religious. For neoconservatives, the liberals' relativism and denial of natural right risks translating into inconstancy in the pursuit of the national purpose, as could be seen during the Cold War and today in the War on Terror.

For the libertarian (and the economic conservative more broadly), liberalism is objectionable because of its reflexive preference for regulation and planning. Liberalism is virtually synonymous with big government.

No efforts to swear off this addiction—including solemn pronouncements that the era of big government is over—can succeed. Liberalism is a repeat offender and perennial antagonist to the "system of natural liberty." The return of ever grander plans of government control, from the Great Society in the 1960s to plans for industrial policy in the 1970s, to the huge projects of government expansion promoted by the Obama administration, is proof, for libertarians, of the "fatal conceit" that animates liberal thinking.

The religious right objects to liberalism's "secularism," also known as "secular humanism" or the "religion of humanity." Secularism goes well beyond the espousal of an interpretation of the Constitution which seeks to erect a famous "wall of separation" between religion and the state. Secularism's fundamental objective is a project in its own right to eliminate any recognized place for biblical faith as the guiding light of the culture. It will not rest content until faith withdraws from playing any public role, direct or indirect. The conflict of secularism and faith is at the heart of the so-called culture war.

THE FUTURE OF THE MOVEMENT

Despite the fact that conservatism in some form helped to set the agenda in American politics for much of the period from 1980 through 2008, many of its critics claim that it can never serve as the philosophy of a truly active force or a "governing party." Doesn't the word "conservative" itself, they ask, connote the very opposite, suggesting a disposition to go slow, to wait upon others to lead, and then to react?

Conservatism can fulfill the role of being the philosophy of a governing party only if its four heads are properly arranged. That arrangement will always depend in part on prevailing circumstances. Traditionalism and libertarianism are apt to be at their most influential when the task at hand involves correcting or undoing errant liberal policies. Traditionalism is sometimes proudly without a positive project; it finds its voice in the critical assessment of others' foolish initiatives and often functions best as the "conscience of conservatism." Libertarianism (including economic conservatism) is most needed in counteracting the excesses brought on by centralized planning. Its strong suit is found in domestic "administration"—not, obviously, in the liberal meaning of building the administrative state, but an older meaning of handling affairs. Today, economic conservatism cannot be passive. It must be concerned with positive plans for managing the economy, reducing budgets, and coping with the massive economic pressures created by the overcommitments of the welfare state in pensions and medical care.

When it comes to the initiating role of charting new courses to steer the nation in the international environment and setting a moral compass, neoconservatives and the religious right must assume the leading roles. The central challenges of high politics that will shape the West in the long term are found in the battle to save civilization from a new barbarism and the effort to sustain a climate hospitable to biblical faith. America's role in influencing the outcome on both of these questions is central. As the most important world power, America has the responsibility to craft the basic strategy for thwarting the new barbarism and for carrying the burden of putting that strategy into effect. As the nation in the West with the largest movement to sustain faith, America has the task of keeping a lamp burning until the tide has turned.

If a partnership in leadership between neoconservatives and the religious right is to succeed, each part needs to be conscious of its role and of the character of its partner. Avoiding misconceptions is crucial, for there are many who advance arguments that have been intended to set these two groups at odds. One contention is that the foundational concept of natural right, given its basis in reason, is hostile to faith. This position is in error. Properly understood, the American conception of natural law assigns to the political power the charge of protecting rights, but it does not demand abandonment of a larger or higher purpose. The respect for and enforcement of rights is a floor for political life, not a ceiling. Projects that are compatible with maintaining natural rights but envision encouraging a higher task are not banned from the life of the political community. Natural right on its own does not require the cultivation of biblical faith in the name of the common good, but neither does it preclude it. Many adherents of natural right have today become convinced that its goals can only be maintained by and with support of the religion. Proof of the alliance may be seen in how neoconservatives have teamed with members of the religious right to work together on key issues such as the composition of the courts, genetic engineering, and school choice.

If proponents of natural right have found much that is compatible in the project of faith, the reverse is also the case. For one thing, it has been sheer calumny on the part of secularists to suggest that proponents of faith are hostile to the protection of natural rights and therefore at odds with neoconservatives (and everyone else). Over the course of its brief career, the religious right has pursued its aims on top of, and not in opposition to, the system of natural rights, which it fully supports. The more important point that bears on a partnership is that the project of faith is concerned with a limited mission, not with managing the whole of a political agenda. For its own sake, it may not want to be more than a powerful influence that works within a coalition, rather than a force that claims responsibility for exercising rule, which is a task that goes far beyond its means and calling. It therefore needs a partner in governing. It would be foolish, of course, to think that the different priorities of these two parts of the coalition may not sometimes create conflict. On a realistic and successful management of these divergences hinges the future of the conservative movement.

APPENDIX: IS CONSERVATISM
A FORM OF LIBERALISM?

American conservatism is devoted to conserving the American republic. It can have no higher or nobler goal. But what is it, more precisely, that conservatism is meant to conserve? Since the American republic is commonly classified as a "liberal" regime, some have asked whether conservatism today should not be considered a synonym for, or a branch of, liberalism. If this is the case, as many believe, it would make the central task of conservatism to be that of conserving liberalism. ("Liberalism" in this context refers to its original eighteenth-century variant, meaning a limited government whose chief aim is to secure individual rights, rather than the modern variant, meaning a positive state that seeks to establish "social justice.")

There is no doubt some pedigree to equating conservatism with liberalism, as two of the greatest American conservatives, Friedrich Hayek and Milton Friedman, at one time preferred the label of liberalism.[8] Yet it is in the end a mistake to think of American conservatism as the same thing as liberalism, even in the original sense. Conservatism may serve liberalism and seek to preserve it, but it often does so in ways that original liberalism hardly conceived of and that modern liberalism usually rejects. And this it does for original liberalism's own good. The fact is that liberal theory never developed adequate tools to sustain itself; it has always required something beyond itself to survive. Conservatism, while endorsing much of liberalism, is the philosophy that recognizes this need. Without conservatism, liberalism would begin to wither away. In fact, it has already begun to do so.

Conservatism conserves the American republic by supporting its theoretical foundation of natural rights. This "abstract truth, applicable to all men and all times" (Lincoln) is something conservatives are not embarrassed to proclaim, even before the United Nations General Assembly. On this point, conservatives are in accord with many of the original liberals. Modern liberals, by contrast, prefer to deny any claims of truths or foundations; they advertise themselves as pragmatists or "nonfoundationalists," all while folding their values inside the process of development or change.

Conservatism conserves the American republic by supporting the idea of the nation. The nation is necessary for security, for the activities of the common political life, and even for the welfare of humanity in general. What entity other than the nation state, after all, defends us, enacts our laws, and provides for the well-being of many beyond its authority? Conservatism not only recognizes the rational case for the nation, but leaves space for justifiable feelings of attachment to it, acknowledging that the heart has its reasons that reason cannot comprehend. Original liberalism was also a friend of the nation and developed such supportive ideas as sovereignty. But it is also the case that liberalism had difficulty from the first in articulating what the nation state was beyond a contract, and it could never make full sense of reasonable feelings of attachment to it.[9] Modern liberalism has grown increasingly uneasy about the nation. It considers patriotism an anachronism and promotes global citizenship and global studies as replacements for American citizenship and education in our own political tradition. The main category of modern liberalism is "humanity."

Conservatism conserves the American republic by giving appropriate support to biblical religion. Biblical religion has been the major source of our ethical system, one of self-restraint and belief in something beyond material existence. Conservatives subscribe to the liberal principles of freedom of religion, nonestablishment, and religious tolerance. But they see no contradiction (why should they?) between holding these principles and promoting reasonable measures—whether these concern immigration, fiscal policy, or education—to preserve the central place of the biblical religions in our culture. Original liberal theory was in some formulations cool to religion, and it often failed to acknowledge or appreciate how much liberal society had borrowed from the storehouse of religious capital. As for modern liberalism (setting aside the important faction that is hostile to biblical religions), it has taken the legal norm of religious freedom and twisted it into a new ideal of neutrality between faith and nonbelief. Liberalism does not require such neutrality, and conservatism does not recommend it.

Conservatism conserves the American republic by promoting "the tradition," which refers, beyond religion and the Enlightenment, to the classical Greek and Roman ideals of virtue and excellence. Conservatives subscribe to the liberal principle of equality of rights, but they do so in no small part because it makes room for the emergence of inequalities and excellences. The tradition also provides a theoretical basis for a hierarchy of standards, allowing conservatives to criticize without apology the vulgarity that pollutes any society and that runs rampant in ours. Original liberalism often had the same inclinations—Jefferson spoke of a "natural aristocracy"—but it engaged too easily in attacks on the classics and, in its rationalist exuberance, went too far in elevating utility at the expense of nobility. Modern liberalism, with its focus on compassion, has had difficulty openly supporting and rewarding excellences. It has also allied itself culturally with relativism, which is the application of the idea of equality to all thought. Relativism makes it harder to support standards. Above all, in our universities, modern liberalism has pushed aside the "old books" in order to make room for diversity and identity politics.

Conservatism is the home today for the few remaining proponents of original liberalism. And rightly so, since the conservative movement is friendly to property rights and markets and is opposed to collectivism. But conservatism is also the home for those who believe that liberalism's defense requires something more than liberal theory. Conservatives of this variety show how the cultivation of tradition, religion, and classical virtue replenish the cultural capital that sustains liberalism. The existence within conservatism of these different strands of thought produces the aforementioned tensions, but it is also a source of the movement's great creativity. That creativity is best expressed in the view that the public good is not to be found in adherence to the simplest principles, but in the blending of different and partly conflicting ideas. By acknowledging this complexity, conservatism shows that it is no mere branch of liberalism.

8

✛

The Social Construction
of the Reagan Legacy

More than thirty years have passed since Ronald Reagan was first elected president, yet his legacy still remains an active force in American politics. Only a handful of presidents besides Reagan succeeded in projecting political influence beyond their term in office: Thomas Jefferson, Andrew Jackson, Abraham Lincoln, and Franklin Roosevelt. To this list might be added two others, Herbert Hoover and Jimmy Carter, whose reputations as failures endured for decades.

The importance of the Reagan legacy was on full display in the 2008 presidential campaign, where it played an important role in the nomination contests of both parties. For the GOP, all of the contenders vied for the right to claim the Reagan mantle. The eventual nominee, John McCain, never tired of reminding his audiences that he had been a "foot soldier in the Reagan revolution," while one of his main rivals, Mitt Romney, declared that "we're in the house that Reagan built." Among Democrats, the power of Reagan's name was hardly less evident, though in a different way. Barack Obama at one point made the slip of mentioning the "R" word: "Ronald Reagan changed the trajectory of America in a way that Richard Nixon . . . and Bill Clinton did not." His competitors immediately pounced on this violation of the Democratic first commandment never to say anything positive about Ronald Reagan. John Edwards reminded Obama that Reagan "caused the middle class and working people to struggle every single day. . . . I can promise you this: this president will never use Ronald Reagan as an example for change." Here was at least one promise that Edwards managed to keep. Despite these rebukes, Barack Obama's secret respect for Reagan as a transformative leader seems to have held firm, and he has made it his own objective as president to end the active force of Reagan's legacy and replace it with a new one of his own making. The politics of the next period may well consist of the contest between the old Reagan legacy and the new vision of President Obama.

THE CONCEPT OF SOCIAL CONSTRUCTIONISM

The notion of a "social construction of a legacy" has a decidedly postmodern ring to it. Social constructionism is a concept very much in vogue in intellectual circles today, especially among literary critics, philosophers, and sociologists. They invoke it to suggest that there is no firm reality. Nothing that is is, except as we humans make it so, and we usually make it so to serve our own ends. The theory of social constructionism applied to politics rests on the maxim that in the beginning, man created spin. Spin, paradoxically, works best when it is not perceived for what it is, but for just the opposite. Nothing challenges the professional political spinner more than being placed in a location designated the "spin room," for the effect is to discount in advance the "sincerity" of whatever is said. The cleverest spinner would prefer to be thought of as operating from a no-spin zone, but, with all apologies to Bill O'Reilly, purveyors of social constructionism remind us that no such thing exists.

Both spinners and biographers treat the lives of political figures and help to fashion the legacy. But the difference between the two professions could not be greater. The genuine biographer seeks to recount the truth about his or her subject, so far as that is possible. The result and even the purpose may be to promote or save a legacy, but that end must never be pursued by massaging the facts or eliding reality. The spinner has a different job. His task is the construction of a legacy, or "legacy management," to serve a political purpose. This effort may try to masquerade as biography, but its credo is spin. It will be content with a facsimile of the truth if that serves best to craft the desired reputation of a political figure and to push the political agenda.

Many will no doubt deplore the activity of legacy management. But candor obliges one to admit that, for better or worse, legacy managers in our democracy today are not only here to stay, but also play a large role in shaping political discussion. Legacy managers would not exist unless there was a market for what they do. This fact may not excuse them, but it at least makes what they do appear more understandable.

LEGACY MANAGERS AND THE BATTLE
FOR POLITICAL IDEAS

Legacy management in the strict sense is limited to only a few presidents. All presidents, of course, go down somewhere in history, even if it is only in rankings made by presidential scholars. There will accordingly always be some people, including the presidents themselves, their families and friends, and perhaps employees in presidential museums, who have a strong interest in these historical judgments. Yet in the case of most presidents, the simple truth of the matter is that the political influence of their image after their service in the White House is negligible. Think, for example, of Chester Arthur or Gerald Ford. Four or eight years after their retirement, debates about these presidencies had no continuing political impact. No self-respecting legacy manager, should one exist, would have an interest in bothering with these men, and there would be no objection if judgments about them were shaped by genuine biographers operating with a scrupulous regard for the truth.

Nor, at the opposite end of the spectrum, are legacy managers much concerned *today* with the grand legacies of a select few presidents—Washington, Jefferson, and Lincoln—whose reputations hover far above the mundane preoccupations of ordinary partisan politics. These legacies are, of course, still active, touching in different ways on understandings of the meaning of America, and as such they can remain of interest to certain thinkers pushing a current cultural agenda. George Washington, for example, has always loomed as a symbol of virtue and dignity in the conduct of the office, which leads some preoccupied with restraint to cultivate his image. It has been said of Jefferson that he has served as "a sensitive reflector . . . of America's troubled search for the image of itself."[1] From this observation, the historian Gordon Wood has concluded that Jefferson "has become someone invented, manipulated, turned into something we Americans like or dislike."[2] (It is almost as if Wood had used the word "constructed.") But this kind of legacy controversy, though suggestive of the kind of activity under discussion here, does not reach the threshold of a concrete political payoff. Legacy managers, *sensu stricto*, are concerned only where a legacy still counts as hard currency in the political marketplace.

Legacies possessing this active status are of different types. One is chiefly stylistic and escapes the bonds of partisanship. It rests on evoking memories of a mood or a feeling that is said to have prevailed under a particular president. The great example is the Kennedy legacy, dubbed "Camelot," which features warm images of youth, hope, and idealism. Few legacies have enjoyed a more skilled set of managers, which included such luminaries as John Kenneth Galbraith, Arthur Schlesinger Jr., and Theodore Sorensen. These men all served under President Kennedy and continued for a long time thereafter to reap enormous dividends from the glow of the Kennedy years. The Kennedy legacy continued to exercise an active influence as recently as the 2008 election, when, much to the dismay of Hillary Clinton, the major figures of the Kennedy family in an elaborate ceremony endorsed Barack Obama for the Democratic nomination. This move was an attempt to wrap the Kennedy mantle around Barack Obama, with daughter Caroline telling the audience that Obama would be able to make people "feel inspired and hopeful about America the way people did when my father was president."[3]

The more typical active legacy is of a more partisan nature. It derives from the reputation of a president's leadership skill and, especially, of the merits of his political program and public philosophy as reflected in the concrete achievements it promoted. A public philosophy, like FDR's liberalism or Reagan's conservatism, after all, can live on and remain politically consequential beyond the president's time in office. In such cases the legacy may be strongly contested, with managers at work on both sides, one seeking to build up the legacy, the other trying to tear it down. The legacy of Ronald Reagan obviously falls into this category.

WHAT MAKES A LEGACY CONSEQUENTIAL?

What makes some legacies become important? No simple answer exists, but four conditions contribute to the result. A legacy will matter when (1) a president prominently sets forth a public philosophy, (2) partisans at the time agree to make a public test of the merits and worth of the new ideas, (3) there is something distinctive or controversial about the personal character of the president, and (4) significant parts of the elite determine afterward that they want to keep the contest alive.

The case of Ronald Reagan fulfills these four conditions more completely—not each one individually, but all four together—than any other president in American history. It is therefore no accident that controversy over Reagan's legacy has continued for so long. Reagan's "competitors" here are Jefferson, Jackson, Lincoln, and FDR. When it comes to the magnitude of the stakes involved, meaning the prominence of the new public philosophy and its consequences, more was at issue when Lincoln, FDR, and (perhaps) Jefferson came to power, but not Jackson. With Jefferson and Lincoln, however, much of the popular political opposition to them collapsed in the immediate aftermath of their presidencies. The anti-Jefferson forces were confined to the rapidly fading Federalist Party, while public opposition to Lincoln after the Civil War became the province mostly of a sector of southern whites. As a consequence, the fourth condition—a desire to keep the battle going—was not met in these instances to nearly the same degree as in Reagan's case. FDR in this respect is closer to Reagan, because the battle over the public philosophy of New Deal liberalism continued to be waged for some time afterward. But part of the hostility to FDR was mitigated as a result of his wartime leadership, which worked across party lines. Reagan never had an occasion to achieve this kind of nonpartisan appeal.

When it comes to the third condition, judgments of the personal factor (especially in the form of negative portrayals by the opposition), all five of these presidents faced significant criticism. Comparisons are difficult, but an estimate can be hazarded that places personal opposition to Reagan (1) "above" that encountered by Lincoln, who was attacked more for his ideas than his character, (2) on a par with that encountered by Jefferson and FDR, who were both highly mistrusted, and (3) below that endured by Andrew Jackson, who was among the most vilified of all presidents. The legacy struggle over Jackson was intense and continued for almost two decades—a period that historians have dubbed the Age of Jackson— although it did not outlast the time already clocked by Ronald Reagan. Because of this fact alone, should not the current era be known as the Age of Reagan?

THE LEGACY STRUGGLE OVER RONALD REAGAN

Quitting these historical speculations, the origin of the legacy struggle over Ronald Reagan can be traced back to the 1980 presidential campaign. Reagan is one of only a few presidential candidates who, prior to election, articulated an important new public philosophy. He was nominated as the head of a popular movement of conservatism that captured his party, an accomplishment that won him the fervent support of a large group of core supporters and that riled and frightened those on the Left. Whatever some historians might now say about the actual magnitude of the changes Reagan sought, both sides during the campaign agreed on the radical character of Reagan's public philosophy. The intellectual elite of the Democratic Party missed no opportunity to label his positions "extreme" and argue that his thinking was primitive and simplistic. Conservatism, they contended, would ruin the country and threaten peace and order in the world.

Democrats upped the ante by adding a personal dimension to the contest. Ronald Reagan was said to be a fool or, in the slightly nicer language of Clark Clifford, "an amiable dunce." Following the assassination attempt on Reagan in 1981, when he showed such remarkable grace under fire, the personal esteem in which he was held grew to such an extent that the most severe attacks on his character became ill advised. But the overall strategy of belittling his intelligence never changed. The most illustrative and influential expression of this view—because it summed up with such consummate pretentiousness what so many were saying and thinking—was a product of Michael Rogin, a well-known professor of political science at Berkeley. In a series of articles and then a book, Rogin argued that Reagan's governing ideas derived from the scripts of the films in which he had acted. Reagan, the actor, could not tell the difference between reality and fiction, and he brought his delusions or illusions from the big screen into American politics.[4] This period was still one in which liberal intellectuals were sufficiently snobbish concerning their pedigrees that they expressed contempt for Hollywood, a position that contrasts with their current thinking, which tends to celebrate the intellectual acumen of the likes of an Alec Baldwin.

Reagan's initial domestic policy plan to cut taxes and limit government spending was met by a strong and hostile reaction from the Left. It was not long before someone—it is still not known whether it was a proponent or opponent—coined the term "Reagan revolution" to describe his program. The language of revolution was surely hyperbolic, but the elite of the Democratic Party gleefully embraced it, and the perception of what was at stake grew larger by the day. The disagreements on questions of foreign policy during this period were, if anything, even more intense. Reagan's advocacy of a large defense buildup, his refusal to accede to the mass hysteria of the nuclear freeze movement, and his frank expressions of anti-Communism—culminating in his provocative identification of the Soviet Union as an "evil empire"—led opponents to label him an ideological extremist and a threat to world peace.

The upshot of these confrontations was that, by 1984, both sides willingly and enthusiastically entered into a solemn covenant. They agreed that Ronald Reagan's conservative programs and public philosophy should be treated as the ultimate test of the principles for governing America. The first three of the four conditions for creating a legacy controversy had been fully satisfied. The prospect of avoiding a full-pitched battle would now depend on one side deciding, after Reagan left office, to stand down. Neither did.

PARADOX AND IRONY IN THE REAGAN LEGACY

Fast-forward now to 1990. Much happened in the previous decade, but four major developments stand out. All of them, at first glance, seem to reflect well on Reagan's presidency, and three appear to have brought huge benefits to the nation. These developments were as follows:

1. The rise of conservatism as a major force in America, not only in the electoral realm but increasingly in the media and in the arena of the production and dissemination of ideas in public policy.
2. An end to the widespread view of the late 1960s and 1970s that the presidency was a broken institution and that the nation could not be governed.
3. A major improvement of economic conditions as measured by almost all of the important macroeconomic indices.
4. A transformation of the world order, marked by the end of the Cold War, the collapse of Communism, the end of the Soviet empire, and the victory of the West.

Supporters of Ronald Reagan were naturally quick to cite these developments as proof of the success of his presidency. Their argument was that, because these things began to occur during Reagan's tenure, and because Reagan was conspicuously involved in each of them, his leadership and policies were in large degree responsible for what had occurred. Taking the argument a step further, they contended that Reagan's conservative philosophy, which favored market approaches and low taxes in domestic affairs and a strong defense and staunch anti-Communist posture in foreign affairs, had been vindicated.

For Reagan's opponents, these developments, especially the last three, posed an enormous challenge. To admit that they resulted from Ronald Reagan's leadership skill and governing philosophy would seem to concede too much: that liberals had lost their grand wager and that Reagan was a success. Yet, damaging as such an acknowledgment sounds, it might not have been fatal. Examples in our history of parties "standing down" in some fashion are not as rare as one might think—indeed, parties could hardly survive if they did not on occasion cut their losses and move on. Nor is it necessary to grant everything to the opposition or engage continually in public acts of penance. It is sufficient to artfully admit a point or two and then change the subject to current issues and problems.

Some in the Democratic Party after 1988 counseled just such a strategy. But much of the party's liberal wing opted to fight on, adopting a scorched-earth policy of denying all credit to Ronald Reagan. This stance fulfilled the final condition for perpetuating a legacy war. Liberal legacy managers proceeded to deploy two general lines of argument. The first was to agree that while certain positive developments had taken place, the results were in no sense due to actions taken by Ronald Reagan. The achievements were a consequence either of luck or of the efforts of others. Success sometimes came in spite of Ronald Reagan's policies. The most notable application of this line of argument was found in discussion of foreign affairs, where the positive outcomes were clearest. The simplest way to deny any achievement was to claim, as so many did, that Reagan just happened to be in office when the moment arrived for the collapse of Communism. According to the analysis of Raymond Moore, "While some presidents are gifted in their conduct of foreign affairs, Reagan was lucky. . . . Reagan was a very fortunate president able to take advantage of forces and trends outside his control (and use them for his benefit)."[5]

At least this position acknowledged that Reagan used fortune to his advantage, which, when one thinks about it, is no small mark of a competent politician. To more fully discredit Reagan, therefore, it was necessary to go one step further. The liberal legacy managers' more robust argument was to attribute events in large measure to human agency, but not to anything Ronald Reagan had done, nor (since it was Reagan's strong anti-Communist views that were at issue) to anything done by anyone who shared Reagan's view of Communism, such as Margaret Thatcher or Pope John Paul II. All the credit for the change instead was assigned to the Soviet leader, Mikhail Gorbachev, who was depicted as acting at his own behest and uninfluenced by any pressures or inducements deriving from Reagan's policies. The apotheosis of Gorbachev was the liberal legacy managers' main strategy for handling the "problem" of a positive assessment of Reagan's presidency.

Even this strategy, however, did not go far enough. Some went on to argue that the fall of Communism confirmed the liberal rather than the conservative understanding of world affairs. Reagan's hard line toward the Soviets made things much worse, and but for his policies, the collapse would have occurred sooner. According to Strobe Talbott, "The Soviet system has gone into meltdown because of inadequacies and defects at its core, not because of anything the outside world has done or not done." In fact, Talbott went on, events showed that the threat posed by the Soviet Union was never as great as conservatives liked to make out: "The doves in the great debate of the past forty years were right all along."[6]

More moderate Democrats, including many in the Democratic Leadership Council such as Joseph Lieberman and Bill Clinton, saw the danger for the Democratic Party in the continuation of a full-scale legacy war against Ronald Reagan. As early as 1991, Clinton signaled his readiness to have the Democratic Party move on. Clinton praised Reagan's "rhetoric in defense of freedom" and his role in "advancing the idea that communism could be rolled back." He continued, "The idea that we were going to stand firm and reaffirm our containment strategy, and the fact that we forced [the Soviets] to spend even more when they were already producing a Cadillac defense system and a dinosaur economy, I think it hastened their undoing."[7]

The liberal legacy managers' second line of argument was that the successes of the 1980s were an illusion. The good that people thought they saw under Reagan's presidency was cosmetic, a result of short-term fixes achieved at the expense of long-term solutions. This rhetorical strategy became the principal approach for handling the "problem" of the economic recovery. After initially denying the notion that tax cuts could improve economic performance, liberals came around to the view that the real source of the economic improvement had not been the tax cuts, but huge budget deficits. The growth that was generated by tax-cutting policy, dubbed "Reaganomics," was not only unsustainable but spurious. It was based on placing the real costs on the backs of future generations, which would have to pay for the current generation's profligacy. Haynes Johnson called the 1980s "an age of illusion when America lived on borrowed time."[8] A far more interesting and important critique, however, contended that even if an economic recovery had taken place, it came at the cost of a profound moral deterioration. The 1980s was "a decade of greed." This phrase, which played on some of the spectacular excesses of this period of rapid growth, was meant to deny the substantiality of the development that had occurred. The wealth that was generated was ill gotten and went to the richest and most rapacious, not to the average American.

The high (or low) point of the efforts to discredit the Reagan presidency were reflected in a poll of selected presidential scholars taken in 1996 for the purpose of ranking American presidents. The scholars, mostly historians of distinction and distinguished liberals, judged Reagan a mediocrity, just above the insignificant Chester Arthur and the hapless Jimmy Carter.[9] The specific grounds of the evaluation are not known. Given their liberal sentiments, it is likely that they would have found fault with many of Reagan's policies in areas other than the four discussed above, including his judicial appointments and his stance on questions of civil rights. And these scholars certainly could have grounds for doubting Reagan's grasp of the management of the office, as revealed in the Iran-Contra affair. Yet, even giving full weight to these objections, the momentous outcome of events in foreign affairs and the economic recovery should arguably have led historians to grant Reagan a "good" ranking. That they did not do so would have to be explained either by the fact that they abused their academic credentials by rating on partisan grounds, or that they accepted the liberal legacy managers' arguments that the positive developments were not of Reagan's doing. Since it is inconceivable to believe that academics could ever behave dishonorably, one is left with the conclusion that they must have been gullible.

Why did liberals insist on unleashing their legacy managers to under-mine Ronald Reagan, when a different policy would better have served the interest of the Democratic Party? One explanation focuses on the bitter factional struggles that had been going on within the Democratic Party. The Left or "peace" faction in foreign policy had invested so much in its criticism of the military after the Vietnam War and in its opposition to staunch anti-Communism that it could not make any concession on these points without relinquishing control of the Democratic Party. If it were not for the interests of this faction, Democrats could easily have taken a different path. They could have claimed that anti-Communism had been the policy of *both* parties (as indeed it once had been under Truman, Kennedy, and Johnson) and that both parties should therefore share credit for the triumph. By attacking Reagan and anti-Communism, they foreclosed this option and chose instead to give all the credit to Gorbachev.

A further explanation for the continuing liberal attacks on Ronald Reagan is found in a psychological pathology. Well into the decade of the 1990s, the liberal intellectual elite not only disagreed with conservatives, but had an irrational contempt for them. Thinkers on the Left had so dominated intellectual discourse for the previous half-century that their notions of who was an intellectual and what constituted thinking left no room for treating conservatism seriously. It was not just that conservative arguments, in their estimation, were wrong; it was that they were not arguments at all. The ready dismissal of Ronald Reagan as a dunce fit perfectly into this frame of reference. Reagan, as a conservative, could not have been giving voice to a genuine alternative intellectual position, because such a position did not exist. To cede to another argument is difficult enough, but to cede to no thought at all was more than the liberal pride or psychology could bear.

THE LIMITS OF SOCIAL CONSTRUCTION

The contest over Ronald Reagan's legacy continued unabated throughout the 1990s. Liberal legacy managers staked their all on trying to diminish and discredit Reagan's reputation rather than to make tactical accommodations and move on. For conservatives, Reagan's greatness was never in doubt, and there was no question for Republicans of the political value of his name and memory. As the 2000 election contest approached, Republicans were openly looking for an heir to Reagan. When George W. Bush rose to the occasion at the Republican convention with a stirring acceptance speech, many in the party were satisfied with his credentials and hailed him as the "little Gipper."

Sometime after 2000, the tide in the Reagan legacy war turned decisively in Reagan's favor. He came to be accepted as an important president by a broad spectrum of the American public. Streets, buildings, and a major airport were all named in his honor. There was even a shift of sorts within the scholarly community. Panels of experts selected to grade presidents gave Reagan a much higher mark than before, elevating him from his earlier ranking as a below average president to the status of a "near great," in the company of the likes of Theodore Roosevelt, Harry Truman, and Dwight Eisenhower.[10] When Reagan died in June 2004, the ceremonial observances in his honor went on for a full four days, in what was the largest national celebration since VJ Day. Old foes for the most part either maintained a decent silence or, in a few instances, expressed a qualified admiration.

The full list of reasons for the changed assessment of Ronald Reagan will never be known. One factor was surely that, after listening to the arguments, the public came around to a settled judgment about Reagan's record that rejected many of the charges of his detractors. Another factor has been the cumulative impact of the work of biographers.[11] Their findings have called into question some of the hagiographic claims of legacy managers on the Right, but they have proven devastating to the case of the legacy managers on the Left. It is known now that Reagan's interests and training during his Hollywood years were far more political (and serious) than had been described in previous caricatures; that, in the years between acting and running for governor of California, he spent an enormous amount of time, almost unprecedented for a modern American political leader, reading, reflecting, and sharpening his political arguments; that he crafted and wrote many of his own speeches and position papers; and finally, that leaders of the Soviet Union in its waning years acknowledged that Reagan's defense buildup and initial hard line influenced their actions and weakened their will.

All legacies are approximations of the truth. They derive from a mixture of honest attempts of biographers to assess the merit of a presidency and politically motivated efforts by legacy managers to spin reality for partisan gain. It is gratifying in Ronald Reagan's case that the most baseless exercises in distortion could only gain so much ground before they foundered on the evidence of the record. The social construction of reality evidently has its limits.

IV

THE AMERICAN
WAY OF LIFE

9

✛

The Theoretical Origins
of Anti-Americanism

One ideology, and one ideology only, has today a truly global reach: anti-Americanism. If not in every country, then certainly on every continent, large numbers of intellectuals and members of the political class organize their political thinking on the basis of anti-Americanism. Anti-Americanism is prominent not only in nations that Americans count as hostile, but also in countries that have traditionally been considered its friends. The authors of a huge Pew Institute Survey on public opinion in thirty-five nations observed in 2002 that "while attitudes toward the United States are most negative in the Middle East/Conflict Area, ironically, criticisms of U.S. policies and ideals such as American-style democracy and business practices are also highly prevalent among the publics of traditional allies."[1]

Anti-Americanism has had its ups and downs in recent decades, but from all evidence these variations have occurred around a fairly strong—and growing—baseline. The variations have to do with policies, parties, and persons. As for policies, anti-Americanism has spiked during long and difficult wars, such as Vietnam and Iraq, and during flare-ups and wars between Israel and its Arab neighbors. As Israel's strongest, and sometimes sole, supporter, America invariably pays a price in world opinion for backing its ally.

When it comes to parties, anti-Americanism has increased when a conservative Republican is president, which was the case with Ronald Reagan and George W. Bush. These presidents employed a more confrontational rhetoric toward their adversaries (the "evil empire" and the "axis of evil") and were unabashed in supporting the nation (America) as the primary unit of action in international relations. Anti-Americanism in the West has sources on both the Right and the Left, but in the contemporary context it is the Leftist variant in Europe that is more prominent, with far greater representation among intellectuals and in the media. Greater opposition to Republican presidents is therefore to be expected. The parties that win power in Europe also have an impact on anti-Americanism, with Leftist parties being more likely to give expression to and validate these opinions. A bridge was crossed in Germany in the national election in 2002, when the socialist chancellor, Gerhard Schröder, ran a campaign with a strong anti-American undercurrent. The expression of such views by the head of a major party in Europe was something new, made possible by the end of the Soviet threat after 1991, and it seems to have legitimated anti-Americanism as an instrument of European politics.[2]

Finally, as for persons, certain American presidents—Reagan and Bush (the two "cowboys") again stand out—have prompted a rise of anti-Americanism. Both were conspicuous for their more American dispositions and for their embrace of American exceptionalism; this provided fodder for many of their foes. The presidency of George W. Bush in particular seems to mark the high point, offering a "perfect storm" for stimulating anti-Americanism. President Bush launched a difficult war (Iraq), was a conservative Republican, spoke strongly of America's determination of its foreign policy (a so-called unilateralist), supported Israel during two wars, faced governments in Europe headed by Leftist parties for much of his presidency, and looked and talked like the caricature of the "provincial" American. He happened to be an evangelical Christian to boot.

Anti-Americanism during the Bush years was so obvious and important a phenomenon that it was not only regularly commented upon in the press, but also became a major topic of social science research. There was an outpouring of articles and books on the subject, and it was the focus of many university courses, both in America and abroad. During the 2008 presidential campaign, Barack Obama made it a priority to reduce anti-Americanism, and since becoming president he has spoken out on the subject on a number of occasions—in one instance, in France in 2009, going even so far as to acknowledge that America had "shown arrogance" and "been dismissive, even derisive" toward Europeans.[3] Whether this approach will permanently reduce anti-Americanism or, what is obviously more important, serve America's interests and promote her purposes remains to be seen.

THE SOURCES OF ANTI-AMERICANISM

Anti-Americanism has both a "natural" and a theoretical source. The natural source derives from the dominant strategic position of the United

States today. America is the only nation in the world with a capacity to project significant force far from its own borders, and it has showed its willingness do so, even without direct backing from the United Nations. It has always been the fate of the world's major power to be regarded with suspicion. There was strong opposition to Rome in the ancient world, especially among the Greeks, who, much like the Europeans today, had a barely concealed contempt for the crude and unsophisticated power from the West that had dislodged them from their position of world preeminence. As for attitudes toward the great world power of the nineteenth century, Great Britain, Americans need look no further than the views of many of their own political leaders of the day, who regularly denounced the British for their arrogance and imperial excesses.

Americans often express bewilderment at being branded an "empire," and react with incredulity when they hear claims, such as those of the editor of *Le Monde Diplomatique*, Ignacio Ramonet, that "America subjugates the world like no other empire has done in the history of humanity."[4] An empire in the traditional definition referred to a nation that occupied and ruled its subordinates. Americans are obviously not holders of an empire in this sense. If they were, it is inconceivable that they would put up with the drumbeat of antagonistic commentary by the likes of a Ramonet, not to mention the scores of anti-American diatribes that take place at the United Nations. But Americans are also in error to think that the milder form of influence and leadership they exercise around the world immunizes the United States from expressions of hostility. That America has the status of the world's primary power, and that others do not, is enough to provoke envy and resentment.

There is a strong psychological aspect as well to the phenomenon of anti-Americanism. People evidently possess a deep-seated impulse to believe that an identifiable entity (be it a person, a god, or a nation) is responsible for what occurs, and that nothing happens by simple accident. America, which many have designated as the world's "hyper-power," serves the function of being its universal talisman. If something goes wrong, or even if something does not go right, others take comfort in declaring it to be America's fault. Foreign leaders of all stripes find it helpful to divert attention from difficult situations or from their own failures by blaming the results on America. So too do many in the public, who indulge in anti-Americanism as a way to alleviate some of their own frustrations. According to one observer of contemporary Europe, it is the "shallowness of post-ideological and post-utopian politics, its subversive dullness, [that] is one of the major reasons for the seductive power of anti-American discourse. People are against America because they are against everything—or because they do not know exactly what they are against."[5]

But the "natural" reactions against American power go deeper, and are more sinister, than this kind of perplexity. Many experience a profound satisfaction in watching the great humbled. The philosopher Jean Baudrillard spoke for a large number when he described his immediate reaction to the attack on the United States of September 11, 2001: "How we have dreamt of this event, how all the world without exception dreamt of this event, for no one can avoid dreaming of the destruction of a power that has become hegemonic. . . . It is they who acted, but we who wanted the deed."[6]

Americans also err in expecting too much from others' gratitude. Gratitude is a sentiment with clear limits in the relations among nations. George Washington famously warned in his Farewell Address of the danger of developing "an habitual fondness" for another nation, which can make a country a "slave . . . to its affection" and can "lead it astray from its duty and its interest."[7] It is true, of course, that many Eastern Europeans, recalling America's opposition to Soviet domination, still remain appreciative of the U.S. position in the Cold War. But memories of American steadfastness during this period are bound to fade as time goes on, and there are indications that this process is already well under way. Some in Western Europe still feel a genuine debt to America for its help in their liberation during World War II. By now, however, most political leaders mention their gratitude as an obligatory ritual at summits and ceremonies, and many probably now resent the exercise. Gratitude, after all, is an emotion that is filled with ambiguity. Feelings of thankfulness are usually mixed with painful reminders either of past defeat or of weakness. Outside of Europe, the United States has provided large amounts of aid to countries such as Turkey, Jordan, and Egypt, which created ties of interest and brought occasional thanks, but which has not generated much popular gratitude.

Yet if anti-Americanism were based just on this "natural" foundation of being the world's greatest power, not only would it be less virulent than it is, but there also would be nothing "special" about it. What differentiates anti-Americanism from the conventional opposition to an empire and gives it its exceptional character is its other, *theoretical* source. America has become a symbol for something to be despised on philosophical grounds. Anti-Americanism rests on the singular idea that something associated with the United States, something at the core of American life, is deeply wrong and threatening to the rest of the world. Over a half-century ago, the French novelist Henry de Montherlant had one his characters (a journalist) speak as follows: "One nation that manages to lower intelligence, morality, human quality on nearly all the surface of the earth, such a thing has never been seen before in the existence of the planet. I accuse the United States of being in a permanent state of crime against humankind."[8] America in this view represents all that is grotesque, obscene, monstrous, stultifying, stunted, leveling, deadening, deracinating, deforming, root-less, and—always in quotation marks—"free."

America so conceived is an intellectual construct that has been built up over a period of more than two centuries by some of the best-known theoretical minds of the West. America has been designed so as to be impervious to refutation by facts. These thinkers have rarely in fact been concerned with the actual qualities of the American people or the American political system; their focus instead has been on modernity. The identification of America with an abstract idea is evident from the development of the neologisms "Americanization" or "Americanism," which are treated nowadays as ordinary terms of intellectual discourse. (By contrast, no one speaks of Venezuelanization or New Zealandism.) "Americanization," for example, is a synonym for the all-powerful social scientific concept of "globalization," differing only in its slightly more sinister connotation. Recent "anti-globalization" rallies easily slipped into protests against "Americanization," with special animus directed against American (mass) culture's hegemony, symbolized by McDonald's, Disney, Microsoft, and, more recently, Google. As two analysts claimed in a book titled *Dangereuse Amérique* (*America the Dangerous*), "America has colonized others' minds, even more than their territories," an assertion that once again leads one to wonder how it is that these purveyors of anti-Americanism have succeeded so well.[9]

Anti-Americanism, then, derives its explosive character from being a result of a mix of "natural" and theoretical causes. This peculiar combination allows a philosophical discourse to invade the political realm in a manner akin to how theological discourse once entered the political world. Anti-Americanism is part of the political religion of modern times; America serves as the negative pole to the positive ideals of the vague "religion of humanity" among advanced European audiences and to the teachings of Islam in areas of Muslim domination.

Because the theoretical aspect of anti-Americanism derives from Western philosophy, one might think that its influence would be limited to those nations where that philosophy is deeply rooted and where anti-Americanism originated. But this is not the case. A theoretical doctrine has the property of being able to travel, and it has no need of a passport. Anti-Americanism has spread from its birthplace in Europe to much of the globe, helping to shape opinion in pre–World War II Japan, where many in the elite had studied German philosophy, and to influence thinking in Latin American and African countries today, where French thought carries so much weight. Most important, Western philosophy's influence has been enormous in the Islamic and Arab world. Well before the attacks of September 11, 2001, Bernard Lewis had traced Muslim views of America to "intellectual influences coming from Europe," especially German philosophy, "which enjoyed a considerable vogue among Arab and some other Muslim intellectuals in the thirties and early forties."[10] Detailed accounts of the intellectual origins of contemporary radical Islamic movements have only added support to this position, showing that the views of many Islamic intellectual leaders about the West and America have been drawn in large measure from various currents of Western thought.[11] These ideas have, of course, been adapted to Islam and set within a theological framework, but the substance of the critique comes from philosophy. It is to this source that we owe the innumerable *fatwahs* and the countless jihads that have been pronounced against America. What has been attributed to a "clash of civilizations" has often been a phase of internecine intellectual warfare within philosophy, conducted with the assistance of mercenary forces recruited from other cultures.

The philosophical source of anti-Americanism has also meant that these ideas have not been excluded from entering the United States, where they now enjoy a very considerable resonance among American intellectuals. American thinkers, who are frequently objects of anti-Americanism, often join with their accusers, displaying a strange disorder known as BAIS (Battered American Intellectual Syndrome). Except for their lack of originality, American intellectuals would probably be among the greatest progenitors of anti-Americanism. As it is, they have had to rest content with repeating and embellishing on what others have said.

NINETEENTH-CENTURY THEORETICAL ANTI-AMERICANISM

The negative image of America developed in several stages that can best be likened to different strata found at an archaeological site. The initial stratum was a product of Europe's nineteenth-century Romantic movement. America became embroiled, almost as an innocent bystander, in its reactions to the French Revolution. As the precursor of the French Revolution, the American Revolution had to be guilty of the same errors. The French Revolution was criticized for its excessively rationalist or metaphysical character, in particular for its belief that political societies could be established on the basis of abstract and universal principles. Conservative Romantics responded that nothing created or fashioned under the guidance of universal principles or with the assistance of rational science—nothing constructed chiefly by "reflection and choice"—was solid or could long endure.[12]

What was true of France had to be true of America as well. Joseph de Maistre, one of the early theoretical opponents of the rationalist revolutions, went so far as to deny the existence of "man" or "humankind," as referred to in the Declaration's claim that "all men are created equal." According to Maistre, "There is no such thing in this world as man; I have seen in my life French, Italians, and Russians . . . but as for man, I declare that I have never met one in my life; if he exists, it is entirely without my knowledge."[13] The problem in America, for Maistre, was not only the flawed foundation of natural rights in the Declaration, with its empty, abstract principles, but also the Constitution, which revealed the folly of people thinking that they could build a successful government on the basis of reflection and choice: "All that is new in [America's] constitution, all that results from common deliberation is the most fragile thing in the world: one could not bring together more symptoms of weakness and decay."[14] Instead of human reason and rational deliberation, Romantic thinkers placed their confidence in the unplanned organic growth of distinct communities; they put their trust in the slow development of the historical process.

By the early nineteenth century, after the French Revolution had failed, the United States became the only functioning society based on an Enlightenment conception of nature. Its existence constituted an affront to many Romantic thinkers, and it accordingly became a primary object of their ire. Yet the grounds of criticism needed to be changed from what Maistre and others had said at the period of the revolutions. By surviving and prospering, the United States had refuted the original charges of the inherent fragility of societies founded with the aid of reason. Some Romantics accordingly shifted ground and began to argue that America's continued existence and prosperity came at the cost of sacrificing everything deep and profound. Success (in the low sense) was proof of superficiality. Nothing constructed on the thin soil of Enlightenment principles could sustain a genuine culture. The poet Nikolaus Lenau, sometimes referred to as the "German Byron," provided the classic summary of the anti-American thought of the Romantics: "With the expression *Bodenlosigkeit* [rootlessness] I think I am able to indicate the general character of all American institutions; what we call Fatherland is here only a property insurance scheme." In other words, there was no real community in America, no real *volk*. America's culture "had in no sense come up organically from within." There was only a dull materialism: "The American knows nothing; he seeks nothing but money; he has no ideas." Then came Lenau's haunting image of America: "the true land of the end, the outer edge of man."[15]

Some Romantics saw America's vaunted freedom as an illusion. American society was the very picture of a deadening conformity. The great poet Heinrich Heine gave expression to this sentiment: "Sometimes it comes to my mind / To sail to America / To that pig-pen of Freedom / Inhabited by boors living in equality." America, as Heine put it in his prose writing, was a "gigantic prison of freedom," where the "most extensive of all tyrannies, that of the masses, exercises its crude authority."[16] It is not as if all such criticisms were built entirely from the imagination; they had some basis in firsthand accounts of perceptive observers, among them Alexis de Tocqueville. Yet the extremity of these Romantic accounts suggests that their aim was not so much actual description as the construction of philosophical symbol to serve in the intellectual battles going on at the time. America has been the bearer of that symbol, with all the consequences that have followed.

Opposition to America also came at this time from another quarter—from a Left that favored the French Revolution and that saw America as an unworthy and regressive rival. Some contemporaries of the French Revolution had already launched this critique. America, they claimed, was flawed because of its understanding of nature, which was too skewed toward the idea of the individual and toward self-interest. American principles failed to stress, as the French Revolution did, the higher and nobler qualities of virtue and fraternity. According to Condorcet, the American founders were tainted by "the prejudices that they imbibed in their youth"; the French Revolution was grounded on principles that were "purer, more precise, and more profound than those that guided the Americans."[17] The attack from the Left grew sharper in the nineteenth century, as revolutionaries targeted not only the old monarchies but also the new liberalism associated with the United States. The problem with America—to use a term of opprobrium made famous by Rousseau—was that it was "bourgeois," meaning contemptible in its accommodation to self-interest and in its depreciation of all erotic, heroic, and artistic impulses.

Following on Condorcet and especially on Marx, the Leftist attack on America was now based in part on a new kind of historical rationalism ("scientific history"). This analysis, supposedly without sentimentality, claimed to know that American principles were only passing phases in the forward movement of history, which would end in the more advanced system of Communism. But scientific history always enjoyed the support of a previous Romantic underpinning. It faulted America for being a society that did not provide for a deeper and more rewarding communal existence. America was capitalist, or, as is said by many soft Marxist critics today, "ultra-liberal."

The next stratum in the construction of anti-Americanism emerged during the era of mass industrialization in the late nineteenth and early twentieth centuries. America was seen as the source of the techniques of mass production and of the methods and the mentality that supported the new modes of production and distribution. Friedrich Nietzsche was an early exponent of this view, arguing that America sought the reduction of everything to the calculable in an effort to dominate and get rich: "The breathless haste with which they [the Americans] work—the distinctive vice of the new world—is already beginning ferociously to infect old Europe and is spreading a spiritual emptiness [*Geistlosigkeit*] over the continent." Long in advance of Hollywood movies or rap music, the spread of American culture was likened to a disease. Its progress in Europe seemed ineluctable. "The faith of the Americans is becoming the faith of the European as well," Nietzsche warned.[18]

It was Nietzsche's disciples, however, who transformed the idea of America into an abstract category. Arthur Moeller van den Bruck, best known for having popularized the phrase "The Third Reich," proposed the concept of *Amerikanertum* (Americanness), which was to be "not geographically but spiritually understood." Americanness marked "the decisive step by which we make our way from a dependence on the earth to the use of the earth, the step that mechanizes and electrifies inanimate material and makes the elements of the world into agencies of human use." It embraced a mentality of dominance, use, and exploitation on an ever-expanding scale, or what came to be called the mentality of "technologism" (*die Technik*): "In America, everything is a block, pragmatism, and the national Taylor system."[19] Another author, Paul Dehns, titled an article, significantly, "The Americanization of the World." Americanization was defined here in the "economic sense" as the "modernization of methods of industry, exchange, and agriculture, as well as all areas of practical life," and in a wider and more general sense as the "uninterrupted, exclusive and relentless striving after gain, riches and influence."[20]

TWENTIETH-CENTURY THEORETICAL ANTI-AMERICANISM

It would be difficult to understate how deeply this current of anti-American thinking penetrated philosophy and social science in the early part of the twentieth century. The works of two thinkers, who were far better known in their own time than today, best illustrate this point: Theodor Lessing (a philosopher) and Richard Müller Freienfels (a psychologist).

Lessing, who might be described as a left-wing follower of Nietzsche, published in 1914 a well-received book titled *Europe and Asia*, which contrasted the cultures and mentalities of people from these two continents.[21] The book enjoyed enough success that Lessing was able to bring out four subsequent editions. On each occasion he added more about a continent he had all but omitted in the original work: America. In the end, and in light of the momentous events of World War I, Lessing felt the need to refocus the entire work: "The contrast with which this work deals [between Europe and Asia] is no longer real or practical. . . . In reality the entire

earth has been for some time becoming one great America." For a philosophical mind, the harshness of his treatment of America seems almost to
defy belief, although he was doing no more really than summarizing the
essence of existing theoretical views of the United States. After compar-
ing everyday life in America to existence in one of the lowest circles of
Dante's *Inferno*, Lessing moved to a more abstract account of the principle
of American society: "The law of her being is called production; her life
is utility. Her faith is the faith in success and in the rule of efficiency. She
symbolizes the subjugation of nature by man and especially of man by
man." Lessing then shifted to the unnatural character of American life,
where everything appeared to him misshapen and deformed, in the direction of the gargantuan: "As grapefruits, strawberries, pineapples, grapes,
chrysanthemums, roses, vegetables, and corn have all been grown too far
over their natural sizes, thus destroying the loveliness and natural goodness of things of the earth, so also has America produced the most beautiful girls and women and the healthiest and most vigorous of youngsters
and men—the first without souls, the other without dreams."[22] This is
Lessing's own *Invasion of the Body Snatchers*, where Americans are aliens
posing as human beings.

This same view worked its way into social science, in the studies of
psychology of Richard Müller Freienfels, whom John Dewey considered
a leading social scientist of the day. One of Freienfels's major works was
Geheimnisse der Seele (*Mysteries of the Soul*), published in 1927, which offered a general history of human psychological development.[23] One chapter, titled "The Americanization of the Soul," treats "the problem of that
Americanism which we shall endeavor to understand as a transformation
of the life of the soul in general." Freienfels at one point clarifies that he is
discussing "Americanism" rather than America itself: Americanism is an
"abstraction" that is "determining the expression of the twentieth century
all the world over." But the move from the concrete to the abstract in no
way lessens the connection to (or the implicit blame for) America. The decisive characteristic of "Americanism," now just a term of social science,
is a flattening of the soul and a loss of depth. The cause lies in a "math-
ematization of life" and a "mechanization of life": "Mass and quantity
are becoming decisive, and they leave no room for quality. . . . From the
standpoint of any non-American, it means a psychological wilderness, an
empty and superficial world." Americanism is clearly the great malady
of our age. It is threatening to spread everywhere: "Even in Europe the
American, or rather the Americanistic spirit, is becoming more and more
prevalent, while . . . depth and individuality and refined intelligence are
disappearing."[24] Parts of Freienfels's argument strikingly parallel the
analysis of America and modernity found in one the most widely studied
philosophic works of the 1960s, Herbert Marcuse's *One-Dimensional Man*.

The next stratum in the construction of anti-Americanism—and the one that still most powerfully influences modern discourse on America—was the creation of two renowned German thinkers, Ernst Jünger and Martin Heidegger. These two established the framework for contemporary anti-Americanism by transforming the theme of technologism into a fully theoretical or metaphysical view. Technologism is a force that Western thought created but that now governs and determines how man lives and thinks. "America" in this thought emerges as the symbol of technologism, but a symbol in a negative sense, as technologism utterly uncontrolled. In different ways these authors suggest a choice or an alternative, not replacing technologism per se, but the American variant.

Jünger's essay on "Total Mobilization" (1930) and then his classic book *The Worker* (1932) were milestones in the elaboration of the argument of technologism. They were, as Heidegger reported, the source for his own famous reflections on the subject. Jünger spoke of all the great modern movements—Fascism, Bolshevism, Americanism—as those designed to deploy the totality of society's resources to achieve an objective. "Progress," or victory at any rate, could be secured only in this way. Modernity was based on "total mobilization": "Esteem for quantity is increasing: quantity of assent, quantity of public opinion has become the decisive factor in politics." Despite its claims of freedom, America no less than the others was a mass society that had found its own way to total mobilization. There was no genuine freedom left in the modern world: "Even the dream of freedom is disappearing as if under a pincer's iron grasp,—the movements of uniformly molded masses trapped in the snare set by the world-spirit comprise a great and fearful spectacle."[25] A terrible beauty was born. America was no more the symbol of this new tyranny than bolshevism, although Jünger in one of his literary works, *The Adventuresome Heart* (1930), revealed a special horror for America when, in contemplating American city life and commercialism, he was reminded of "my old doubts of whether Americans are really human."[26] Jünger was the cool and calm observer of this modernity, which he accepted as an unalterable reality. Still, he suggested a third way between the other two—a German way—that might "bring victory of the soul over the machine." His portrayal of Americanism was in part a call to action on behalf of a different alternative.

Like some of his predecessors, Martin Heidegger offered a technical or philosophical definition of the concept of Americanism, apart, as it were, from the United States. Americanism, he wrote, is "the still unfolding and not yet full or completed essence of the emerging monstrousness of modern times."[27] But Heidegger in this case clearly was less interested in definitions than in fashioning a symbol—something more vivid and human than "technologism." In a word, America was *katestrophenhaft*, the site of catastrophe.[28]

In one his earliest and perhaps best-known passages on America, Heidegger in 1935 echoed the prevalent view of Europe being in a "middle" position between Americanism and Bolshevism:

> Europe . . . lies today in a great pincer, squeezed between Russia on the one side and America on the other. From a metaphysical point of view, Russia and America are the same, with the same dreary technological frenzy and the same unrestricted organization of the average man.[29]

Even though European thinkers, as the originators of modern science, were largely responsible for this development, Europe, with its pull of tradition, had managed to stop well short of its full implementation. It was in America and Russia that the idea of quantity divorced from quality had taken over and grown, as Heidegger put it, "into a boundless et cetera of indifference and always the sameness." The result in both countries was "an active onslaught that destroys all rank and every world creating impulse. . . . This is the onslaught of what we call the demonic, in the sense of destructive evil."[30]

In Heidegger's view, America and the Soviet Union comprised the axis of evil. But America represented the greater and more significant threat, for "Bolshevism is only a variant of Americanism." In a kind of overture to the Left after World War II, Heidegger spoke of entering into a "dialogue" with Marxism, which was possible because of its sensitivity to the general idea of history.[31] A similar encounter with Americanism was out of the question, as America was without a genuine sense of history. Americanism was "the most dangerous form of boundlessness, because it appears in a middle class way of life mixed with Christianity, and all this in an atmosphere that lacks completely any sense of history." When the United States declared war on Germany, Heidegger wrote, "We know today that the Anglo Saxon world of Americanism is resolved to destroy Europe. . . . The entry of America into this world war is not an entry into history, but is already the last American act of American absence of historical sense."[32]

In creating this symbol of America, Heidegger managed to include within it many of the problems or maladies of modern times, from the rise of instantaneous global communication, to an indifference to the environment, to the reduction of culture to a commodity for consumption. He was especially interested in consumerism, which he thought was emblematic of the spirit of his age: "Consumption for the sake of consumption is the sole procedure that distinctively characterizes the history of a world that has become an unworld. . . . Being today means being replaceable."[33] America was the home of this way of thinking; it was the very embodiment of the reign of the ersatz, encouraging the absorption of the unique and authentic into the uniform and the standard. Heidegger cited a passage from the German poet Rainer Maria Rilke:

> Now is emerging from out of America pure undifferentiated things, mere things of appearance, sham articles. . . . A house in the American understanding, an American apple or an American vine has nothing in common with the house, the fruit, or the grape that had been adopted in the hopes and thoughts of our forefathers.[34]

Following Nietzsche, Heidegger depicted America as an invasive force taking over the soul of Europe, sapping it of its depth and spirit: "The surrender of the German essence to Americanism has already gone so far as on occasion to produce the disastrous effect that Germany actually feels herself ashamed that her people were once considered to be 'the people of poetry and thought.'"[35] Europe was almost dead, almost Americanized, but not quite. By its consciousness of the problem, Europe might still ready itself to receive what Heidegger called "the Happening," but only if it were able to summon its interior strength and "push [America] back to the other hemisphere."[36] The path to salvation, if there was one, lay in anti-Americanism.

Heidegger's political views are commonly deplored today on account of his open support of Nazism in the 1930s. Because of this connection, some have supposed that his influence on subsequent political thought (as distinct from general intellectual thought) has been meager. Yet nothing could be further from the truth. Heidegger's ideas proved sufficiently protean that with a bit of tinkering they could easily be adopted by the Left. And this is exactly what happened. Following the war, Heidegger's thought, shorn of its National Socialism but fortified in its anti-Americanism, was embraced by influential thinkers like Jean-Paul Sartre and was married to Communism. This coupling became the core of the intellectual Left in Europe for the next generation, raising anti-Americanism to new levels of respectability. Propagandists for the Communist parties in Europe joined with intellectuals to make regular use of anti-American sentiments.

The connection between Communism and anti-Americanism led some favoring America to think that if Communism should ever cease, anti-Americanism would end with it. These hopes too were based on a misdiagnosis of the phenomenon. The collapse of European Communism after 1989 has served, on the contrary, to reveal the true depth of anti-Americanism. Uncoupled from Communism, which gave it a certain strength but also placed limits on its appeal, anti-Americanism more easily worked its way into the mainstream of political thought. With the Soviet Union dead, only one of the infamous Heideggerian pincers remains to threaten Europe and the world. If Europe once found its identity in being in "the middle" (or a "third force"), many began to argue that its new identity lay in becoming a "pole of opposition" to America (or the leader of a "second force").

Variants of the Heideggerian view of America have become integral themes of modern and postmodern thought. One of the most influential treatments is found in the writings of the philosopher Alexandre Kojève, best known for his revival of the fantastic notion of "the end of history." Kojève presented his views in a spirit of cool observation and detachment, offering no open value judgments. Yet his picture of the "end of history" can leave no doubt as to where he stands. The "end" is characterized by what Kojève calls "the disappearance of man." Although a biological creature in the form of man will continue to exist, man properly speaking—an agent who acts on the world and struggles to create something new—will cease to exist. Man will be replaced by "an animal of the species of Homo sapiens" that will engage in many activities analogous to those of humans: it will practice a kind of art but in the way that "spiders weave their webs"; it will construct edifices, but after the fashion of "birds building their nests"; it will engage in discussion in the manner of the "discourse of bees"; and it will perform music but with noises that resemble those of "frogs and cicadas."[37] In 1947 Kojève considered the end of history as a future possibility, but after a trip to America a few years later, he concluded that its outline was already fully present and visible in America: "The American way of life is the type of life proper to the posthistoric period, and the presence today of the United States in the World prefigures the future 'eternal present' of humanity in its entirety. Thus the return of man to an animal nature appeared no longer as a possibility to come, but as a certitude already present."[38]

The postmodern French philosopher Jean Baudrillard sketched this picture in more detail in 1986.[39] It came in the form of an ironic travel log, *America*, meant ostensibly to describe America as it is, without value judgment. The mere fact that Baudrillard characterized Americans as fat, dumb, primitive, and uncultured was surely no reason to think that he harbored anti-American sentiments. On the contrary, he professed to be utterly charmed by the "inspired banality" of America, whereas he faults his fellow Europeans for their "art of thinking about things, of analyzing them, and of reflecting on them." As a result, Europeans are paralyzed and unfit for modernity. Unlike Americans, they get nothing done. America is history's final stop. It is "utopia achieved": "America is the original version of modernity . . . and Americans make up the ideal material for an analysis of all the variants possible of the modern world." Americans are happily ahistorical, living without "a past or a founding truth"; this allows them to adapt perfectly to the modern world of signs and simulacra, which is the world one finds in Disneyland. The "distinctly American miracle" is that of the "obscene," meaning of tastelessness, which allows Americans to progress without qualms by constructing things like suburbs. America is a happy mass society "where the quantitative is exalted without apology."[40]

Baudrillard proved incapable of sustaining this ironic posture in the face of subsequent events and fell more squarely into the mold of a "conventional" Heideggerian critic. During the first Gulf War in 1991, he expressed his hopes for an American defeat, not on any mere political or strategic ground, but for a deeper, metaphysical reason. American technologism, he argued, is premised on controlling, ordering, homogenizing, dominating, and eliminating "the other." America is a vast despotism practicing a "consensual integrism (of Enlightenment, of rights of man . . . of sentimental humanism) that is just as ferocious as that of any tribal region or primitive society."[41] The failure of the American military effort in Kuwait, even if it meant victory for the tyrant Saddam Hussein, would be a first step in rescuing the world from this Enlightenment barbarism.

The 1999 Kosovo War served as a further occasion for the expression of this radical strain of anti-Americanism. European governments took the lead in asking for American leadership to oust the Serbians from Kosovo, and much of Europe's intelligentsia supported the war in the name of the common cause of "humanitarian intervention." The war created a temporary alliance of liberal intellectuals on both sides of the Atlantic. Radicals were therefore compelled to attack not only America, but also American hegemony of Europe. That hegemony was the explanation for Europe's defection to America and to Enlightenment barbarism. Régis Debray, the former Third World revolutionary, argued that Europe had been "deprogrammed" to adopt American ways of thinking. A mind becomes Americanized, he contended, when "the notion of time is replaced by that of space, when historical thinking is replaced by technological calculation, and political thinking by moralistic thinking." America found its purest expression in a media-saturated world: "With CNN, all the planet becomes America." For Debray, the Kosovo War presented a great opportunity, provided that it would end in a NATO failure, an outcome that might awaken Europeans to the realization that they had become "as uncultured and shortsighted as their leader."[42]

CONTEMPORARY ANTI-AMERICANISM

Some of the harshest expressions of anti-Americanism came in the first decade of the twenty-first century. Following an initial outpouring of sympathy for America after the September 11 terrorist attacks, large parts of the world joined together a year later to oppose the American-led effort to oust Saddam Hussein in the second Gulf War. Much of the opposition in Europe stemmed from a judgment that the war was a strategic mistake, but a significant component also reflected and drew on theoretical anti-Americanism. This element became stronger as the war continued and grew into an indictment of the Bush presidency and of America in general.

The anti-Americanism of the twenty-first century maintained many of the older themes, but it added new elements that differed and in some ways even contradicted past claims. In accord with most symbols, anti-Americanism has always had a protean character allowing things to be added or deleted without changing the overall valence. In the current version, America, which was previously condemned for being too modern, was now faulted for not keeping up with Europe and taking the next step into postmodernity. America, as Jacques Derrida claimed, continued to embrace a religious culture, while the European nations had moved into a post-Christian world. From this perspective, the crisis in international relations was not, as many in America defined it, the conflict between Islamic terrorism and the West, but instead the clash between two equivalent "fundamentalisms," one American and Christian, the other Islamic.[43] Europe represented the superior third option. America was also accused—this time by Jürgen Habermas as well as Derrida—to be atavistic in another sense.[44] It clung to the old idea of a nation anchored in an identity based on a metaphysical proposition. Alone in the West, Americans continued to speak without shame or embarrassment of "Laws of Nature." Only as the advanced nations abandoned the concern for such "truths" and adopted a new doctrine of political nonfoundationalism could a plural and peaceful world come into being. America was now a great impediment to this new order.

In a speculative passage in his *History of the Decline and Fall of the Roman Empire*, Edward Gibbon raised the question of whether barbarism could ever again destroy the citadel of civilization as it had done when the Germanic tribes overran and conquered Rome. Gibbon concluded that the power and resources of the Europe of his day (the late eighteenth century) made the success of another such onslaught highly unlikely. He then added a caveat which contained further point of assurance: "Should the Barbarians carry slavery and desolation as far as the Atlantic Ocean . . . Europe would revive and flourish in the American world, which is already filled with her colonies and institutions. . . . Whatever may be the changes of their political situation, they [the Americans] must preserve the manners of Europe."[45]

Gibbon's argument assumed a harmony in the "manners"—we might say values—of the West. Defining the West, of course, has never been an easy task. It has evolved from an uneasy combination of three elements: Jerusalem (the biblical religions), Athens (classical philosophy), and the modern Enlightenment. The depiction of America in the ideology of anti-Americanism not only calls into question the community of interests between Europe and America, but threatens the very idea of the West itself by pulling apart its different elements and setting them at odds with each other. Anti-Americanism is the Trojan horse that has been introduced to destroy Western civilization.

Notes

CHAPTER 1: THE DOCTRINE
OF POLITICAL NONFOUNDATIONALISM

1. John Rawls, *Political Liberalism* (New York: Columbia University Press, 1993), especially 48–54; Richard Rorty, *Contingency, Irony, and Solidarity* (Cambridge: Cambridge University Press, 1989).

2. For the differences between Rorty and Habermas, see Jürgen Habermas, Richard Rorty, and Leszek Kolakowski, *Debating the State of Philosophy* (Westport, Conn.: Praeger, 1996). Rawls and Habermas carried out an extensive debate in the *Journal of Philosophy* 92, no. 3 (1995). See Jürgen Habermas, "Reconciliation through the Public Use of Reason: Remarks on John Rawls's *Political Liberalism*," 109–31, and John Rawls, "Reply to Habermas," 132–80.

3. Alexander Hamilton, James Madison, and John Jay, *The Federalist Papers* (New York: New American Library Press, 1961), 279 (no. 43). Because of the variety of editions of *The Federalist* that are in use, all citations will hereafter be to the number of the paper.

4. Abraham Lincoln, letter to Henry L. Pierce, April 6, 1859, in *Selected Speeches and Writings* (New York: Library of America, 1992), 215; Rorty, *Objectivity, Relativism, and Truth* (Cambridge: Cambridge University Press, 1991), 187.

5. Rorty, *Contingency, Irony, and Solidarity*, 51–52.

6. Rorty, *Essays on Heidegger and Others* (Cambridge: Cambridge University Press, 1991), 132–33.

7. Rawls, *Political Liberalism*, 63.

8. *Philosophy in a Time of Terror: Dialogues with Jürgen Habermas and Jacques Derrida*, ed. Giovanna Borradori (Chicago: University of Chicago Press, 2003), 117. Derrida puts "European" inside quotation marks to indicate that this position is not quite official. In actual fact, there is much more legal involvement between church and state in many European countries than there is in the United States.

9. Jürgen Habermas, "La statue et les revolutionnaires," *Le Monde*, May 3, 2003.

10. Pierre Rosanvallon, "Europe—les Etats-Unis, les deux universalismes," *Le Monde*, February 22, 2005.

11. Barack Obama, "Remarks by the President at the Acceptance of the Nobel Peace Prize," December 10, 2009, at www.whitehouse.gov/the-press-office/remarkspresident-acceptance-nobel-peace-prize.

12. Lincoln, speech of March 6, 1860, at New Haven, Connecticut, in *Selected Speeches and Writings*, 257.

13. Rorty, *Contingency, Irony, and Solidarity*, 86.

14. Rorty, *Essays on Heidegger*, 135.

15. Auguste Comte, *Cours de Philosophic Positive* (Paris: Bachelier, 1830), 1:40–41.

16. Alexander Stephens, "Cornerstone" speech, in Henry Cleveland, *Alexander H. Stephens in Public and Private* (Philadelphia: National Publishing, 1866), 721; Lincoln, speech on the Kansas-Nebraska Act, October 16, 1854.

17. John Stuart Mill, "Coleridge," in *Collected Works*, ed. John Robson et al. (Toronto: University of Toronto Press, 1963–1991), 10:133–34.

18. *The Works of John Adams* (Boston: Charles C. Little and James Brown, 1850), 2:371 (emphasis added).

19. Woodrow Wilson, *The New Freedom* (New York: Doubleday, Page, 1913), 42.

20. Thomas Jefferson, letter to Major John Cartwright, June 5, 1824, in *The Portable Thomas Jefferson*, ed. Merrill D. Peterson (New York: Viking Penguin, 1975), 578.

21. John Hugginson, "Election Sermon," cited in Alexis de Tocqueville, *Democracy in America*, trans. and ed. Harvey C. Mansfield and Delba Winthrop (Chicago: University of Chicago Press, 2000), 688–89.

22. Winston Churchill, *The Gathering Storm* (Boston: Houghton Mifflin, 1948), 345–46.

23. Thomas Jefferson, "A Summary View of the Rights of British America," in *The Portable Thomas Jefferson*, 4.

24. Locke in this period was widely seen, perhaps incorrectly, as a thoroughgoing materialist. See Merle Curti, "The Great Mr. Locke: America's Philosopher, 1783–1861," in *Probing our Past* (Gloucester, MA: P. Smith, 1962), 69–118.

25. George Bancroft, oration of February 18, 1840, at Hartford, Connecticut; Bancroft, speech to the New York Historical Society, 1858.

26. Jean Antoine Nicolas Condorcet, *Esquisse d'un Tableau Historique des Progres de L'Esprit Humain* (Paris: Flammarion, 1998), 88 (my translation). Published in English as *Sketch for a Historical Picture of the Progress of the Human Mind* (London: Weidenfeld and Nicolson, 1955).

27. William Graham Sumner, "Socialism," in *On Liberty, Society, and Politics*, ed. Robert C. Bannister (Indianapolis: Liberty Fund, 1992), 172.

28. John Dewey, *Freedom and Culture* (New York: Prometheus, 1989), 120; *Reconstruction in Philosophy* (Boston: Beacon Press, 1957; orig. 1920), 44.

29. *The Political Writings of John Dewey*, ed. Debra Morris and Ian Shapiro (Indianapolis: Hackett Publishers, 1993), 45.

30. See Mark Noll, *America's God* (Oxford: Oxford University Press, 2002) and Nathan Hatch, *The Democratization of American Christianity* (New Haven, CT: Yale University Press, 1989).

31. Cited by Mark Noll in "The Contingencies of Christian Republicanism," Tom Engeman and Michael Zuckert, eds. *Protestantism and the American Founding* (Notre Dame, IN: University of Notre Dame Press, 2004), 240.

32. Sidney Fine, *Laissez faire and the General Welfare* (Ann Arbor: University of Michigan Press, 1956), 180–81.

33. Charles Beard, "Written History as an Act of Faith," American Historical Association Presidential Address, 1933, *American Historical Review* 39, no. 2 (1934), 219–31, www.historians.org/info/AHA_History/cabeard.htm (accessed March 13, 2008).

34. See Francois Lyotard, *The Postmodern Condition* (Manchester, UK: Manchester University Press, 1984).

35. Leo Strauss, "The Crisis of Our Time," in *The Predicament of Modern Politics*, ed. Harold J. Spaeth (Detroit, MI: University of Detroit Press, 1964), 44.

36. See especially Leo Strauss, *Natural Right and History* (Chicago: University of Chicago Press, 1953), and Walter Lippmann, *Essays in the Public Philosophy* (Boston: Little, Brown, 1955).

37. Rorty, *Contingency, Irony, and Solidarity*, 63.

38. See Peter Lawler's excellent analysis of this issue in *Postmodernism Rightly Understood* (Lanham, MD: Rowman & Littlefield, 1999), 41–76.

39. Bradley Center for Philanthropy and Civic Renewal, "What's the Big Idea?," Bradley Symposium, May 25, 2006, http://pcr.hudson.org/index.cfm?fuseaction=publication_details&id=4044 (accessed March 13, 2008), 26.

40. Rorty, *Objectivity, Relativism, and Truth* (New York: Cambridge University Press, 1991), 212, 211, 219.

41. Rorty, *Contingency, Irony, and Solidarity*, 86, 91.

42. Rorty, *Achieving Our Country* (Cambridge, MA: Harvard University Press, 1998), 11.

43. Iris Marion Young, *Justice and the Politics of Difference* (Princeton, NJ: Princeton University Press, 1990), 98–99.

44. "What's the Big Idea?" 28–29.

CHAPTER 2: POLITICAL FOUNDATIONS IN TOCQUEVILLE'S *DEMOCRACY IN AMERICA*

1. Timothy Pitkin, *A Political and Civil History of the United States of America* (New Haven, CT: Hezekiah Howe and Durrie & Peck, 1828), I:3. For an overview of the historiography of the early period, related to the Founding, see Lester Cohen, *Revolutionary Histories* (Ithaca, NY: Cornell University Press, 1980).

2. Alexis de Tocqueville, *Democracy in America*, trans. Harvey C. Mansfield and Delba Winthrop, (Chicago: University of Chicago, [1835] 2000), 31, 32. Hereafter cited as *DA*.

3. This term was coined by Michael Zuckert in *The Natural Rights Republic* (Notre Dame, IN: Notre Dame University Press, 1996).

4. This term is derived from J. G. A. Pocock, *The Ancient Constitution and the Feudal Law* (New York: Norton Books, 1957), 36, 37.

5. *DA*, 143, 144. Tocqueville lauds the character of the Founders, who were "remarkable for their enlightenment, more remarkable still for their patriotism," and he judges the framework they produced to be "superior to all the state constitutions" (143). His greatest praise of the Founders' originality comes in his account of their invention of what we know as federalism: "This constitution . . . rests on an entirely new theory that will be marked as a great discovery in the political science of our day" (147).

6. *DA*, 106, 107 (emphasis added).

7. *Federalist* 38.

8. *DA*, 399.

9. *DA*, 295. "I am convinced that the happiest situation and the best laws cannot maintain a constitution despite mores, whereas the latter turn even the most unfavorable positions and the worst laws to good account" (295).

10. DA, 29. I include the term *germe*, translated variously as "germ," "seed," or "kernel," because of its importance in other accounts of Customary History.

11. *DA*, 56.

12. *Federalist* 43.

13. *DA*, 56

14. For one of the early treatments of these thinkers, see Isaiah Berlin, *Against the Current* (London: Hogarth Press, 1980).

15. *DA*, 7, 56.

16. See Thomas West, "Misunderstanding the American Founding," in *Interpreting Tocqueville's Democracy in America*, ed. Ken Masugi (Lanham, MD: Rowman & Littlefield, 1991). Although careful to point out that Tocqueville eloquently defends the importance of individual rights, West notes that he does not do so by reference to the standard of natural rights. Tocqueville discusses the importance of individual rights, among other places, in *Democracy in America* at pages 672 and 227–28. The latter passage is reminiscent of John Locke's ([1692] 1996) treatment, especially in its references to children.

17. G. K. Chesterton, *What I Saw in America* (London: Hodder and Stoughton, 1922), 7.

18. In addition to West, see Paul Rahe, *Soft Despotism, Democracy's Drift: Montesquieu, Rousseau, Tocqueville, and the Modern Prospect* (New Haven, CT: Yale University Press, 2009).

19. John Phillip Reid, "The Irrelevance of the Declaration," in *Law in the American Revolution and the Revolution in the Law*, ed. Hendrik Hartog (New York: New York University Press, 1981), 46–89. Reid's view is that "natural law principles played a relatively minor role . . . in motivating Americans to support the Whig cause" (48). For a summary of the republican school's position, see Alan Gibson, *Interpreting the Founding* (Lawrence: University of Kansas Press, 2006), 22–36.

20. See Daniel Rodgers, "Republicanism: The Career of a Concept," *Journal of American History* 79 (1992), 11–38; and Gibson, *Interpreting the Founding.* Carl Becker's *The Declaration of Independence* (New York: Harcourt Brace, 1922) was for many years considered the major work in this area. It stressed the centrality of the ideas of the Declaration, in particular the importance of the natural rights doctrine.

21. Daniel Rodgers develops this point in his survey of discourse on political concepts in early America in *Contested Truths* (Cambridge, MA: Harvard University, 1987). Rodgers explains (69–71) that natural rights discourse, having served in a perfunctory way in the early decades of the century, had been revived by the late 1820s, not only because of the celebrations attached to the fiftieth anniversary of the Declaration in 1826, but also because elements of the Jacksonian movement began to employ natural rights claims in political debates relating to economic issues.

22. Tocqueville provided his description of the event in a letter to Ernest de Charbol, July 16, 1831, in which he commented that the reading of the Declaration was "really a fine spectacle . . . it seemed that an electric current made the hearts [of the audience] vibrate." Alexis de Tocqueville, *Lettres choisies, Souvenirs*, ed. Françoise Mélonio and Laurence Guellec (Paris: Gallimard, 2003), 205–6. For further account of this event, see George Wilson Pierson, *Tocqueville in America* (Baltimore: Johns Hopkins University Press, [1938] 1996), 179–84; and Rahe, *Soft Despotism, Democracy's Drift*, 195–96.

23. *DA*, 249. See also Tocqueville's characterization of Jefferson as "the greatest democrat who has yet issued from within American democracy" (193). In addition, there are whole passages of *Democracy in America*, especially in I:10, in which Jefferson's analysis lies in the background, though it is not explicitly cited.

24. From Jefferson's letter to Richard Henry Lee, May 8, 1825.

25. Alexis de Tocqueville, *The Old Regime and the Revolution*, Alan S. Kahan, trans. (Chicago: University of Chicago Press [1856] 1998), 196.

26. *DA*, 415, 416.

27. *DA*, 407. He goes on: "In order that there be a society . . . it is necessary that all the minds of the citizens always be brought and held together by some principal ideas."

28. *DA*, 225. In another passage, Tocqueville expresses some doubts about whether the modern theoretical basis of solidarity can ever work entirely: "What maintains a great number of people under the same government is much less reasoned will than the instinctive and in a way involuntary accord resulting from similarity of sentiments and resemblance of opinions" (358).

29. *DA*, 32.

30. The interpretation that follows develops one aspect of Montesquieu's thought, not the whole of it. More perhaps than any other political theorist, Montesquieu articulated his thought in different "parts," the harmony among which has long been a subject of debate. For example, certain chapters of the work indicate that Montesquieu also favored a public doctrine of natural law. He should perhaps be seen as providing a number of alternative foundations, the choice (or mixing) among which must be at the discretion of the legislator, as context would dictate. For arguments on the importance of history as a standard along with or in place of natural law, see James Stoner, *Common Law and Liberal Theory* (Lawrence: University of Kansas, 1992), 154; and Pierre Manent, *The City of Man* (Princeton, NJ: Princeton University, 1998).

31. Edward Gibbon, *The Decline and Fall of the Roman Empire* (New York: Modern Library, [1776] 1995), 167.

32. Because many readers use different editions of *The Spirit of the Laws*, the references are to the chapters rather than the page numbers in the Cambridge 1989 edition. *The Spirit of the Laws*, trans. Anne M. Cohler, Basia Carolyn Miller, and Harold Samuel Stone (Cambridge: Cambridge University, [1748] 1989).

33. For an account of "Gothic history" and its use in America, see Trevor Colbourn, *The Lamp of Experience* (Chapel Hill: University of North Carolina Press, 1965).

34. The term "historical sense" comes from the German historian, Friedrich Carl Von Savigny, *Vom Beruf unserer Zeit für Gesetzgebung und Rechtwissenschaft* (Hildesheim: Georg Olms Verlagsbuchandlung, [1814] 1967), 5.

35. In a letter to his friend Louis de Kergolay (November 10, 1836), Tocqueville spoke of the three thinkers who influenced him most ("the three men with whom I live a bit every day"): Pascal, Montesquieu, and Rousseau. Scholars have disputed the degree of influence among the three, but I follow Raymond Aron and Jean Claude Lamberti in assigning the prize to Montesquieu.

36. *DA*, 7. Virginia helped to form the general mores of a romantic and more aristocratic slave nation in the South (31). Although the book's central theme is democracy, Tocqueville provides extensive treatment of the South's national character.

37. *DA*, 315, 29.

38. The only connection Tocqueville makes between America and the Goths is not between the Goths and the European settlers, but between the Goths and the Indians. Tocqueville speaks of the "resemblance that exists between the political institutions of our fathers, the Germans, and those of the wandering tribes of North America, between the customs recounted by Tacitus and those I was sometimes able to witness" (315).

39. *DA*, 28.

40. His is the first fully rational Customary History. As for other options—for example, treating Pennsylvania as the most influential colony (as George Bancroft would shortly do)—Tocqueville either did not know enough about these possibilities or found the arguments unconvincing. The greater part of historical work in America at that time concentrated on New England.

41. *DA*, 31–32. This is a point many historians today might dispute and was also called into question in George Bancroft's famous nineteenth-century history, which develops the thesis of multiple traditions in the American colonial period.

42. *DA*, 43.

43. Montesquieu appeared quite content to omit religion from the principal narrative of the early development of liberty. But when he directly takes up the theme of religion (especially in Book X), he supports a moderate form of Christianity.

44. *DA*, 39.

45. *DA*, 43.

46. *DA*, 62.

47. Tocqueville never offers a full, discursive treatment of his understanding of natural right, which must be pieced together from various portions of his work. Instances can be found at pages 98, 184, 282, 284, 348, and 510. Natural right often appears in passages having a poetic quality, as when Tocqueville speaks

of men building monuments to history, of the Indians being driven from their native lands, and of the strivings of those with great souls and great ambition. Tocqueville leaves open the question of how revealed religion helps man to understand right in all of its dimensions.

48. Rufus Choate, *The Works of Rufus Choate with a Memoir of His Life*, ed. Samuel Gilman Brown (Boston: Little, Brown and Company, 1862), volume 1.

49. *DA*, 43.

50. Rahe, *Soft Despotism, Democracy's Drift*, 195.

51. Tocqueville, *The Old Regime*, 201.

52. Other versions of the two-founding thesis were already under discussion or had been sketched. Included here was Daniel Webster's "Plymouth Oration," December 22, 1820.

53. Choate, *Works*, 414–38.

54. Abraham Lincoln, address before the Young Man's Lyceum of Springfield, January 27, 1838.

55. *DA*, 415.

56. *DA* 15, 416.

57. See especially Tocqueville's letters to Theodore Sedgwick, Edward Childe, and Jared Sparks from 1857 in Aurelian Craiutu and Jeremy Jennings, eds. and trans., *Tocqueville on America after 1840: Letters and Other Writings* (Cambridge: Cambridge University, 2009), 226, 224, 240. In addition, Tocqueville took the unprecedented step (for him) of publishing a public testimony in America against slavery in 1855, which appeared first in *The Liberty Bell* and was reprinted elsewhere. In this testimony he inches toward a natural law position, though the final source he cites is God's conception of man (Craiutu and Jennings, 169).

CHAPTER 3: AMERICAN POLITICAL FOUNDATIONS IN THE THOUGHT OF LEO STRAUSS

1. Leo Strauss, *Natural Right and History* (Chicago: University of Chicago Press, 1950), 2, 289–90.

2. Strauss, *Natural Right and History*, 314.

3. Strauss, *Natural Right and History*, 2.

4. Strauss appears here to be reversing Martin Heidegger's technique of claiming that Americanism ("pragmatism") had taken over German thinking.

5. Strauss, *Natural Right and History*, 1.

6. Strauss, *Natural Right and History*, 241. This statement is roughly in line with the only other quotation from an American Founder that appears in the book, James Madison's statement that "[t]he protection of [different and equal faculties of acquiring property] is the first object of government." A highly instructive comment on this quotation is provided by Wilson Carey McWilliams in his fine article, "Strauss and the Dignity of American Political Thought," *Review of Politics* 60, no. 2 (Spring 1988), 231–36.

7. The subsequent references to things about or related to America in the period after the Revolution include the following: Lincoln, 70, note 29 (Charnwood's

discussion of Lincoln's views on John Brown, bearing on Strauss's critique of the adequacy of the Weberian distinction between the ethics of intention and the ethic of responsibility); Beard, 92 (on the eighteenth-century revolutionists in general); James Madison, 245 (on the importance of the protecting the right of *acquiring* property); and Burke, 295 (on his support for the American Revolution).

8. Leo Strauss, *What Is Political Philosophy? And Other Studies* (Chicago: University of Chicago Press), 55.

9. Dewey condemns philosophy (old style) just because "it beckons men away from the world of relativity and change into the calm of the absolute and the eternal." *Reconstruction in Philosophy* (Boston: Beacon, 1957; orig. 1920), 179.

10. Strauss, *Natural Right and History*, 32.

11. Strauss, *Natural Right and History*, 146.

12. Locke is treated in depth in a section devoted to him, but perhaps the most damaging discussions of modern natural right are to be found in the sections on Rousseau and Burke, where Strauss presents a summary of the romantic and idealistic critiques of modern natural rights. See Strauss, *Natural Right and History*, 202–51, 252–323.

13. See also Leo Strauss, "Letter to the Editor," *National Review*, January 5, 1956: 23–24, in which Strauss writes, "A conservative, I take it, is a man who believes that 'everything good is heritage' . . . who despises vulgarity . . . who knows that the same arrangement may have very different meanings in different circumstances." It should be pointed out that Burke supported the American colonists while opposing the French revolutionaries. Strauss, *Natural Right and History*, 295. The modern conservative insight about the importance of unique situations inside the political world was a truism of classical political philosophy. Strauss, *What Is Political Philosophy?*, 61.

14. Strauss, *Natural Right and History*, 100; Strauss, *What Is Political Philosophy?*, 297.

15. Another surface message, more relevant to political philosophy, is this: American thinkers should try to replace the unfruitful dialogue between historicism and modern natural right, which turns out to be nearly a quarrel within the same family, with a new dialogue between the modern and premodern forms of natural right.

16. To simplify the discussion, I will not speak much here of faith-based Straussians who have sought to combine his philosophy with the insights and teachings of religion.

17. Strauss, *What Is Political Philosophy?*, 65–66. There are several versions of this thesis: that the correction is in the American Founding but not in Locke, whom Americans thankfully read exoterically rather than esoterically; that Locke, if read differently than Strauss does, already contains the correction; and that the way in which the problem is stated was transformed by Christianity, so that if Aristotle would have returned in the seventeenth century he would have stated matters roughly in the same way as John Locke.

18. As prudence must always weigh circumstances, it was one thing to distance Americans from their origins in the 1950s, when few were genuinely anti-American, but something quite different thereafter, when, following the emergence of the New

Left in the 1960s and a left-wing Heideggerianism thereafter, attacks on America became more pronounced.

19. Edmund Burke, "Letter to Sheriffs of Bristol."

20. Strauss, *Natural Right and History*, 4.

21. Strauss, *Natural Right and History*, 6. This view of the effect of the dominant strain of intellectual historicism in America proved to be a fairly accurate assessment of its course in the postwar period in America. See Richard Rorty, *Achieving Our Country* (Boston: Harvard University Press, 1998).

22. Strauss, *What Is Political Philosophy?*, 10–16.

23. This is a close paraphrase of Strauss's account of Burke's view of the use of principles.

24. Charles Beard, *The Republic* (New York: Viking, 1943), 38. According to Carl Becker, "To ask whether the natural rights philosophy of the Declaration of Independence is true or false is essentially a meaningless question." The effect of posing this meaningless question was, of course, to make readers think that a grounding of natural rights, indeed any idea of nature, was silly. Doctrines of higher law were myths created by men at certain points in history to justify their actions. Carl Becker, *The Declaration of Independence* (New York: Knopf, 1951; orig. 1922), 277.

25. John Burgess, "The American Commonwealth: Changes in Its Relation to the Nation," *Political Science Quarterly* 1, no. 1 (March 1886), 17. Such views were commonplace in advanced academic discourse by the early part of the twentieth century. See Charles Wright, "American Interpretations of Natural Law," *American Political Science Review* 20, no. 3 (August 1926), 524–47.

26. Dewey, *Reconstruction*, 26.

27. For discussions of the distinction between the old individualism and the new individualism (individuality), see Dewey's *Reconstruction in Philosophy, and Individualism Old and New* (New York: Beacon Press, 1971); and Herbert Croly, *The Promise of American Life* (New York: MacMillan, 1909).

28. Dewey, *Reconstruction*, 24. See Strauss, "Letter to Helmut Kuhn," *Independent Journal of Philosophy* 2 (1978), 23; and the discussion of this point by Susan Shell, "Natural Right and the Historical Approach" (paper presented at the conference "Leo Strauss's *Natural Right and History*: A Reassessment," LeFrak Forum, Michigan State University, April 20–22, 2001). Dewey's view of nature later underwent considerable revision, but his position in *Reconstruction in Philosophy* deserves attention, as it was his most influential general book on philosophy and the greatest statement of the pragmatic viewpoint.

29. Dewey, *Reconstruction*, 17: "Metaphysics is a substitute for custom as the source and guarantor of higher moral and social values—that is the leading theme of the classic philosophy of Europe, as evolved by Plato and Aristotle."

30. Dewey, *Reconstruction*, 59.

31. See especially his elucidation of the Aristotelian understanding of natural right in *Natural Right and History*, 157–63.

32. Strauss, *Natural Right and History*, 174, 175; Strauss, *What Is Political Philosophy?*, 279–81; Leo Strauss, *Liberalism Ancient and Modern* (Ithaca, NY: Cornell University Press, 1968), 57–58. Nominalism is the only philosophical category that is listed in the index of *Natural Right and History*, 325. Every other entry is a name.

33. Strauss, *What Is Political Philosophy?*, 281.

34. In Carl Becker's case, see his "What Is Still Living in the Political Philosophy of Thomas Jefferson?" *American Historical Review* 48, no. 4 (July 1943), 691–706. Becker writes, "[T]he incredible cynicism of Adolf Hitler's way of regarding man . . . has forced men everywhere to reexamine the validity of half-forgotten ideas and to entertain once more half-discarded convictions as to the substance of things not seen . . . the 'inalienable rights of man' are generalities, whether glittering or not, that denote realities—the fundamental realities that men will always fight and die for rather than surrender" (705). Or see John Dewey's reappreciation of the founding in works such as *Freedom and Culture* (New York: Putnam, 1939), where he "translates" Jefferson's word "natural" into "moral," and then goes on to say that Jefferson's "fundamental beliefs remain unchanged in substance if we forget all special associations with the word *NATURE* and speak instead of aims or values to be realized" (155, emphasis in the original). For a discussion of this point, see James Nichols, "Pragmatism and the U.S. Constitution," in *Confronting the Constitution*, ed. Allan Bloom (Washington, DC: American Enterprise Institute, 1990), 381–84.

35. Strauss, *Natural Right and History*, 2.

CHAPTER 4: FAME AND *THE FEDERALIST*: THE AMERICAN FOUNDERS AND THE RECOVERY OF POLITICAL SCIENCE

1. Douglass Adair, "Fame and the Founding Fathers," in *Fame and the Founding Fathers: Essays by Douglass Adair*, ed. Trevor Colbourn (New York: Norton, 1974), 3–27 (originally published in 1967).

2. Vernon Parrington, *Main Currents in American Thought I* (New York: Harcourt, Brace, and Co., 1927), 279–91.

3. *Federalist* 72. Hamilton clearly based his analysis here on David Hume's discussion of "the love of fame," which is the title of a section in his *Treatise of Human Nature*. A fine "discussion" of Hume's views on fame can be found in Robert Manzer's "Hume on Pride and Love of Fame," *Polity* 28, no. 3 (Spring 1996), 333–55.

4. Montesquieu made this allegation even against the sober-minded Aristotle: "Aristotle wanted to indulge sometimes his jealousy against Plato." *The Spirit of the Laws* II, trans. Thomas Nugent (New York: Hafner, 1949), 170.

5. Abraham Lincoln, address to the Young Man's Lyceum of Springfield (1838), in *Abraham Lincoln, Selected Speeches, Messages and Letters*, ed. T. Harry Williams (New York: Holt Reinhart and Winston, 1957), 12.

6. *Federalist* 72.

7. David Hume, *Essays: Moral, Political and Literary*, ed. Eugene Miller (Indianapolis: Liberty Press, 1987), 82.

8. See Mark Landy and Sydney Milkis, *Presidential Greatness* (Lawrence: University of Kansas Press, 2001).

9. *Federalist* 14.

10. For an excellent overview of this question of the authorship of *The Federalist*, see Douglass Adair, "The Authorship of the Disputed Federalist Papers," in *Fame and the Founding Fathers*, 21–74.

11. *Federalist* 72.

12. See *Federalist* 9, 37, and 47.

13. I am using the word "science" in its looser eighteenth-century sense to refer to a rational body of knowledge that covers a certain field.

14. See Michèle Duchet, *Anthropologie et histoire au siècle des lumières* (Paris: Maspero, 1971).

15. *Federalist* 11.

16. Buffon wrote a forty-three-volume set, beginning in 1749, titled *Natural History*; Raynal was the author of *Histoire Philosophique et Politique des établissements et du Commerce des Européens dans les deux Indes* (1770); and De Pauw wrote *Recherches Philosophiques sur les Américains*, a three-volume opus first published in 1768. De Pauw's book is cited in *Federalist* 11.

17. Ernst Cassirer, *The Philosophy of the Enlightenment* (Princeton, NJ: Princeton University Press, 1968), 77. A similarly high judgment of Buffon's importance is adopted by Michel Foucault, *Les Mots et Les Choses* (Paris: Gallimard, 1966), 137–76. In America at the time, Jefferson discussed Buffon at length in the first part of *Notes on the State of Virginia*, calling him "the best informed naturalist who has ever written." *Notes on the State of Virginia*, Query 6 (90). Page numbers are from Merrill Peterson, *The Portable Thomas Jefferson* (New York: Viking Press, 1975).

18. Cited in Antonello Gerbi, *The Dispute of the New World* (Pittsburgh: University of Pittsburgh Press, 1955), 17.

19. Gerbi, *Dispute of the New World*, 30.

20. *Federalist* 15.

21. *Federalist* 14 (emphasis added).

22. Thomas Jefferson, insofar as he embraced natural history, adopted the racialist view in his *Notes on the State of Virginia*.

23. The Founders do not actually assign a distinct name to this body of thought. The term "new philosophy" is the one used by Condorcet in his *Sketch for an Historical Picture of the Progress of the Human Mind*.

24. *Federalist* 6.

25. *Federalist* 6.

26. *Federalist* 34.

27. *Federalist* 37.

28. See especially *Federalist* 8.

29. *Federalist* 1.

CHAPTER 5: DEMAGOGUERY, STATESMANSHIP, AND PRESIDENTIAL POLITICS

1. The most important work in this field is Jeffrey Tulis's *The Rhetorical Presidency*. See also James Ceaser, Glenn Thurow, Jeffrey Tulis, and Joseph Bessette, "The Rise of the Rhetorical Presidency," *Presidential Studies Quarterly* 11 (1981), 158–71; Theodore Lowi, *The Personal Presidency* (Ithaca, NY: Cornell University Press, 1985); and George Edwards, *The Public Presidency* (New York: St. Martins Press, 1983).

2. Woodrow Wilson, *Constitutional Government in the United States* (1908; repr. New York: Columbia University Press, 1961), 68.

3. Although presidents did not generally give policy speeches, many pre–Civil War presidents did go on tours and deliver speeches of greeting. See Jeffrey Tulis, *The Rhetorical Presidency* (Princeton, NJ: Princeton University Press, 1987), 64.

4. "Proceedings of the Senate Sitting for the Trial of Andrew Johnson," February 24, 1868. The text can be found at www.law.umkc.edu/faculty/projects/ftrials/impeach/articles.html.

5. A few candidates nevertheless did conduct campaigns. See Tulis, *Rhetorical Presidency*; Gil Troy, *See How They Ran* (New York: Free Press, 1991).

6. Woodrow Wilson, *Congressional Government: A Study in American Politics* (Boston: Houghton Mifflin, 1885), 85.

7. *Populism* is another term that was once used—and still is—to characterize dangerous popular leadership appeals. For example, the current Venezuelan president, Hugo Chavez, is often referred to, usually in a derogatory sense, as a politician who uses populist methods. But in American politics the term has recently been sanitized, and it often carries today, for both the Left and the Right, a favorable connotation. Thus, the 2004 Democratic vice-presidential candidate, John Edwards, was regularly described as having a positive "populist" message, while many conservative Republicans have proudly sought office on populist themes.

8. A few political scientists who use these models have introduced some normative elements under the names of "shirking," "pandering," and "manipulation." The terms *pandering* and *manipulation* have parallels to certain elements of demagoguery. For discussion of these issues from different viewpoints, see in particular Brandice Canes-Wrone, *Who Leads Whom? Presidents, Policy, and the Public* (Chicago: University of Chicago Press) 2005; Brandice Canes-Wrone and Kenneth W. Shotts, "The Conditional Nature of Presidential Responsiveness to Public Opinion," *American Journal of Political Science* 48, no. 4 (2004), 690–706; and Lawrence Jacobs and Robert Shapiro, *Politicians Don't Pander* (Chicago: University of Chicago Press, 2000). Some of the limitations of the modern approaches to leadership are discussed by Randall Strahan, "Personal Motives, Constitutional Forms, and the Public Good: Madison on Political Leadership," in *James Madison: The Theory and Politics of Republican Government*, ed. Samuel Kernell (Palo Alto, CA: Stanford University Press, 2003).

9. Aristotle, *Nichomachean Ethics*, 1094b, 11–13.

10. George Mason, from his speech at the ratification debate in Virginia, June 17, 1788. It can be found at http://press-pubs.uchicago.edu/Founders/documents/a2_1_1s16.html (emphasis added).

11. *Federalist* 10.

12. *Federalist* 71.

13. *Federalist* 1.

14. From James Madison, "Vices of the Political System of the United States," as cited in Bryan Garsten, *Saving Persuasion* (Cambridge, MA: Harvard University Press, 2006), 202. According to Garsten, Madison arrived at the Convention holding the view that "the demagogy of ambitious men was a major cause of disorder and civil strife in his own day" (202).

15. *Federalist* 58.

16. Hugh Heclo, "The Permanent Campaign," in *Understanding the Presidency*, sixth edition, eds. James Pfiffner and Roger Davidson (Boston: Longman, 2009), 167.

17. Plutarch, "Life of Caius Gracchus," in *The Lives of the Noble Grecians and Romans*, trans. John Dryden (New York: Modern Library, 1957), 1011.

18. *Federalist* 63.

19. Tulis, *The Rhetorical Presidency*, 45–47.

20. David Nichols, *The Myth of the Modern Presidency* (University Park: Pennsylvania State University Press, 1994).

21. In the original plan of the Constitution, there was no separate vote for the vice president. The vice president was selected as the runner-up in the presidential vote.

22. *Federalist* 68.

23. This change also raised the threshold for being elected at the electoral stage, increasing it from a number equal to a quarter of the electors to a number equal to a half of the electors.

24. Thomas Ritchie, *The Virginia Enquirer*, January 1, 1824. See also *The Virginia Enquirer*, December 23, 1823. Cited in James Ceaser, *Presidential Selection* (Princeton, NJ: Princeton University Press, 1979), 137.

25. Letter from Martin Van Buren to Thomas Ritchie, January 13, 1827. Cited in Ceaser, *Presidential Selection*, 138.

26. Troy, *See How They Ran*, 45.

27. See Andrew Busch, *Outsiders and Openness in the Presidential Nominating System* (Pittsburgh: University of Pittsburgh Press, 1997).

28. To avoid the negative implications we attach to the term, Carnes Lord in his translation of Aristotle's *Politics* renders *demagogos* as "popular leader." See *Politics* (Chicago: University of Chicago Press, 1984), 278.

29. I rely here on Melissa Lane's "The Evolution of the 'Demagogue' and the Invention of the 'Statesman' in (Reflections on) Ancient Athens" (paper delivered at a conference at Yale University, "Statesmen and Demagogues: Democratic Leadership in Political Thought," March 31–April 1, 2006).

30. Thucydides, *History of the Peloponnesian War* (Loeb translation), 2.65.9.

31. It was part of Plato's divine genius that he challenged the judgment that Pericles was a statesman. He concluded instead that Pericles had in fact artfully corrupted the Athenians during his tenure, making them more unjust and less virtuous (see *Gorgias*, 515c–516d). Aristotle, staying slightly closer to the surface, argued that Pericles managed to enjoy "good repute with the better sorts" and that Athens remained in "fairly good condition" as long as he was on the scene; however, Aristotle concurred with Plato that Athens became worse afterward, due largely to Pericles' policy of introducing wages for the people. Aristotle praises Pericles as a leader, but suggests he descended at times into demagogy, perhaps inevitably or necessarily so. It would appear that no leader of the popular party, perhaps no leader of any kind in a thoroughly democratic system, can eschew all aspects of demagoguery and survive or thrive. See Aristotle, *Constitution of Athens*, trans. Kurt Von Fritz (New York: Hafner, 1950), 97–98; Aristotle, *Politics*, 1274a 6–10.

32. Online version, 1989, http://dictionary.oed.com/cgi/entry/50060328?query_type=word&queryword=demagogue&first=1&max_to_show=10&sort_type=alpha&result_place=1&search_id=BHDy-fJY4gF-11374&hilite=50060328.

33. Walter Lippmann, *Public Opinion* (New York: Free Press, 1955), 157.

34. *Federalist* 71.

35. If one wished to include the more difficult and problematic criterion of intention, the demagogue is one who employs his demagoguery with pure malice aforethought, that is, with the chief aim or end of boosting his power, without regard for the public good.

36. Victor Ehrenberg, *From Solon to Socrates* (New York: Methuen, 1973), 266.

37. After being defeated in the governor's race in Alabama in 1958, George Wallace is reliably reported to have told one of his campaign aides, "I was out-niggered, and I will never be out-niggered again" (www.pbs.org/wgbh/amex/wallace/sfeature/quotes.html).

38. Aristotle, *Constitution of Athens*, 99.

39. Plutarch, *Moralia: Quomodo Adult*, 52E.

40. Tim Duff, *Plutarch's Lives: Exploring Virtue and Vice* (Oxford: Clarendon Press, 1999), 303.

41. *Federalist* 1.

42. *Federalist* 1.

43. Alexis de Tocqueville, *Democracy in America*, trans. Harvey Mansfield and Delba Winthrop (Chicago: University of Chicago Press, 2000), 377.

44. Aristotle, *Rhetoric*, 1108b.

45. Plutarch, "Life of Pericles," in *Lives*, 195.

46. Samuel Taylor Coleridge, "A Lay Sermon," in *Coleridge's Writings on Politics and Society*, ed. John Beer, four volumes (Princeton, NJ: Princeton University Press, 1991), 1:101–2.

47. See also Jeremiah 23:16. The "demagogues" in this case refer not just to "false prophets" but also to certain priests and political figures.

48. 23 and 5:31.

49. Machiavelli, *Discourses* I:11. According to historian Guicciardini, "If he was good, we have seen a great prophet in our time; if he was bad, we have seen a great man. For, apart from his erudition, we must admit that if he was able to fool the public for so many years on so important a matter without ever being caught in a lie, he must have had great judgment, talent and power of invention" (Guicciardini, *History of Florence*, chap. 16).

50. Hobbes's warnings duplicate the biblical criticism of false prophecy, although without allowing for the idea of true prophecy. See Thomas Hobbes, *Leviathan*, ed. Richard Tuck (Cambridge: Cambridge University Press, 1996), 297. I am following here the arguments of Garsten, *Saving Persuasion*, 43.

51. David Hume, "Of Superstition and Enthusiasm," in *Essays: Moral, Political, and Literary*, ed. Eugene Miller (Indianapolis: Liberty Fund, [1742] 1987).

52. This well-worn phrase, which Blackstone used in his *Commentaries*, was picked up by Jefferson and used in his letter to Roger Weightman, June 24, 1826.

53. Woodrow Wilson, *Leaders of Men* (1890; repr. Princeton, NJ: Princeton University Press, 1952), 42.

54. I rely here on the analysis of Clifford Orwin, found in his Bradley lecture, "Moist Eyes: Political Tears from Rousseau to Clinton," delivered on April 14, 1997, at the American Enterprise Institute, www.aei.org/publications/pubID.18967,filter.all/pub_detail.asp.

55. See Larry Sabato, *The Rise of Political Consultants* (New York: Basic Books, 1981); Joe Klein, *Politics Lost* (New York: Doubleday, 2006); and Dennis Johnson, *No Place for Amateurs* (London: Routledge, 2001).

56. Garsten, *Saving Persuasion*, 13.

57. Woodrow Wilson, "Cabinet Government in the United States," in *College and State*, ed. Ray Stannard Baker and William E. Dodd, two volumes (New York: Harper Brothers, 1925), 1:37.

58. Adam Sheingate, "'Publicity' and the Progressive-Era Origins of Modern Politics," *Critical Review* 19, nos. 2–3 (2007), 465, 466.

59. See the works of Harold Lasswell, Walter Lippmann, and, much later, the authors of the *American Voter*.

60. Lippmann, *Public Opinion*, 158. For a discussion of the rise of consultancy, see Sheingate, "'Publicity' and the Progressive-Era Origins of Modern Politics."

61. *The Scientific Study of Politics*, ed. Herbert J. Storing (New York: Holt, Rinehart & Winston, 1962).

62. Joseph Bessette, "Deliberative Democracy: The Majority Principle in Republican Government," in *How Democratic Is the Constitution?*, ed. Robert A. Goldman and William A. Schambra (Washington, DC: AEI Press, 1980); Joseph Bessette, *The Mild Voice of Reason* (Chicago: University of Chicago Press, 1994).

63. Besides Jürgen Habermas, some of the others who have contributed to the theme of discursive democracy include John Rawls, Joshua Cohen, Amy Gutmann, Dennis Thompson, and Seyla Benhabib.

64. Tocqueville devoted a famous chapter in his volume on the *Old Regime and the French Revolution* to showing how this process operated in eighteenth-century France, with the spread of ideas from the theorists, to the "men of letters," to many of those who made the Revolution: "When we closely study the French Revolution we find that it was conducted in precisely the same spirit as that which gave rise to so many books expounding theories of government in the abstract" (author's translation, part 3, chap. 1).

65. John Adams claimed, "Every man of a crowded audience appeared to me to go away as I did ready to up arms against the writs of assistance. Then and there was the first scene of the first act of the opposition to the arbitrary claims of Great Britain. Then and there the child of Independence was born." Available at www.mass.gov/courts/stc/john-adams-b.html.

66. David Hume, "On the Liberty of the Press," *Essays: Moral, Political, and Literary*, 604.

67. Alexis de Tocqueville, *The Old Regime and the French Revolution*, part 3, chap. 1, which is titled, "How Towards the Middle of the Eighteenth Century Men of Letters Took the Lead in Politics and the Consequences of This New Development."

68. See especially Michael Schudson, *Discovering the News* (New York: Basic Books, 1978).

69. For Aristotle, persuasion by showing one's character and credibility (*ethos*) is one of the three basic types of proof in rhetoric. The other two are *pathos* (emotional appeals) and *logos* (rational argumentation). A notable example of a decisive failure of ethos was Al Gore's performance during his first debate with George Bush in 2000, when he exaggerated a story and was observed to sigh and

smirk, thereby displaying an unmerited arrogance. This performance was widely regarded as turning the campaign against him.

70. Almost as direct are the replays of large sections of the speeches on news programs in subsequent days and throughout the campaign.

71. John Marshall put it this way: "By weakening the office of President he [Jefferson] will increase his personal power"; quoted in Raymond Tatalovich and Thomas S. Engeman, *The Presidential Political Science: Two Hundred Years of Constitutional Debate* (Baltimore: Johns Hopkins University Press, 2003), 38.

72. Martin Van Buren to Thomas Ritchie, January 13, 1827. Cited in Ceaser, *Presidential Selection*, 160.

73. Cited in Paul F. Boller, *Campaigns from George Washington to George W. Bush* (Oxford: Oxford University Press, 2004), 66.

74. Robert Gunderson, *The Log Cabin Campaign* (Lexington: University of Kentucky Press, 1957), 7.

75. Seymour Martin Lipset and Earl Raab, *The Politics of Unreason* (New York: Harper & Row, 1970), 50–55.

76. Harry Jaffa notes that Douglas's supposed indifference to slavery, not caring whether it was voted up or down, "may then in fact have been an act of prudence of the highest kind. . . . from this point of view, Douglas's suppression of the morality concerning slavery would be a higher act of virtue than Lincoln's gratification of his feelings on the subject." Harry Jaffa, "Abraham Lincoln," in *American Political Thought*, ed. Morton Frisch and Richard Stevens (Dubuque, IA: Kendall Hunt, 1971), 130.

77. Lincoln made two comments that shed light on his view of the role of abstract principles. First, from his speech at New Haven (1860): "Whenever the question of [slavery] shall be settled, it must be settled on some philosophical basis. No policy that does not rest on some philosophical public opinion can be permanently maintained." Second, from his letter to Henry L. Pierce and others (1859): "All honor to Jefferson—to the man who . . . had the coolness, forecast, and capacity to introduce into a merely revolutionary document, an abstract truth, applicable to all men and all times." Abraham Lincoln, *Selected Speeches and Writings* (New York: Library of America, 1992), 216, 257.

78. From the Lincoln-Douglas debates (first debate at Ottawa, Illinois). Lincoln went on, "I ask you to consider whether, so long as the moral constitution of men's minds shall continue to be the same, after this generation and assemblage shall sink into the grave, and another race shall arise with the same moral and intellectual development we have—whether, if that institution is standing in the same irritating position in which it now is, it will not continue an element of division?" The debates are online at www.nps.gov/archive/liho/debates.htm.

79. Taft's speech at Cambridge, Ohio, is available at http://ehistory.osu.edu/osu/mmh/1912/content/TRSeeksGOPNomination.cfm.

80. As cited in Jonathan Alter, *The Defining Moment: FDR's Hundred Days and the Triumph of Hope* (New York: Simon and Schuster, 2006), 220–21.

81. Morton Frisch, "Franklin Roosevelt," in Frisch and Stevens, *American Political Thought*, 236.

82. Andrew Young, *The Politician* (New York: Thomas Dunne, 2010).

CHAPTER 6: DOCTRINES OF
PRESIDENTIAL-CONGRESSIONAL RELATIONS

1. For a summary and commentary on this dispute, see Stephen Skowronek, "The Conservative Insurgency and Presidential Power: A Developmental Perspective on the Unitary Executive" 22 *Harvard Law Review* 2070 (2009).

2. *Federalist* 47.

3. See, for example, Alexander Hamilton, James Madison, and John Jay, *The Federalist Papers*, introduction by Clinton Rossiter (New York: New American Library, 1961), nos. 37, 47, 48, 66, and 71.

4. *Federalist* 48.

5. See *Federalist* 37: "Experience has instructed us that no skill in the science of government has yet been able to discriminate and define, with sufficient certainty, its three great provinces the legislative, executive, and judiciary; or even the privileges and powers of the different legislative branches. Questions daily occur in the course of practice, which prove the obscurity which reins in these subjects, and which puzzle the greatest adepts in political science."

6. In addition, in accord with English common law, the Americans understood the judicial power to play a role in interpreting and applying the law. When Americans "invented" the idea of written constitutions, the judicial power was understood by most to include a power of interpreting and applying the fundamental law, or what is referred to now as "judicial review." Judicial review is thus an American addition to separation of powers theory; it was not part of the original theory for the simple reason that written constitutions did not previously exist or figure in the thought of Locke or Montesquieu. Significantly, too, judicial review has become one of the most problematic elements of separation of power theory, for in its most extensive application judicial review has been said to make one power—the judicial power—superior to all others.

7. *Federalist* 47.

8. This is a well-known formulation by Richard Neustadt, *Presidential Power* (New York: Wiley, 1960), 33. Neustadt here was not directly denying the idea of the separation of powers, but his description may nicely be expanded to present an alternative view.

9. The Founders, in line with Montesquieu's teaching, also argued that the placement of one of the powers—the judicial power to punish—in its own branch, wholly independent of the power to execute or legislate, is by itself an essential guarantee of liberty that gives citizens the feeling that their rights are secure from arbitrary power.

10. *Federalist* 47.

11. The legislative power is chiefly in the hands of the Congress, but it is divided between two institutions, the House and the Senate, the leaders of which do not control the whole process and may often be rivals.

12. *Federalist* 68. The phrase is repeated in *Federalist* 77.

13. "Letter of an 'Old Whig,'" published in the *Philadelphia Independent Gazetteer*, December 4, 1787; reprinted in *The Power of the Presidency*, third edition, ed. Robert Hirschfield (New York: Adeline, 1982), 28–29.

14. See Gary J. Schmitt, "Thomas Jefferson and the Presidency," in *Inventing the American Presidency*, ed. Thomas Cronin (Lawrence: Kansas University Press, 1989), 326–47.

15. Cited in Wilfred E. Binkley, *President and Congress*, third edition (New York: Random House, 1962), 63.

16. *Federalist* 49.

17. For an account that argues that Jefferson sought to establish a popular base for the presidency, see Jeremy Bailey, *Thomas Jefferson and Executive Power* (Cambridge: Cambridge University Press, 2007). If Bailey is correct, Jefferson's theory nevertheless did not entirely take hold with his party and had to be restated and revived by Jackson. Bailey also argues that Jefferson had a view of strong presidential leadership that operated outside of the Constitution as a form of prerogative. Again, if true, it is difficult to argue that this was part of a public doctrine as defined here. Other presidents of his party did not reiterate this position.

18. Richard Harlow, *The History of Legislative Methods in the Period before 1825* (New Haven, CT: Yale University Press, 1917), 196.

19. Binkley, *President and Congress*, 74.

20. The reverse no doubt was also thought to be true: a limited or weak president would make more likely a smaller national government.

21. Ralph Ketcham, "James Madison and the Presidency," in *Inventing the American Presidency*, ed. Thomas Cronin, 351.

22. Schmitt, "Thomas Jefferson and the Presidency," 342.

23. Ketcham, "James Madison and the Presidency," 360. Ketcham stops short, however, of taking this argument to its conclusion that Madison would never have sanctioned extraordinary executive actions. Madison "probably would also have approved of Lincoln's understanding and defense of the Union in 1861."

24. Cited in Binkley, *President and Congress*, 97.

25. Binkley, *President and Congress*, 96.

26. The Whigs, by contrast, argued not only that the veto could not be used as a mere instrument of policy, but also that, in matters of constitutional judgment, the president was obliged to accept the interpretations of the Congress and the Court.

27. Leonard D. White, *The Jacksonians: A Study in Administrative History, 1829–1861* (New York: The Macmillan Company, 1954), 24.

28. David Nichols is the first to have shown that the Jacksonian step should be seen in substantial part as a step *back* in the direction of the original constitutional view.

29. American Political Science Profession, "Toward a More Responsible Two-Party System: A Report of the Committee on Political Parties," *APSR* 44, No. 3, Part 2, Supplement (1950).

30. Woodrow Wilson, *Constitutional Government in the United States* (New York: Columbia University Press, 1961), 126.

31. Wilson, *Constitutional Government*, 55, 157, and 192. See Christopher Wolfe, "Woodrow Wilson: Interpreting the Constitution," *Review of Politics* 41, no. 1 (January 1979), 121–35.

32. This is the thesis of David Nichols in *The Myth of the Modern Presidency*.

33. This scholarship begins with Charles Thatch, Herbert Storing, Martin Diamond, Louis Fisher, and Harvey Mansfield, who were followed by a group

of scholars of the next generation that included Joseph Bessette, Gary Schmitt, and David Nichols, and finally by a new generation among whom are Benjamin Kleinerman, Jeremy Bailey, and George Thomas; this body of scholarship has recovered an understanding of the issues of executive and legislative powers that, for polemical and doctrinal reasons, had long been obscured.

CHAPTER 7: FOUR HEADS AND ONE HEART: THE MODERN CONSERVATIVE MOVEMENT

1. A perfect example in this genre is Sam Tanenhaus, *The Death of Conservatism* (New York: Random House, 2009).

2. Samuel Huntington, *Who Are We? The Challenges to American National Identity* (New York: Simon and Schuster, 2004).

3. John Henry Newman, "Who's to Blame?" (1855), in *Discussions and Arguments on Various Subjects* (New York: Longmans, Green, 1891), 315.

4. Some libertarians, such as Murray Rothbard, begin from a premise of nature in the form of natural rights.

5. Friedrich A. Hayek, "Our Moral Heritage," *Heritage Lectures No. 24* (Washington, DC: The Heritage Foundation, 1982), 3.

6. The phrase is from Adam Smith's *The Wealth of Nations*.

7. Samuel Sherwood, "The Church's Flight into the Wilderness" (1776), in *Political Sermons of the American Founding Era 1730–1805*, ed. Ellis Sandoz (Indianapolis: Liberty Fund, 1990), 503.

8. Hayek stated in *The Constitution of Liberty*, "I will nevertheless continue for the moment to describe as liberal the position which I hold and which I believe differs as much from true conservatism as from socialism. Let me say at once, however, that I do so with increasing misgivings, and I shall later have to consider what would be the appropriate name for the party of liberty. The reason for this is not only that the term 'liberal' in the United States is the cause of constant misunderstandings today, but also that in Europe the predominant type of rationalistic liberalism has long been one of the pacemakers of socialism."

9. By creating a vacuum, liberalism in other places may bear some responsibility for encouraging a reaction that went well beyond conservatism to extreme attachments to the nation or the *volk*.

CHAPTER 8: THE SOCIAL CONSTRUCTION OF THE REAGAN LEGACY

1. Merrill D. Peterson, *The Jefferson Image in the American Mind* (New York: Oxford University Press, 1960), 234.

2. Gordon S. Wood, *Revolutionary Characters: What Made the Founders Different* (New York: Penguin Press, 2006), 94.

3. Caroline Kennedy, "A President like My Father," *New York Times*, January 27, 2008.

4. Michael Paul Rogin, *Ronald Reagan, the Movie and Other Episodes in Political Demonology* (Berkeley: University of California Press, 1987).

5. Raymond Moore, "The Reagan Presidency and Foreign Policy," in *The Reagan Presidency: An Incomplete Revolution?*, ed. Dilys M. Hill, Raymond A. Moore, and Phil Williams (New York: St. Martin's Press, 1990), 197.

6. Kennan and Talbott as quoted in Dinesh D'Souza, "How Reagan Won the Cold War," *National Review*, November 24, 1997, republished in *National Review Online*, June 6, 2004, www.nationalreview.com/flashback/ dsouza200406061619.asp.

7. Clinton as quoted in E. J. Dionne, "Clinton's Depressing Assault on Obama," *Washington Post*, January 25, 2008.

8. Haynes Johnson, *Sleepwalking through History: America in the Reagan Years* (New York: Norton, 1991), 13.

9. Arthur Schlesinger Jr., "The Ultimate Approval Rating," *New York Times Magazine*, December 15, 1996, 46–51; Arthur Schlesinger Jr., "Rating the Presidents: Washington to Clinton," *Political Science Quarterly* 112 (Summer 1997), 179–90.

10. See "The Rankings," www.opinionjournal.com/extra/?id=110007243. The poll in question was conducted in 2005 by the *Wall Street Journal* and the Federalist Society and surveyed 130 professors from the fields of history, law, political science, and economics.

11. There are now too many to list, but a recent biography that cites the other sources and carefully discusses the Reagan years is Steven Haywood, *The Age of Reagan* (New York: Crown Forum, 2009).

CHAPTER 9: THE THEORETICAL ORIGINS
OF ANTI-AMERICANISM

1. *What the World Thinks in 2002*, p. 1, A Report of the Pew Research Foundation. Available at the website of the Pew Foundation.

2. The Schröder campaign was imitated in 2004 by Jose Zapatero, also a socialist, who ran successfully for prime minister of Spain in 2004.

3. Speech of President Obama, April 3, 2009. Obama went on to call some Europeans to task for indulging "an anti-Americanism that is at once casual, but can also be insidious."

4. Ignacio Ramonet, *Guerres du XXIe siècle* (Paris: Galilée, 2002), 88–89.

5. Ivan Krastev, "The Anti-American Century?" *The Journal of Democracy* 15, no. 2 (2004), 8.

6. Jean Baudrillard, "L'esprit du terrorisme," *Le Monde* (November 3, 2001), 1.

7. George Washington, Farewell Address, at http://earlyamerica.com/early america/milestones/farewell/text.html.

8. Henry de Montherlant, *Le Chaos et la Nuit* (Paris: Gallimard, 1963), 265.

9. Noel Mamčre and Patrick Farbiaz, *Dangereuse Amérique* (Paris: Ramsey, 2002), 63.

10. Bernard Lewis, "The Roots of Muslim Rage," *Atlantic* (September 1990), 52.

11. Paul Berman, *Terror and Liberalism* (New York: Norton, 2003); Waller Newell, "Postmodern Jihad," *Weekly Standard* (November 26, 2001), 26.

12. Alexander Hamilton, James Madison, and John Jay, *The Federalist* (New York: New American Library, 1961), 33 (*Federalist* 1).

13. Joseph de Maistre, *Considérations sur la France* (Geneva: Slatkine, 1980; orig. 1797), 133–34.

14. Joseph de Maistre, *Oeuvres complètes* (Geneva: Slatkine, 1979), 1:87.

15. Nikolaus Lenau, *Samtliche Werke und Briefe* (Frankfurt: Insel Verrl, 1971), 2:216, 2:213.

16. Heinrich Heine, "Jetzt Wohin?" cited in Ernst Fraenkel, *Amerika: Im Spiegel des Deutschen politischen Denkens* (Cologne: Westdeutschef Verlag, 1959), 106–7.

17. Antoine-Nicolas de Condorcet, *Sketch for a Universal Picture of the Progress of the Human Mind*, trans. June Barraclough (New York: Noonday Press, 1955; orig. 1795), 147.

18. Friedrich Nietzsche, *The Gay Science*, trans. Walter Kaufmann (New York: Vintage, 1974), 258–59, 303.

19. Arthur Moeller van den Bruck, *Die Zeitgenossen* (Minden: Bruns, 1906), 13.

20. Cited in Otto Basler, "Americanismus: Geschichte des Schlagwortes," in *Deutsche Rundschau* (August 1930), 144.

21. Theodor Lessing, *Europa und Asien*, fifth edition (Leipzig: Felix Meiner, 1930).

22. Lessing, *Europa und Asien*, 100, 206, 209.

23. Richard Müller Freienfels, *Geheimnisse der Seele* (Munich: Delphin, 1927), translated by Bernard Miall as *Mysteries of the Soul* (New York: Knopf, 1929).

24. *Mysteries of the Soul*, 8, 240, 252, 269.

25. Ernst Jünger, "Total Mobilization," translated by Richard Wolin in *The Heidegger Controversy*, ed. Richard Wolin (Boston: MIT Press, 1933), 137–38.

26. Ernst Jünger, "Das Abenteuerliche Herz," in *Samtliche Werke* (Stuttgart: Klett-Cotta, 1979), 102.

27. Martin Heidegger, *Holzwege* (Frankfurt: Vittorio Klostermann, 1957), 103.

28. Martin Heidegger, "Holderins Hymne," in *Gesamtausgabe* (Frankfurt: Vittorio Klostermann, 1975), volume 53, 179.

29. Martin Heidegger, *An Introduction to Metaphysics*, trans. Ralph Manheim (New Haven, CT: Yale University Press, 1959; orig. 1935), 37.

30. Heidegger, *An Introduction to Metaphysics*, 45–46.

31. For his discussion of a "productive dialogue" with Marxism, see Martin Heidegger, "A Letter on Humanism," in *Basic Writings*, ed. David Krell (New York: Harper & Row, 1977), 220–21.

32. Heidegger, "Holderins Hymne," volume 53, 68.

33. Martin Heidegger, "Overcoming Metaphysics," in *The Heidegger Controversy*, 84; Martin Heidegger, "Seminars" in *Questions III and IV* (Paris: Gallimard, 1976).

34. Heidegger, *Holzwege*, 268.

35. Martin Heidegger, "Andenken, Erlauterungen zu Holderlins Dichtung," in *Gesamtausgabe*, 52:134.

36. Heidegger, "Andenken," 52:37.

37. Alexandre Kojève, *Introduction a la Lecture de Hegel,* ed. Raymond Queneau (Paris: Gallimard, 1968), 436.

38. Kojève, *Introduction a la Lecture de Hegel,* 437.

39. Jean Baudrillard, *Amérique* (Paris: B. Grasset, 1986).

40. *New York Times,* December 12, 1988, A44; *Amérique,* 23, 50, 58, and 151.

41. Jean Baudrillard, *La Guerre du Golfe n'a pas eu lieu* (Paris: Galilée, 1991), 90, 100.

42. Régis Debray, "L'Europe somnambule," *Le Monde* (April 1, 1999), 1.

43. *Philosophy in a Time of Terror: Dialogues with Jürgen Habermas and Jacques Derrida,* ed. Giovanna Borradori (Chicago: University of Chicago Press, 2003), 117.

44. *Philosophy in a Time of Terror: Dialogues with Jürgen Habermas and Jacques Derrida,* ed. Giovanna Borradori; Jürgen Habermas, "La statue et les révolutionnaires," *Le Monde* (May 3, 2003).

45. Edward Gibbon, *The Decline and Fall of the Roman Empire* (New York: Modern Library, 1995), 1223.

Index

Absalom, 92

Adair, Douglass, 61, 64

Adams, John, 7, 99, 127–28

Adams, John Quincy, 82, 106

The Adventuresome Heart (Jünger), 177

Agnew, Spiro, 112

Alcibiades, 90

America (Baudrillard), 180

The American Dilemma (Myrdal), 28

American party, 107

anti-Americanism: aim of, 52;
contemporary, 181–83; factors
affecting, 167–68; nineteenth-
century theoretical, 172–75; sources
of, 168–72; twentieth-century
theoretical, 175–83

Anti-Federalists, 120, 123, 126–27

Apology (Plato), 89

Aristotle: on Cleon, 89; Dewey and,
193n29; Montesquieu and, 33–34,
194n4; natural right and, 49; on
Pericles, 197n31; political science
and, 68; on rhetoric, 96–97, 199n69

Bancroft, George, 9, 190n40, 190n41

Baudrillard, Jean, 170, 180

Beard, Charles, 13, 53, 57

Becker, Carl, 194n34

Bellow, Saul, 112

Bessette, Joseph, 98

Bible, 92–93, 99. *See also* religion

Bryan, William Jennings, 109–10

Buchanan, Patrick, 88

Buffon, Count de, 70

Burgess, John, 53

Burke, Edmund, 48, 51, 99, 192n12

Burr, Aaron, 66, 81, 105

Bush, George H. W., 114

Bush, George W.: anti-Americanism
and, 167–68, 182; Gore's
debate with, 199n69; political
nonfoundationalism and, 5; as
successor to Reagan, 162; unitary
executive and, 119; Whigism and,
138

Caesar, Julius, 90

Caius Gracchus, 79

Carter, Jimmy, 114, 153, 161

Cassirer, Ernst, 70

Charbol, Ernest de, 28–29

Chavez, Hugo, 196n7

checks and balances, 124–25. *See also*
separation of powers

207

About the Author

James W. Ceaser is professor of politics at the University of Virginia and a visiting fellow at the Hoover Institution, where he is a member of the Boyd and Jill Smith Task Force on Virtues of a Free Society. Professor Ceaser is author of a number of works on American politics and American political thought, including *Nature and History in American Political Development*, *Reconstructing America*, *Liberal Democracy and Political Science*, and *Presidential Selection*.